# SUMMIT

## English for Today's World

# 2

Joan Saslow • Allen Ascher

with Silvia Carolina Tiberio

Pronunciation Booster by Bertha Chela-Flores

PEARSON
Longman

**Summit: English for Today's World   2**

Pearson Education, 10 Bank Street, White Plains, NY 10606

**Staff credits:** The people who made up the *Summit 2* Student's Book team—representing editorial, production, design, and manufacturing—are Rhea Banker, Aerin Csigay, Dave Dickey, Pamela Fishman, Ann France, Aliza Greenblatt, Mike Kemper, and Marian Wassner.

**Text composition:** Kirchoff/Wohlberg
**Text font:** Palatino 11/13
**Cover Photograph:** "Apex" by Rhea Banker, Copyright ©2005 by Rhea Banker
**Text credits:** Page 22 "The Silent Couple." Adapted with the permission of Simon & Schuster Adult Publishing Group from *The Book of Virtues*, edited, with commentary by William J. Bennett. Copyright © 1993 William J. Bennett; p. 68 "A Valuable Lesson." Christopher Elliott/National Geographic Image Collection; p. 106 "World's First 'Green' Dealership." Courtesy of Ford Motor Company; p. 116 Pew Global Attitudes Survey. Pew Global Attitudes Project.
**Illustration credits:** Steve Attoe, pp. 14, 45, 66, 89, 90, 94; Francois Escalmel, pp. 18, 62; Oki Han, p. 23; Marc Mongeau, p. 22; Dusan Petricic, pp. 16, 30, 93, 95; Anna Veltfort, p. 67; Carl Wiens, p. 55.
**Photo credits:** All original photography by David Mager. Page 2 (top left) AP/Wide World Photos, (top middle) Woods Hole Oceanographic Institution, (top right) AP/Wide World Photos, (middle) AGE Fotostock America, Inc., (bottom left) Galen Rowell/Peter Arnold, Inc., (bottom middle) Frans Lanting/Minden Pictures, (bottom right) Al Giddings Images, Inc.; p. 3 (top) Frans Lanting/Getty Images, (middle) Frans Lanting/Getty Images, (bottom left) Charlotte Thege/Peter Arnold, Inc., (bottom right) Computer Associates International, Inc.; p. 4 Cary Wolinsky/Aurora & Quanta Productions, Inc.; p. 6 (left) AP/Wide World Photos, (right) Woods Hole Oceanographic Institution; p. 7 (1) Al Giddings Images, Inc., (2) Dr. Madan Kataria, (6) AP/Wide World Photos, (8) R. Scott Martin/Corbis Sygma; p. 8 Michael K. Nichols/National Geographic Image Collection; p. 9 (left) Lilly Dong/Getty Images, (middle) Michael McQueen/Getty Images, (right) Digital Vision/Getty Images; p. 10 Diaphor Agency/Index Stock Imagery; p. 21 (top) AP/Wide World Photos, (middle) Bill Irwin/Pearson Education, (bottom) Tony Freeman/PhotoEdit; p. 26 (background) Getty Images, (top) Bettmann/Corbis, (middle) Louie Psihoyos/Corbis, (bottom) Jacques M. Chenet/Corbis; p. 28 (left & right) Kelsey Adventures Ltd.; p. 31 Ghislain & Marie David de Lossy/Getty Images; p. 32 Bettmann/Corbis; p. 34 (top) Ki Ho Park/Kistone Photography, (bottom) AP/Wide World Photos; p. 35 (left) AP/Wide World Photos, (right) Jeffrey Markowitz/Corbis Sygma, (bottom) Doug Perrine/Pacific Stock; p. 37 (1) Michael Newman/PhotoEdit, (2) Mary Kate Denny/PhotoEdit, (3) ThinkStock/Index Stock Imagery; p. 38 (Carl) MedioImages Fresca Collection/Alamy, (Karen) AbleStock/Index Stock Imagery, (Bill) Vic Bider/PhotoEdit, (Kate) Michael Newman/PhotoEdit; p. 41 (top left) David Young-Wolff/PhotoEdit, (bottom left) Michael Newman/PhotoEdit, (top right) Michael Newman/PhotoEdit, (bottom right) Andersen Ross/Getty Images; p. 43 (top left) Vicky Kasala/Getty Images, (top right) Michael Newman/PhotoEdit, (middle) Elena Rooraid/PhotoEdit, (bottom left) Stockbyte, (bottom right) Stockbyte; p. 44 Giantstep Inc./Getty Images; p. 50 Jack K. Clark/The Image Works; p. 51 (background) Jeff Greenberg/PhotoEdit, (bird) Dennis MacDonald/PhotoEdit; p. 52 (1) Shoot Pty. Ltd./Index Stock Imagery, (2) John Sann/Getty Images, (3) Stockbyte, (4) M. Nader/Getty Images; p. 56 Erik Simonsen/Getty Images; p. 59 Stephen Alvarez/National Geographic Image Collection; p. 63 AP/Wide World  Photos; p. 68 www.Elliott.org; p. 70 AP/Wide World Photos; p. 71 (city) Romilly Lockyer/Getty Images, (cruise) Tom Bean/Getty Images, (beach) MedioImages/Getty Images, (woods) Ty Allison/Getty Images, (tour) Tim Hall/Getty Images; p. 74 (left to right) David Gould/Getty Images, Photodisc Collection/Getty Images, Stuart Dee/Getty Images, Ryan McVay/Getty Images, Adam Jones/Getty Images, (man) Mark  Harmel/Photo Researchers, Inc.; p. 75 (background) Adam Jones/Getty Images, (man) Mark  Harmel/Photo Researchers, Inc.; p. 76 (top) Michael Newman/PhotoEdit, (1) SuperStock, Inc./SuperStock, (2) Bettmann/Corbis, (3) SPL/Photo Researchers, Inc., (4) Bettmann/Corbis, (5) Bettmann/Corbis, (6) Lynn Gilbert/Pace/MacGill Gallery, (7) Bettmann/Corbis; p. 77 (top) Dennis Degnan/Corbis, (bottom) Jose Luis Pelaez, Inc./Corbis; p. 83 Hulton Archive/Getty Images; p. 86 (1) ©2001 by Randy Glasbergen/www.glasbergen.com, (2) ©The New Yorker Collection 1997 Aaron Bacall from cartoonbank.com. All Rights Reserved, (3) ©The New Yorker Collection 2002 Mick Stevens from cartoonbank.com. All Rights Reserved, (4) ©The New Yorker Collection 1970 Robert Day from cartoonbank.com. All Rights Reserved; p. 87 (1) Meredith Parmelee/Getty Images, (2) Jose Luis Pelaez, Inc./Corbis, (3) Walter Hodges/Getty Images, (4) Frederick Tousche/Getty Images, (5) Photofest, (6) Henry Horenstein/Getty Images; p. 98 Sanford/Agliolo/Corbis; p. 99 John Lamb/Getty Images; p. 101 Johan Visschedijk/1000aircraftphotos.com; p. 102 Gabe Palmer/Corbis; p. 104 Rainer Grosskepf/Getty Images; p. 105 Richard Green/Mira.com; p. 106 Lester Lefkowitz/Getty Images; p. 110 (Gates) Chris Farina/Corbis, (Welch) Najlah Feanny/Corbis Saba, (Klein) McPherson Colin/Corbis Sygma, (Noor) AP/Wide World Photos, (Roy) Torsten Blackwood/AFP/Getty Images/NewsCom, (Annan) AP/Wide World Photos, (Clinton) Wally McNamee/Corbis; p. 111 Paul Conklin/PhotoEdit; p. 112 (left) Emmanuel Faure/Getty Images, (middle) Stephen Marks/Getty Images, (right) Brooke Slezak/Getty Images; p. 113 (top to bottom) Paul Chesley/Getty Images, Steve Raymer/Corbis, Paul Barton/Corbis, Shao Xian/Photocome/ NewsCom; p. 114 Chen Shuhui/Photocome/ NewsCom; p. 116 Paul Morrell/Getty Images; p. 118 Steve Mason/Getty Images.

**The Library of Congress has cataloged the earlier edition as follows:**

Saslow, Joan M.
Summit 2 : English for today's world / Joan Saslow, Allen Ascher, with Silvia Carolina Tiberio.
    p. cm.
ISBNs: 0-13-110697-X (pbk.)
    **0-13-232012-6 (Student's Book with Take-Home Super CD-ROM)**
1. English language—Textbooks for foreign speakers.  2. English language—Rhetoric.  I. Ascher, Allen.  II. Title: Summit two.  III. Title.
PE1128.S2757 2006
428.2'4--dc22

2005032366
Printed in the United States of America
2 3 4 5 6 7 8 9 10–CRK–11 10 09 08 07

# Contents

# Scope and Sequence OF CONTENT AND SKILLS

| UNIT | Vocabulary* | Conversation Strategies | Discussion Topics | Grammar |
|---|---|---|---|---|
| **1**<br><br>**Dreams come true**<br><br>*Page 2* | • Life choices and plans<br>• Dreams and goals<br><br>**Word Skill:** using collocations with *have* for job qualifications | • Use *You know* to ease into a conversation<br>• Respond with *That's great* to convey enthusiasm or encouragement<br>• Preface a statement with *I guess* to soften an opinion<br>• Begin a response with *True, but* to present an alternate view | • A famous person you admire<br>• Dreams and plans for the future<br>• Achievements and beliefs<br>• Qualifications of job applicants<br>• A "dream job" | • The present perfect for past events related to the present<br>• The present perfect and the present perfect continuous for unfinished or continuing actions |
| **2**<br><br>**Character counts**<br><br>*Page 14* | • Taking and avoiding responsibility<br>• Expressing admiration and compassion<br>• Story-telling expressions | • Use *I hate to tell you this, but* to soften bad news<br>• Use word stress to convey meaning<br>• Begin a sentence with *Well* to allow time to think<br>• Use expressions such as *I feel terrible* to convey regret<br>• Ask *Are you sure . . . ?* to confirm information<br>• Use *That's not necessary* to decline help politely | • Proverbs from around the world<br>• The social uses of lying<br>• Helping others<br>• The purpose of a story with a moral | • Adjective clauses with *whose, where,* and *when*<br>• Relative pronoun as the object of a preposition |
| **3**<br><br>**Dealing with adversity**<br><br>*Page 26* | • Sequence words<br>• Expressing frustration and empathy<br>• Encouragement and discouragement<br><br>**Word Skill:** using parts of speech | • Use expressions such as *I give up* and *I've had it* to get a listener's attention<br>• Soften a suggestion with *Maybe*<br>• Use expressions like *I know what you mean* to encourage the listener to say more | • Dangerous or frightening experiences<br>• Giving advice and encouragement<br>• Attitudes toward adversity<br>• Heroism | • Describing the relationship of past events and actions to each other<br>• Clauses with *No matter* |
| **4**<br><br>**Personality and life**<br><br>*Page 38* | • Comparing oneself with others<br>• Problematic attitudes and behaviors<br>• Expressing and controlling anger<br><br>**Word Skill:** distinguishing meaning | • Ask a rhetorical question to grab someone's attention<br>• Provide an example or clarifying statement to support a point of view<br>• Say *Really?* to introduce a contrasting statement<br>• Use expressions such as *I'm like that myself* and *I'm just the opposite* to establish common ground | • Describing your shortcomings<br>• Managing stress<br>• Handling anger<br>• Values and priorities | • The subjunctive |
| **5**<br><br>**It's all in your mind**<br><br>*Page 50* | • Ways to express disbelief<br>• Expressions with *mind*<br><br>**Word Skill:** using participial adjectives | • Use *It says here* to share information from an article<br>• Use expressions such as *That's impossible* to invite someone to reconsider a belief<br>• Ask *Why not?* to defend a position | • Superstitious beliefs and practices<br>• Suspicious claims<br>• Fears and phobias<br>• Interpretation of dreams | • Non-count nouns made countable<br>• Indefiniteness and definiteness: article usage |

*Vocabulary presentations include individual words, phrases, and collocations.

| Grammar and Pronunciation Boosters | Listening Tasks | Readings | Writing |
|---|---|---|---|
| **Grammar Booster** • Stative verbs: non-action and action meanings | • Summarize people's future plans • Take notes • Infer speakers' attitudes | • An online magazine table of contents • A profile of Dr. Robert Ballard • A biographical article about Jane Goodall • A job advertisement • Resumés | • Write a biography **Writing Skill:** avoiding sentence fragments |
| **Pronunciation Booster** • Sentence stress and intonation: review | | | |
| **Grammar Booster** • Adjective clauses: overview • Adjective clauses with quantifiers **Grammar for Writing:** adjective clauses reduced to adjective phrases | • Evaluate people's responses • Associate speakers with specific actions • Identify speakers' concerns and courses of action | • A magazine article about why people tell lies • A traditional tale • Fables | • Describe an experience that taught you a lesson **Writing Skill:** punctuating adjective clauses |
| **Pronunciation Booster** • Emphatic stress and pitch to express emotion | | | |
| **Grammar Booster** • Describing past actions and events: review | • Rephrase advice given in response to different problems • Summarize a news report • Paraphrase people's descriptions of problems | • Quotations on dealing with adversity • A newspaper article about a rescue • A biographical article about Helen Keller • Profiles of three heroes | • Narrate past events logically **Writing Skill:** time relationships |
| **Pronunciation Booster** • Vowel reduction to /ə/ | | | |
| **Grammar Booster** • Infinitive and gerund phrases in place of the subjunctive | • Infer purpose from a description • Identify main ideas • Summarize information | • A catalogue of self-help workshops • An advice column about coping with stress • A magazine article about identifying priorities | • Provide tips for solving a problem **Writing Skill:** supporting sentences |
| **Pronunciation Booster** • Shifting emphatic stress | | | |
| **Grammar Booster** • More phrases that make non-count nouns countable • More non-count nouns with both a countable and an uncountable sense • Article usage: overview | • Focus on details • Compare differing interpretations • Summarize information • Infer point of view | • A website homepage on superstitions • "Sensationalist" ads • A magazine article about phobias | • Describe a superstition **Writing Skill:** subject-verb agreement |
| **Pronunciation Booster** • Linking sounds | | | |

# *Scope and Sequence* OF CONTENT AND SKILLS

SCOPE AND SEQUENCE

# International Advisory Board

**Reviewers and Piloters** Many thanks also to the reviewers and piloters all over the world who reviewed *Top Notch* and *Summit* in their final forms.

# To the Teacher

## What is *Summit*?

- *Summit* is a two-level high-intermediate to advanced communicative series for adults and young adults that can follow any intermediate course book.
- *Summit* is designed to follow the *Top Notch* series, forming the top two levels of a six-level course.
- Each *Summit* Student's Book is designed for 60 to 90 instructional hours with options and extensions that enable it to fulfill the needs of longer courses.

## Key Elements of the *Summit* Instructional Design

### Concise two-page lessons

Each easy-to-teach two-page lesson is designed for one class session and begins with a clearly stated communication goal and ends with free communication practice. Each lesson integrates all four skills with a focus on conversation, grammar, reading, or listening, keeping the pace of a class session lively and varied.

### Daily confirmation of progress

Adult students need to observe and confirm their own progress. In *Summit*, students conclude each class session with a culminating productive activity that demonstrates their ability to use new vocabulary, grammar, word skills, and social language in order to perform the communication goal of the lesson. This motivates students and keeps them eager to continue their study of English, and it builds their pride in being able to speak and write accurately, fluently, and authentically.

### Real language

Carefully exposing students to authentic, natural, corpus-informed English, both receptively and productively, is a necessary component of building understanding and expression. All Conversation Snapshots and Sound Bites feature the language people *really* use; nowhere to be found is "textbook English" written merely to exemplify grammar.

### Memorable model conversations

Even at the advanced levels, learners need models of social language plus strategies they can use conversationally. The full range of social and functional communicative needs as well as a wealth of conversation strategies are presented through practical model conversations that are intensively practiced and applied to the learner's own life experience. Rhythm and intonation practice and an optional Pronunciation Booster provide targeted practice to ensure clear expression.

### High-impact vocabulary syllabus

In order to ensure students' solid acquisition of vocabulary essential for communication, *Summit* contains explicit presentation and practice of words, collocations, and expressions appropriate at each level of study. A focus on word skills, such as using parts of speech and participial adjectives, builds students' ability to cope with and expand on new vocabulary. Meaning is conveyed in a variety of ways: through captioned photographs and illustrations, within the context of realia and readings, in definitions and contextualized sentences, and in authentic dictionary entries from the *Longman Advanced American Dictionary*. These presentations provide a permanent in-book reference that builds learner independence and helps students prepare for tests.

### Learner-supportive grammar

Grammar is approached explicitly and cognitively, through form, meaning, and use, in the following places in *Summit*: in every Student's Book unit, in the bound-in Grammar Booster, in the *Summit* Workbook, in the optional worksheets provided on the Teacher's Resource Disk (found in the Teacher's Edition and Lesson Planner), and on the *Summit* companion website. Grammar charts provide examples and paradigms enhanced by simple usage notes at students' level of comprehension. This takes the guesswork out of meaning, makes lesson preparation easier for teachers, and provides students with comprehensible charts for permanent reference and test preparation. All presentations of grammar, both in the Student's Book and in the Grammar Booster, include exercises to ensure adequate practice.

## Detailed writing syllabus

The *Summit* Student's Book contains a writing syllabus that includes rigorous practice and clear models of important rhetorical and mechanical writing skills, such as supporting sentences, comparison and contrast, and punctuation. Each lesson provides practice in the writing process, from prewriting to revision.

## Unique discussion syllabus

All students want and need to participate in real discussions. *Summit* systematically goes beyond conversation model practice through unique step-by-step Discussion Builders that enable students to prepare for successful discourse. This preparation results in increased accuracy, increased fluency, greater complexity of expression, richer use of vocabulary, and much less fossilization. The Teacher's Resource Disk offers further optional practice with Discourse Strategies to ensure successful communication.

## Components of *Summit 2*

### Student's Book with Take-Home Super CD-ROM

The Student's Book contains a bound-in Grammar Booster, a bound-in Pronunciation Booster, and a Take-Home Super CD-ROM. The Super CD-ROM provides a variety of exciting interactive activities, including speaking practice, listening comprehension, reading comprehension, an interactive workbook, and games and puzzles. The disk can also be played on an audio CD player to listen to the conversation models and for intensive pronunciation practice.

### Teacher's Edition and Lesson Planner

The Teacher's Edition and Lesson Planner offers complete lesson plans for each class session. Suggested teaching times are included for each activity to take the guesswork out of planning. Bound into each Teacher's Edition and Lesson Planner is a free Teacher's Resource Disk with the following optional printable activities to personalize your teaching style:

- Vocabulary-Building Strategies
- Discourse Strategies
- Listening Strategies
- Reading Strategies
- Grammar Self-Checks
- Conversation Prompts
- Extra Writing Skills Practice
- Pronunciation Activities

- A Reading Speed Calculator
- Extra Reading Comprehension Activities
- Graphic Organizers

## Complete Class Audio Program

The Class Audio Program contains listening comprehension activities, rhythm and intonation practice, and targeted pronunciation activities that focus on accurate and comprehensible pronunciation.

Because *Summit* is a course for international communication, a variety of native *and* non-native speakers are included to prepare students for the world outside the classroom.

## Workbook

The tightly linked, illustrated Workbook contains exercises that provide additional practice and reinforcement of language concepts and skills from *Summit* and its Grammar Booster.

## Complete Assessment Package with Exam*View*® Software

Ten easy-to-administer and simple-to-score unit achievement tests assess listening, vocabulary, grammar, social language, reading, and writing. Two review tests, one mid-book and one end-of-book, provide additional cumulative assessment. A speaking test and a writing test are included with each review. In addition to the photocopiable achievement tests, Exam*View*® software enables teachers to tailor-make tests to best meet their needs by combining items any way they wish.

## *Summit TV*

An engrossing and informative video offers excerpts from authentic TV documentaries as well as unrehearsed on-the-street interviews with English speakers from around the world. Both the documentaries and the interviews are thematically tied to the *Summit* units in order to initiate and promote classroom discussion.

## *Summit* Companion Website

The *Summit* Companion Website www.longman.com/summit provides numerous additional resources for students and teachers. This no-cost, high-benefit feature includes opportunities for further practice of language and content from the *Summit* Student's Book.

# *Welcome to Summit!*

# About the Authors

**JOAN SASLOW** is author of a number of textbook series for adults and young adults, including *Ready to Go: Language, Lifeskills, and Civics*, a four-level adult ESL series; *Workplace Plus: Living and Working in English*, a vocational English series; *Literacy Plus*, a two-level series that teaches literacy, English, and culture to adult pre-literate students; and *English in Context: Reading Comprehension for Science and Technology*, a three-level series for English for special purposes.

Ms. Saslow is co-author, with Allen Ascher, of *Top Notch: English for Today's World*. She was the Series Director of *True Colors: An EFL Course for Real Communication* and of *True Voices*, a five-level EFL video course. Ms. Saslow's special interest is in distinguishing the needs of the EFL and the ESL learner and creating materials appropriate for each.

Ms. Saslow has taught in Chile and the United States in a variety of programs. In Chile, she taught English and French at the Binational Centers of Valparaíso and Viña del Mar, and at the Catholic University of Valparaíso. In the United States, Ms. Saslow taught English as a Foreign Language to Japanese university students at Marymount College's intensive English program as well as workplace English at the General Motors auto assembly plant, both in Tarrytown, New York. Ms. Saslow is also an editor, a teacher-trainer, a language learner, and a frequent speaker at gatherings of English teachers throughout the world. Ms. Saslow has an M.A. in French from the University of Wisconsin.

**ALLEN ASCHER**, formerly Director of the International English Institute at Hunter College in New York, has been a teacher, a teacher-trainer, an author, and a publisher. He has taught in language and teacher-training programs in both China and the United States. Mr. Ascher specialized in teaching listening and speaking to students at the Beijing Second Foreign Language Institute, to hotel workers at a major international hotel in China, and to Japanese students from Chubu University studying English at Ohio University in the United States. In New York, Mr. Ascher taught students of all language backgrounds and abilities at the City University of New York, and he trained teachers in the TESOL Certificate Program at the New School. Mr. Ascher has an M.A. in Applied Linguistics from Ohio University.

Mr. Ascher is co-author, with Joan Saslow, of *Top Notch: English for Today's World*. He is author of *Think About Editing: A Grammar Editing Guide for ESL Writers*. As a publisher, Mr. Ascher played a key role in the creation of some of the most widely used materials for adults, including *True Colors, NorthStar, Focus on Grammar, Global Links*, and *Ready to Go*. Mr. Ascher has provided lively workshops for teachers throughout the United States, Asia, Latin America, Europe, and the Middle East.

**SILVIA CAROLINA TIBERIO** has taught English as a Foreign Language at all levels to adults, young adults, and children for twenty years. She was a co-director of Wayland School of English in the province of Buenos Aires, Argentina. Ms. Tiberio taught English at Wayland for over ten years, specializing in training students for the Cambridge First Certificate and TOEFL examinations. She has also led numerous teacher-training workshops and seminars.

Ms. Tiberio has written teacher's manuals for *Top Notch 3* and *Summit 1* as well as for the *Worldview* and *Focus on Grammar* series. She is the co-author of a number of widely used series for young adults and children and of a variety of online English language-learning materials.

# Dreams come true

**A**   **Topic Preview.** Look at the Online Edition of *Global Voyager Magazine.* What types of articles would you expect to find on this website?

http://www.globalvoyager.com

## Global Voyager Magazine

ONLINE EDITION     Contact us  |  Shop  |  Subscribe

▶ **Archives**
Back issues of
the Online Edition

▶ **Features List**
Table of contents for
this month's stories

▶ **Final Cut**
Outtakes of photos
that didn't make it

▶ **Blasts from the Past**
Prize-winning photos
from the archives

▶ **Forum**
Readers' opinions

▶ **Voyager Hot Picks**
The editors' must-sees

▶ **Resources**
Links for this month's features

▶ **Our Advertisers**
The best of the best

**Dr. Robert Ballard**—the man who discovered the *Titanic.* Learn how he turns sunken ships into underwater museums.

**Primatologist and ethologist Jane Goodall.** Insights into her life, her work, and her dreams.

**This Month's Features**
Mysteries of the Underwater World

Among the Hmong

The Ancient Fertile Crescent

Pirate Ships of the Future

Airline Food: Ups and Downs

Working in Patagonia

**Exotic Jobs**
Tour guide Gonzalo Tejeda shares breathtaking photos and scenes of matchless beauty. Download spectacular wallpaper images of Tejeda's "outdoor office."

**Monthly Photo Contest**

Register to enter

The emperor penguin

**Photo Gallery**
Experience a penguin parent-and-chick family reunion through the lens of wildlife photographer Frans Lanting.

Sylvia Earle

**Online Explorer**
Explore the Gulf of Mexico seascape in a mini-submarine with the marine biologist *Time Magazine* named its first "hero for the planet."

**B**   **Discussion.** What would you click on first? Why? What does your choice "say" about you?

**C** 🎧 **Sound Bites.** Read and listen to a conversation between two friends about a career change.

**MAX:** Well, I gave notice at the bank. In two weeks, I'll be working as a full-time photographer.

**SAM:** Way to go! You've been talking about doing that for years! What made you finally take the plunge?

**MAX:** Frans Lanting, believe it or not.

**SAM:** You mean the guy that took those penguin pictures on your wall?

**MAX:** Right. I read that in order to get those shots he camped out on the ice in Antarctica for a month.

**SAM:** Wow! You know, I could really see you doing that.

**MAX:** So could I. After seeing those photos, I realized I didn't want to spend the rest of my life in a bank. I want to get out and see the world.

**King penguins in Antarctica**
*F. Lanting*

**D** **In Other Words.** Read the conversation again. Then say each of these statements another way.

1. "I gave notice at the bank."
2. "Way to go!"
3. "What made you finally take the plunge?"
4. "You know, I could really see you doing that."

**Zebras in the wild**
*F. Lanting*

---

## STARTING **POINT**

**Pair Work.** Think of a famous person you admire. Tell your partner why you admire that person.

Wangari Maathai

*"Have you heard of Wangari Maathai? She won the Nobel Peace Prize in 2004. I really admire her. She's spent her whole life working to protect the environment. I read she helped plant more than 10 million trees in Kenya."*

Charles Wang

*"One person I really respect is Charles Wang, the guy who founded Computer Associates. He ran this hugely successful software company, and he's given a lot of money to help sick kids."*

# 1 Explain life choices and plans

CONVERSATION

## A ∩ CONVERSATION **SNAPSHOT**

**A:** You know, I've always wanted to take up fashion design.

**B:** That's great. What's stopping you?

**A:** Well, I guess big changes are a little scary.

**B:** True, but life's short. Go for it!

∩ **Rhythm and intonation practice**

**PAGES P2–P3**
Sentence stress
and intonation

## B ∩ Vocabulary. Expressions to describe life choices and plans. Listen and practice.

**take up** something you're interested in
*Joe was so inspired by the Frans Lanting exhibit that he decided to take up wildlife photography.*

**decide on** a course of study or a career
*She decided on a career as a veterinarian because she is interested in medicine and loves animals.*

**apply for** a position or an opportunity to study
*He wants to work in the field of conservation, so he applied for a job at the Forest and Wildlife Center.*

**be accepted to / into** a school or a program
*When Ann heard she was accepted to medical school, she called all her friends.*

**be rejected by** a program or a school
*It was very difficult for Dan to hide his disappointment when he was rejected by the law school.*

**sign up for** a course or an activity
*Over a hundred people signed up for that course because the teacher has such a great reputation.*

**enroll in** a school, organization, or program
*Matt plans to enroll in flight school to fulfill his dream of becoming a pilot.*

**switch to** a new course of study or career
*People who are unhappy in their career often switch to a completely different field.*

## C ∩ Listening Comprehension. Listen to the conversations. Then listen again. After each conversation, summarize the person's situation by completing each sentence with the vocabulary. Use each expression only once.

**1.** She has _____ engineering school.

**2.** She has _____ a career in music.

**3.** He has _____ meditation.

**4.** She has _____ two graduate programs.

**5.** He has _____ teaching.

**6.** She has _____ a position in a medical lab.

## D Grammar. The present perfect for past events related to the present

Although the present perfect expresses a past event or state, it is used to convey information that has relevance to the present.

I love animals and the outdoors, so **I've decided** to become a naturalist.

The following adverbs and expressions are often used with the present perfect: <u>ever</u>, <u>never</u>, <u>already</u>, <u>yet</u>, <u>so far</u>, <u>still</u> (with the negative), <u>once</u>, <u>twice</u>, <u>(three) times</u>.

Have you **ever** thought about a career in law?
We've **never** considered that course of action.
She's **already** decided on a career in business.
I **still** haven't made up my mind about what I'll do after school.
He's been rejected by medical school **three times**.

The adverbs **just**, <u>recently</u>, and <u>lately</u> describe past events that have occurred in recent time.

She's **just** been accepted to a top business school.
They've **recently** made plans to get married.
Have you made any progress with your job search **lately**?

**NOTE:** The adverb <u>lately</u> is rarely used in affirmative statements in the present perfect.

### REMEMBER

Use the simple past, not the present perfect, to talk about a specific time in the past.

She applied for the position at the Science Institute last week.

**NOT** She ~~has applied~~ for the position at the Science Institute last week.

## E Pair Work. Write questions that you could ask someone about his or her life plans and choices, using the vocabulary in Exercise B and the present perfect.

### IDEAS

educational training
career
personal growth
marriage and family
change of studies
change of job or career

**Example:** *Have you decided on a career yet?*

1. ................................................................
2. ................................................................
3. ................................................................
4. ................................................................
5. ................................................................
6. ................................................................

## CONVERSATION **STARTER** • *Now explain your life choices and plans.*

On your notepad, answer the questions you wrote in Exercise E with true information about yourself.

**Pair Work.** Explain your plans for the future to each other. Use the Conversation Snapshot on page 4 as a guide. Start like this: "I've always wanted to ..."

Your life choices and plans

1.

2.

3.

4.

5.

6.

5

# 2 *Describe a person's continuing activities*

**A** ⌖ GRAMMAR **SNAPSHOT.** Read the article and notice the use of the present perfect continuous.

# Dr. Robert Ballard
## DISCOVERER OF THE *TITANIC*

Scientist, historian, and adventurer Dr. Robert Ballard has in his professional life participated in over 100 deep-sea missions and spent innumerable hours exploring deep ocean waters. His expeditions have led to the discovery of a wide variety of shipwrecks ranging from ancient Roman ships to the *Titanic*; the latter has rested at a depth of 4,000 meters in the icy North Atlantic since hitting an iceberg and sinking in 1912.

Dr. Ballard, who **has been searching** for shipwrecks for over 30 years, has said that "there's probably more history preserved underwater than in all the museums in the world combined." However, he has rejected the pleas of those who would like him to remove artifacts from shipwrecks so others can study them. His respect for the people who perished has caused Ballard to take a stand against disturbing the wrecks, which he has come to see as monuments to the dead. So that we may observe these monuments, Ballard has designed a high-tech robot equipped with cameras to photograph their interiors.

The 1985 discovery of the *Titanic* made Ballard an instant celebrity and has generated thousands of letters from students of all ages. Ballard has been involved in educational projects since then and **has been giving** speeches, **writing** books, and **working** on educational TV programs shown widely across the world.

*A high-tech robot designed by Dr. Ballard photographs the* Titanic, *which sank after a catastrophic collision in 1912 with an iceberg.*

Information sources: www.pbs.org and www.lordly.com

**B** **Grammar. The present perfect and the present perfect continuous for unfinished or continuing actions**

**REMEMBER**
The present perfect is also used for finished actions.

Use either the present perfect or the present perfect continuous to describe unfinished or continuing actions. Speakers often choose the present perfect continuous instead of the present perfect when they want to suggest that the action will continue. Note that this is not a sharp distinction or rule.

Ballard **has searched** for shipwrecks for many years.
(The speaker is not necessarily suggesting that Ballard will continue to search.)

He **has been searching** for shipwrecks for many years.
(The speaker may be suggesting that Ballard will continue to search.)

**BE CAREFUL!** Certain stative (non-action) verbs are not used in the present perfect continuous: be, believe, hate, have (for possession), know, like, love, own, seem, understand.
I've known about his research for many years.
NOT I've been knowing about his research for many years.

Grammar Booster

PAGE G1
For more …

**C** Complete the following biographical notes about people who have had an impact on the world. Use the present perfect continuous for unfinished actions, except with the stative verbs that are not used in the continuous. Use the present perfect for finished actions.

**❶ Sylvia Earle** .................... (study) the plant and animal life of the world's oceans for close to forty years. She .................... (be) fascinated by the ocean ever since she moved to the Gulf of Mexico as a young girl. For more than twenty years, she .................... (design) equipment for exploring the ocean floor.

**❷** For many years **Madan Kataria** .................... (understand) that laughter can have health benefits. Since 1995, when he started the Laughter Club of India, he .................... (teach) "laughter yoga," a technique for making people laugh in order to improve their health.

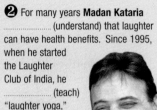

**❸** Ever since her childhood, when she accompanied her physician mother into remote areas of Venezuela and Colombia, **Magdalena Hurtado** .................... (have) a great curiosity about different cultures. For many years now, she and her husband, anthropologist Kim Hill, .................... (educate) people about the influence of biology and ecology on human life.

**❹ Millard and Linda Fuller** created Habitat for Humanity, a worldwide organization that for almost thirty years .................... (help) people build houses for themselves. Since its founding in 1976, Habitat for Humanity .................... (build) more than 175,000 houses around the world.

**❽ Chiaki Mukai**, a medical doctor as well as Japan's first female astronaut, .................... (participate) in space flights since 1994. John Glenn, the famous U.S. astronaut, and many others .................... (express) admiration for her achievements.

**❺ Wangari Maathai**, who won the Nobel Peace Prize in 2004, .................... (plant) trees in Kenya for nearly thirty years. Since she was a young woman, she .................... (believe) that the environment should be the number one priority in her life.

**❻** For a long time **Zahi Hawass**, an Egyptian archeologist, .................... (know) that many great monuments still lie buried beneath the ground. Dr. Hawass .................... (make) many important discoveries that .................... (contribute) significantly to our knowledge of ancient Egypt. Since 1987 he .................... (work) on conserving and restoring the Pyramids.

**❼** For many years **Charles Wang**, the successful businessman who founded Computer Associates, .................... (believe) that people with means should help others in need. He .................... (donate) money to worthy causes for many years.

## GRAMMAR **EXCHANGE** • *Now describe someone's continuing activities.*

Complete the questionnaire about your life, achievements, and beliefs.

Strongest-held belief about life *I believe if people communicated better, the world would be a better place.*

Name .................... Address ....................
How long have you lived there? .................... Where did you live before? ....................
Educational history ....................
Highest degree or grade completed ....................
Marital status .................... If married, when were you married? ....................
Travel history ....................
Awards or prizes ....................
Strongest-held belief about life ....................
When did you develop that belief? ....................

**Pair Work.** Get to know your partner. Use the questionnaire as a guide to ask questions. Use appropriate verb forms.

*"Have you traveled outside of the country anytime in the last year?"*

**Project.** Write a one-page biography of your partner, using the information from your pair work. Either make a scrapbook of all your classmates or post the biographies on a bulletin board. Include pictures if you can.

## 3 Share your dreams and goals in life

A **Reading Warm-up.** Have you ever heard of Jane Goodall? What do you know about her work?

B ⌂ **Reading.** Read the biography of Jane Goodall. What were her goals?

# JANE GOODALL

Born in London on April 3, 1934, world-renowned primatologist Jane Goodall got an early start on animal study, spending much of her childhood observing animals that lived right in the backyard of her house. Later, Kipling's *Jungle Book* and the Tarzan stories fascinated her as well, and those, coupled with her love for animals, led her to plan a life in the African jungle. When she finally ventured into Africa at the age of 23, Goodall was fulfilling her childhood dream.

Goodall worked as a secretary for a year in Kenya until, having learned that anthropologist Louis Leakey was doing research in Zaire, she made a trip to meet him. Leakey had been searching for someone to carry out a field study on chimpanzees at the Gombe National Reserve in Tanzania and decided Goodall would be ideal for the project because her lack of formal training would prevent prior knowledge from interfering with her observations and conclusions. Leakey told her the research might take ten years; she thought it might take just three. They were both mistaken. Goodall has been researching chimps at Gombe for over 40 years now.

Progress in the first months at Gombe was slow and discouraging, as the chimps would not let Goodall approach. Complicating matters, Goodall spent weeks in bed, sick with malaria. But one day Goodall observed a chimp in the camp looking at a banana on the table inside a tent. This was Goodall's first chance to get close to a chimp, and from that day on, bananas were always kept nearby for

any curious visitors. Patience enabled Goodall to win the chimps' trust and gradually make friends with them.

In a lifetime of study, Goodall has discovered many interesting and formerly unknown similarities between chimps and humans. Among those discoveries: chimps are not herbivorous—they also eat meat, just like humans; chimps make and use tools; they adopt orphan infants; they know and use medicinal plants (by chewing).

Today Goodall divides her time between traveling and lecturing about her findings at Gombe and running the Gombe Stream Research Center, where she has been the director since 1967. She has also established a home for injured or orphaned chimps and created a program for schoolchildren to learn about wild animals and conservation of the environment.

Information source: *Jane Goodall*, by Adrian G. Weiss

C Complete the chart, based on information in the biography.

| Difficulties at Gombe | Discoveries at Gombe | Other achievements |
|---|---|---|
| | Chimps eat meat. | |

D **Discussion.** What steps did Jane Goodall take to fulfill her dreams? Based on the information in the biography, what do you think were some of the goals Goodall set for herself?

**E** 🎧 **Vocabulary. Dreams and goals.**
Listen and practice.

> **childhood / lifelong dream**
> *Living in the jungles of Africa had been her childhood dream.*
>
> **fulfill / realize a dream**
> *She finally fulfilled her dream of setting up a home for injured or orphaned chimpanzees.*
>
> **short-term / long-term goal**
> *Her short-term goal was to get to Africa. Her long-term goal was to have an impact on science.*
>
> **set goals for oneself**
> *When she heard that Leakey was in Zaire, she set a goal for herself to meet him.*
>
> **take steps to achieve / reach a goal**
> *It was clear that she needed to take some difficult steps to reach her goal.*

**F** Use the vocabulary to complete the paragraph about Jane Goodall's dreams and goals. In some cases, more than one word is possible.

> Jane's Goodall's _____ dream was to live
> (1)
> in Africa. She _____ this dream when she
> (2)
> was only in her twenties. She was able to do
> this because she _____ goals for herself at the
> (3)
> beginning of her research. When she started
> her field study, her _____ goal was to win
> (4)
> the chimps' trust, and her _____ goal was
> (5)
> to discover new similarities between chimps
> and humans. It was not easy for Goodall to
> _____ her goals, but she was able to do so
> (6)
> because she _____ all the necessary steps.
> (7)

## DISCUSSION **BUILDER** • *Now share your dreams and goals in life.*

**Step 1.** Complete the chart. Use the pictures for ideas.

|  | Goal or dream | Steps taken to achieve it |
|---|---|---|
| **a short-term goal** |  |  |
| **a long-term goal** |  |  |
| **a lifelong dream** |  |  |

**Step 2. Pair Work.** Share the information in your chart with a partner.

**Step 3. Discussion.** Tell the class about your partner's dreams and goals.
Your classmates ask questions to find out more.

# 4 Discuss job qualifications and work experience

**A** 🎧 **Word Skills.** Using collocations with <u>have</u> for job qualifications

> **have experience** doing something
> **have experience with** equipment, a process
> **have experience in** a field
> **have training in** a field
> **have the ability to** do something
> **have knowledge of** a skill, a field

*"Tell me something about your experience."*

*"I've had some training in IT\* and a fair amount of experience managing technical staff."*

\*IT = information technology

**B** **What About You?** Read the ad and explain why you would or wouldn't apply for this job. Use the collocations with <u>have</u>.

> *"I wouldn't apply for this job because I've had no experience planning large events."*

## ASSISTANT CRUISE DIRECTOR

***Have you ever dreamed of seeing the world?*** Here's your opportunity to get paid to do it! One-World Vacation Lines has a number of openings for Assistant Cruise Directors, responsible for all shipboard entertainment. Interested candidates will have experience in the travel or hotel industry and will have the ability to arrange parties, games, and other events for large groups of people. You should love being around people from different cultures. Experience planning recreational activities a plus. Knowledge of languages desirable but not necessary.

**C** 🎧 **Listening Comprehension.** Listen to the job interview with Marcos Ferrante. Then listen again and take notes about his qualifications for the job.

> Experience:
>
> Abilities:
>
>
> Training:
> Goals:

**D** **Discussion.** Do you think Ferrante is a good candidate for the job? Why or why not?

**E** **Pair Work.** Look at the resumés of the two candidates for the assistant cruise director job. Discuss their qualifications. Who is better qualified for the job? Use the collocations with <u>have</u>.

Ivan Urban
Václavské nám. 32
11 525, Praha 1
Czech Republic

| | |
|---|---|
| *Goal:* | Seeking a position in the travel business in which I can use my knowledge of languages and ability to motivate people. |
| *Experience:* | |
| *Sept 05–present:* | East Euro Airlines (Prague, Czech Republic): Customer Service Representative Handle customer inquiries about flight schedules. Book flights and assist customers with other travel arrangements. |
| *June–Aug 05:* | Camp Friendship (Quebec, Canada): Assistant Director of international summer camp for teens. Organized daily activities and weekly trips. |
| *Languages:* | Fluent in Czech, English, German; some Spanish and Japanese. |
| *Special Training:* | Lifesaving procedures |

Alice Shanker
28 Lancer Street
Winter Park, FL 32793 USA

GOAL: To use my ability to work with people from different cultures and gain experience in the tourism industry.

EXPERIENCE:

(Feb 05–present) *Front Desk Clerk, Beachfront Hotel and Resort, Miami Beach, Florida.* Check in hotel guests and assist them during their stay.

(Jan 04–Jan 05) *Executive Assistant, International Print Associates, Miami, Florida.* Organized conferences, sales meetings, and customer events worldwide. Helped solve customers' problems.

## DISCUSSION **BUILDER** • *Now discuss your qualifications for your dream job.*

**Step 1.** On your notepad, write notes to describe the details of your dream job.

Position:
Type of employer:
Responsibilities:
Qualifications you might need:
Qualifications you already have:
Desired salary:
Other:

**Ways to become qualified**
**get** (some) **experience** (doing something)
**get training in** (something)
**learn how to** (do something)
**get a degree / certificate in** (something)
**get certified in** (something)

**Step 2. Discussion.** Take turns describing your dream jobs. Encourage each other by suggesting steps you can take to become qualified for those jobs.

"You may want to get some experience writing articles for your school newspaper."

"It seems like you might need to get a certificate in nursing first."

"I'd suggest you let them know you have the ability to build websites."

# Writing: Write a biography

## Avoiding sentence fragments

A **clause** is a group of words that has a subject and a verb. There are two types of clauses: independent and dependent.

An **independent clause** expresses a complete thought and can stand alone as a sentence. Two or more independent clauses can be joined together with coordinating conjunctions or semicolons.

> Isabel Carter has painted many portraits, **and** people admire her work very much.
>
> Isabel Carter has painted many portraits; people admire her work very much.

A **dependent clause** doesn't express a complete thought and cannot stand alone as a sentence. Subordinating conjunctions or relative pronouns introduce dependent clauses. A dependent clause alone is one kind of **sentence fragment**.

> FRAGMENT: ~~Although Isabel Carter has painted many portraits.~~
>
> FRAGMENT: ~~Who has painted a lot of portraits.~~

**Coordinating Conjunctions**

| | |
|---|---|
| and | for |
| but | so |
| or | yet |
| nor | |

**Relative Pronouns**

who
which
that

**Subordinating Conjunctions**

because
although
even though
if

### ERROR CORRECTION

Find and correct five sentence fragments.

### An Artist in Our Community

Isabel Carter is a talented portrait painter. Who is much admired in our community. Although she is quite young. She has already achieved a great deal. Her portraits, which have been exhibited in local galleries and art shows, use bold strokes of color to express character and mood. Everyone in our community is familiar with Ms. Carter's portraits. Because many of them depict people we all know. Her vision and technique make you see a person you thought you knew in a completely different way, which is quite remarkable. Ms. Carter has painted many beautiful portraits of people. Whom she has encountered around the world, and they are as fascinating to us as the portraits of people we know. If she can get financial support. She will study painting in Italy next year.

To make this kind of sentence fragment into a complete sentence, attach it to an independent clause. Use a comma if the dependent clause comes first.

> Although Isabel Carter has painted many portraits, she hasn't yet sold any.
>
> Isabel Carter hasn't yet sold any paintings, although she has painted many portraits.
>
> Isabel Carter is an artist who has painted a lot of portraits.

**Step 1. Prewriting. Clustering ideas.** Look at the idea cluster. On a separate sheet of paper, create your own idea cluster about a living person you admire. Write ideas in circles and expand each new idea. Include jobs, achievements, hobbies, places traveled to, interests, etc.

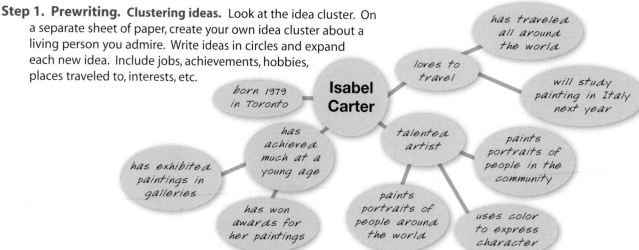

**Step 2. Writing.** On a separate sheet of paper, write a biography of the person you chose, using your ideas.

**Step 3. Self-Check.**

☐ Did you write any sentence fragments? If so, correct them.

☐ Did you use correct verb forms?

# UNIT 1 CHECKPOINT

SUMMIT WEBSITE
For Unit 1 online activities, visit the *Summit* Companion Website at www.longman.com/summit.

**A** 🎧 **Listening Comprehension.** Listen to the conversations. Then read the questions in the chart and listen again. Complete the chart after each conversation.

| | What is the speaker's dream or goal in life? | Is the speaker confident about achieving his / her dream or goal? | |
|---|---|---|---|
| 1 | | ☐ yes | ☐ no |
| 2 | | ☐ yes | ☐ no |
| 3 | | ☐ yes | ☐ no |
| 4 | | ☐ yes | ☐ no |

**B** Complete the sentences with the correct prepositions from the box.

1. She has always wanted to take _____ the piano and has enrolled _____ a program that teaches the basics of music.

2. Anyone applying _____ a job in the newspaper business should have training _____ journalism.

3. He has decided _____ a career as a chef and has been accepted _____ a world-renowned cooking school in France.

4. Her experience _____ the diplomatic service and her knowledge _____ international law make her an excellent candidate for the position at the UN.

5. People who switch _____ a different line of work in mid-career must be prepared to start at the bottom.

6. The ability _____ solve problems is a valuable skill in all professions.

7. There is almost no field in which experience _____ computers is not important.

> for
> in
> of
> on
> to
> up
> with

**C** Complete the biographical notes about people who have had an impact on the world. Use the present perfect continuous for unfinished actions, except with the stative verbs that are not used in the continuous. Use the present perfect for finished actions.

1. Robert Ballard's achievements as a deep-sea explorer and inventor are impressive. He _____ (publish) over 50 scientific articles and _____ (receive) more than 30 awards. He _____ (design) a robot that can enter sunken ships and photograph them. Ballard _____ (always believe) that more history is preserved underwater than in museums.

2. Frans Lanting _____ (document) wildlife from the Amazon to Antarctica for more than two decades. His photographs _____ (dazzle) people for just as long, and he _____ (be) an inspiration for nature photographers and environmentalists all over the world. Lanting _____ (have) a deep love of the natural world ever since he was a child.

3. Arundhati Roy _____ (win) worldwide acclaim and literary prizes for her novel, *The God of Small Things*. Since its publication, however, she _____ (devote) her energies to political writing on a number of global issues. For example, she _____ (speak) at various events worldwide, such as at protests against nuclear weapons tests and against large hydroelectric dam projects.

# UNIT 2

## Character counts

**A** **Topic Preview.** Look at the proverbs and try to explain what each one means. Do you know any similar proverbs in your own language? Can you translate those proverbs into English?

1. A sleeping cat will not catch a rat. (India)

2. Write injuries in sand, kindnesses in marble. (France)

3. Because we focused on the snake, we missed the scorpion. (Egypt)

4. Tell the truth—and run. (Serbia)

5. People who live in glass houses shouldn't throw stones. (Germany)

**B** **Pair Work.** Classify the proverbs according to their themes.

| Themes | Proverb Number |
|---|---|
| Being honest | |
| Being lazy | |
| Criticizing others for faults we also have | |
| Paying too much attention to one thing while neglecting another | |
| Being mindful of the lasting effects of praise and criticism | |

**C** **Discussion.** Which proverbs do you like best? Why?

**D** 🎧 **Sound Bites.** Read and listen to a conversation between two colleagues about the difficulty of saying no.

**SANDY:** Why are you doing all that xeroxing? Isn't that procedures memo due today?

**FRANK:** Yeah, but Chris is in a real bind, and he asked me to help him out. I guess I have a hard time saying no.

**SANDY:** You really are a pushover, you know.

**FRANK:** But Chris helped me out last week. I figure I owe him one.

**SANDY:** I suppose. But don't go overboard. If you don't get that memo in on time, you're going to be in hot water.

**E** **In Other Words.** Read the conversation again. Then say each of these statements another way.

1. "Chris is in a real bind."
2. "You really are a pushover."
3. "I figure I owe him one."
4. "Don't go overboard."
5. "You're going to be in hot water."

**F** **Discussion.** Do you ever find it difficult to say no? Explain the situations in which you have this difficulty.

## STARTING **POINT**

**Pair Work.** Tell your partner about some favors others have asked you to do. How easy is it for you to ask others for favors? Are you a pushover?

### Some favors people ask for

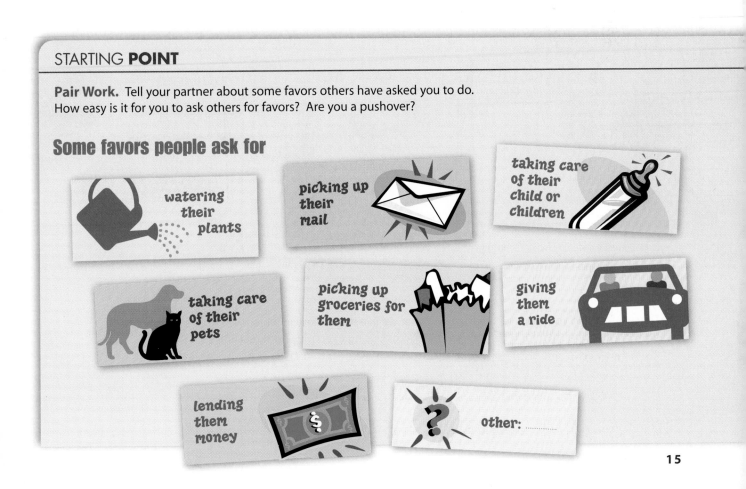

watering their plants

picking up their mail

taking care of their child or children

taking care of their pets

picking up groceries for them

giving them a ride

lending them money

other: _____

# 1 *Discuss the social uses of lying*

**A**  🎧 GRAMMAR **SNAPSHOT.** Read the article. Notice how adjective clauses are introduced.

## To Tell the Truth

Lying is part of everyday life, says psychologist Bella DePaulo, **who** carried out a study **in which** 147 people were asked to keep a diary of the lies they told over the course of a week. Here is what their diaries revealed:

- There wasn't a day **when** the participants didn't tell at least one lie.
- Over the week they deceived about 30 percent of the people **with whom** they interacted.

The most common lies **that** people tell are those **in which** they pretend to like something to avoid hurting others or those **in which** they make up excuses to get out of trouble.

According to psychologist Leonard Saxe, we live in a world **where** we are often rewarded for lying and punished for telling the truth. "If we admit we just overslept, we're punished much more than if we lie and say we were stuck in traffic."

Professor Jerald Jellison of the University of Southern California did an experiment. He proved that the people **whose** professions require the most social contacts—for example, shop assistants, salespeople, politicians, and journalists—tell the most lies.

The truth is, we *all* tell lies. Occasionally, one of the participants in Dr. De Paulo's study would insist that he or she could be entirely truthful for three or four weeks. None of them ever succeeded.

Information source: www.psychologytoday.com

**B**  **Pair Work.** Discuss and then make a list of times in your life when you . . .

told a lie to avoid hurting someone else's feelings.

told a lie to make an excuse.

were punished after telling the truth.

**C**  **Discussion.** Do you agree with Saxe's view that we live in a society in which we are often rewarded for lying and punished for telling the truth? Explain, using examples from real life if possible.

## D Grammar. Adjective clauses

<u>Whose</u>, <u>where</u>, and <u>when</u> introduce adjective clauses about possession, location, and time.

> People **whose jobs require frequent social contact** have the most opportunity to lie. (possession)
> There's no place in the world **where people are completely honest all the time**. (location)
> There has never been a time **when some form of lying wasn't a part of everyday life**. (time)

In formal English, when a relative pronoun is the object of a preposition, the preposition appears at the beginning of the clause. In informal English, the preposition usually appears at the end.

> FORMAL:   The participants in the study deceived many of the people **with whom** they interacted.
> INFORMAL: The participants in the study deceived many of the people **who** (or **that**) they interacted **with**.
>
> FORMAL:   Money is a subject **about which** people are rarely honest.
> INFORMAL: Money is a subject **which** (or **that**) people are rarely honest **about**.
>
> FORMAL:   The researcher **from whom** we received the survey is studying attitudes about lying.
> INFORMAL: The researcher **who** (or **whom**) we received the survey **from** is studying attitudes about lying.
>
> FORMAL:   Most people save their biggest lies for the person **to whom** they are closest.
> INFORMAL: Most people save their biggest lies for the person **who** (or **whom**) they are closest **to**.

**BE CAREFUL!** Use <u>whom</u>, not <u>who</u>, directly after a preposition. Use <u>which</u>, not <u>that</u>, after a preposition.

**Grammar Booster**

**PAGES G2–G4**
For more …

---

## E Complete the sentences with one of the words from the box.

| | |
|---|---|
| who | whom |
| which | whose |
| where | when |

1. The workplace is the place ............. people tend to tell the most lies.

2. The people ............. lies are discovered lose the trust of those they work with.

3. The people with ............. I work are trustworthy.

4. People ............. break their promises cannot be trusted.

5. There are situations in ............. it's impossible to tell the truth.

6. There are times ............. being honest can cause you problems.

7. The people to ............. I never lie are the people ............. are really close to me.

8. There are times ............. I lie to avoid getting into trouble and times ............. I lie to avoid hurting others.

9. Telling the truth is an action for ............. there is sometimes no reward.

10. The people ............. lies were recorded said they would tell about 75 percent of the lies again.

---

## GRAMMAR **EXCHANGE** • *Now discuss the social uses of lying.*

Write examples for each category.

| Situations in which we shouldn't tell lies | Situations in which lying is the best solution | People to whom I'd never lie |
|---|---|---|
| | | |
| | | |
| | | |
| | | |

**Discussion.** Do you think it's possible to be entirely truthful all the time? Do you think it would be desirable? Compare your views.

**Writing.** Write three paragraphs about lying, with each paragraph based on one of the categories above. Use the examples from your notepad and the discussion for support. Use the formal forms with adjective clauses.

# 2 Express regret and take responsibility

## A ⌒ CONVERSATION **SNAPSHOT**

**A:** Tim, I hate to tell you this, but I dropped the camera you lent me, and it can't be fixed.

**B:** Oh, no. How did *that* happen?

**A:** Well, I tripped, and it fell out of the bag. I feel awful about it.

**B:** Are you sure it can't be fixed?

**A:** Pretty sure. I took it to the camera shop, and they said to forget it. But I can replace it with a newer model.

**B:** That's really not necessary.

**A:** No, I insist. And please accept my apology.

⌒ **Rhythm and intonation practice**

Pronunciation Booster

**PAGES P3–P4**
Emphatic stress and pitch

> ⌒ **Ways to express regret**
> I'm so sorry.
> I feel awful (about it).
> I feel (just) terrible.

## B ⌒ Vocabulary. **Ways to take and avoid responsibility.** Listen and practice.

| Statement | | Attitude or action |
|---|---|---|
| He said, "I'm sorry. I'll pay for the damage." | → | He **took responsibility** for the damage. |
| He said, "It wasn't my fault. I'm not paying for it!" | → | He **avoided taking responsibility** for the damage. |
| He said, "I'm sorry. It was my fault." | → | He **admitted making a mistake.** |
| He lied and said, "It was Bob's fault." | → | He **shifted the blame** to someone else. |
| He overslept but said, "Sorry. The train was late." | → | He **made up an excuse.** |
| After he broke the camera, he said, "I'll buy you a new one." | → | He **made up for it.** (He **made up for** breaking the camera by buying a new one.) |

## C ⌒ Listening Comprehension. Listen to the conversations. Then listen again. After each conversation, choose the expression that best completes each statement.

**1.** She ........ the damage.
   **a.** took responsibility for        **b.** avoided taking responsibility for

**2.** He ........ the damage.
   **a.** took responsibility for        **b.** avoided taking responsibility for

**3.** He ........ .
   **a.** admitted making a mistake      **b.** shifted the blame to someone else

**4.** She ........ .
   **a.** admitted making a mistake      **b.** made up an excuse

**5.** She ........ for being late.
   **a.** made up an excuse          **b.** made up

**6.** She ........ losing the scarf.
   **a.** avoided taking responsibility for    **b.** made up for

**Pair Work.** Discuss each question in the survey and fill in the answer that best describes what you would do.

| How hard is it for you to accept responsibility? | | | |
|---|---|---|---|
| **What would you do if you ...** | | | |
| ✳ made a serious mistake at work? | Ⓐ | Ⓑ | Ⓒ |
| ✳ broke or lost something you had borrowed? | Ⓐ | Ⓑ | Ⓒ |
| ✳ forgot to give back something you had borrowed? | Ⓐ | Ⓑ | Ⓒ |
| ✳ forgot to do an assignment at work or in school? | Ⓐ | Ⓑ | Ⓒ |
| ✳ fell behind schedule at work? | Ⓐ | Ⓑ | Ⓒ |
| ✳ were late for an appointment? | Ⓐ | Ⓑ | Ⓒ |
| ✳ were stopped for exceeding the speed limit? | Ⓐ | Ⓑ | Ⓒ |
| ✳ were reminded about a promise you hadn't kept? | Ⓐ | Ⓑ | Ⓒ |
| ✳ were caught telling a lie? | Ⓐ | Ⓑ | Ⓒ |
| ✳ forgot a friend's birthday? | Ⓐ | Ⓑ | Ⓒ |

Ⓐ = I would tell the truth.

Ⓑ = I would make up an excuse.

Ⓒ = I would shift the blame to someone else.

**Group Work.** Choose two situations from the survey that have actually happened in your life. Make notes about what happened and what you said and did. Then meet in small groups and tell your classmates about one of the situations.

Situation:

*I forgot a friend's birthday.*

| Situation: | Situation: |
|---|---|
| What I said: | What I said: |
| What I did: | What I did: |

**Role Play.** Role-play a conversation in which you express regret and take responsibility for having lost or broken something of your partner's. Then change roles. Use the Conversation Snapshot on page 18 as a guide. Start like this: "I hate to tell you this, but ..."

# 3 *Discuss helping others*

**A** 🎧 **Vocabulary. Expressions related to compassion and admiration.** Listen and practice.

| | |
|---|---|
| **do (someone) a favor** do something someone has asked you to do for him or her | **feel sorry for / have compassion for (someone)** feel sympathy for someone because something bad has happened to that person or because he or she is suffering |
| **help (someone) out** do a kind or useful thing for someone | **look up to (someone)** admire or respect someone for his or her experience or achievements |
| **give (someone) moral support** give someone encouragement by expressing approval or interest, rather than by giving practical help | **be proud of (someone)** feel pleased with someone's achievements |
| **find (something) rewarding** feel happy and satisfied because you feel you did something useful or important | |

**B** Complete the sentences with the vocabulary, using the correct verb forms. More than one answer may be possible.

1. They _____ their daughter because she has achieved so much already.

2. She _____ her father because he worked hard to send his children to college.

3. Mike's a nice guy. Whenever I ask him for a ride to work he always says yes, even if it's out of his way. He's always willing to _____.

4. I _____ my cousin Mary. Her father died and her family has suffered.

5. When someone is upset about something, you can help by _____. Often just being a good listener is enough to help someone through a time of trouble.

6. I volunteer at a camp for children with disabilities. Whenever I have a free weekend, I _____ by setting up the equipment or preparing snacks for the kids. When I see the big smiles on their faces, it makes me feel really good. I _____.

**C** 🎧 **Listening Comprehension.** Listen to a radio program in which two people talk about helping others. Then read the statements and listen again. Check <u>Vivian</u> and/or <u>James</u>.

| | Vivian | James | |
|---|---|---|---|
| **1.** | | | work(s) with children. |
| **2.** | | | work(s) with the aged. |
| **3.** | | | volunteer(s) two days a week. |
| **4.** | | | work(s) in a public library. |
| **5.** | | | do(es) favors and run(s) errands. |
| **6.** | | | provide(s) snacks. |
| **7.** | | | was (were) inspired by a family member. |
| **8.** | | | has (have) compassion for others. |

**D** **Discussion.** Summarize what Vivian and James do. Explain how and why they got involved in their programs. Listen again if necessary.

## DISCUSSION **BUILDER** • *Now discuss helping others.*

**Step 1.** If you were to volunteer to help other people, what types of activities would you be most interested in? Discuss and explain your choices with a partner.

| | |
|---|---|
| ○ | Visiting sick children in a hospital |
| ○ | Visiting elderly people in a nursing home |
| ○ | Running errands or doing favors for people who are sick or shut in |
| ○ | Tutoring children who are having trouble in school |
| ○ | Driving an ambulance |
| ○ | Cooking and serving meals to the needy |
| ○ | Collecting money or clothing to help the poor |
| ○ | Donating money to a charity |
| ○ | Raising money for a charity |
| ○ | Traveling to another city or country to help out in a relief effort |
| ○ | Other: ............................................ |

Raising money for disaster relief

Visiting an elderly person in a nursing home

Tutoring a young child

**Step 2. Pair Work.** Discuss what kinds of people you admire and look up to and what kinds of people you have compassion for. Use the expressions from the vocabulary on page 20.

*"I admire people who give up everything to help people who have nothing. I could never do that myself, but I really **look up to** them for their sacrifice."*

*"The people I **have** the most **compassion for** are those who are sick. If you don't have your health, everything is more difficult! It's important to **give** these people the most **moral support** you can."*

**Step 3. Discussion.** What do you think motivates people to help others, especially people they don't know? Provide specific examples from your own or others' experiences.

# 4 *Explain the moral of a story*

**A** **Reading Warm-up.** Are you influenced in any way by fables and other stories that teach a lesson?

**B** 🎧 **Reading.** Read the story about a newlywed couple. Do you think they will have a good marriage?

# The Silent Couple

here was once a very stubborn young man and an equally stubborn young woman who met, fell in love, and got married. After the wedding ceremony, they had a grand feast at their new house. The celebration lasted all day.

When all the guests had left, the husband noticed that the last guest had failed to close the door.

"My dear," he said, "would you mind getting up and shutting the door?"

"Why should I shut it?" yawned the wife. "I've been on my feet all day. You shut it."

"So that's the way it's going to be!" snapped the husband. "Just as soon as you get the ring on your finger, you turn into a lazy good-for-nothing!"

"How dare you!" shouted the bride. "We haven't even been married a day, and already you're calling me names and ordering me around!"

They sat glaring at each other for a full five minutes. Then an idea popped into the bride's head.

"My dear," she said, "neither of us wants to shut the door, and both of us are tired of hearing the other's voice. So I propose a contest. The one who speaks first must get up and close the door."

"It's the best idea I've heard all day," replied her husband.

So they made themselves comfortable and sat face-to-face without saying a word.

They had been that way for about two hours when a couple of thieves passed by and saw the open door. They crept into the house, which seemed perfectly deserted, and began to steal everything they could lay their hands on. They took tables and chairs, pulled paintings off walls, even rolled up carpets. But the newlyweds neither spoke nor moved.

"I can't believe this," thought the husband. "They'll take everything we own, and she won't make a sound."

"Why doesn't he call for help?" the wife asked herself.

Eventually the thieves noticed the silent, motionless couple and, mistaking them for wax figures, stripped them of their jewelry, watches, and wallets. But neither husband nor wife uttered a sound.

The robbers hurried away with their loot, and the newlyweds sat through the night. At dawn a policeman walked by and, noticing the open door, stuck in his head to ask if everything was all right. "Is this your house? What happened to all your furniture?" And getting no response, he raised his hand to hit the man.

"Don't you dare!" cried the wife, jumping to her feet. "That's my new husband, and if you lay a finger on him, you'll have to answer to me!"

"I won!" yelled the husband. "Now go and close the door."

Source: Traditional tale adapted from *The Book of Virtues,* 1993

**C** **Discussion.** Do you think the wife should have closed the door when her husband first asked her to? Do you agree that the husband "won"? If you had to write a moral for this story, what would it be?

**D   Pair Work.** Which proverb do you think gives the same message as the story? Explain your answer.

"A sleeping cat will not catch a rat."

"Write injuries in sand, kindnesses in marble."

"Because we focused on the snake, we missed the scorpion."

"Tell the truth—and run."

"People who live in glass houses shouldn't throw stones."

---

## DISCUSSION **BUILDER** • *Now tell a story with a moral.*

**Step 1. Pair Work.** Read the stories. What do you think is the moral of each story? Which one do you prefer? Why?

### The Frogs and the Well
#### from Aesop's Fables

Two frogs lived together in a pond. One hot summer the pond dried up, and they set out to look for a new place to live. Eventually they passed by a deep well, and one of them looked down into it and said, "There's plenty of water here, and it looks like a nice cool place! Let's jump in and make this our home."

But the other, who was wiser and more cautious, replied, "Not so fast, my friend. If this well dried up like the pond, how would we get out?"

### A Traditional Chinese Tale

There was a young man living in the north of China whose horse ran away. Everyone felt sorry for him.

"Perhaps this will soon turn out to be a blessing," said his father.

After a few months, the horse came back followed by another, very beautiful, horse. Everyone congratulated the man for his good fortune.

"Perhaps this will soon turn out to be a cause of misfortune," said his father.

The man loved to go riding, and one day he fell from the beautiful horse and broke his leg. Everyone felt sorry for him.

"Perhaps this will soon turn out to be a blessing," said his father.

A month later, war broke out, and there was a big invasion in the north. All able-bodied young men had to join the army to fight the invaders. Nine out of ten men died in the terrible battles that were fought. The man had not joined in the fighting because of his injured leg, and so he survived.

**Step 2. Group Story.** With a small group, create a story that teaches a lesson. (It can be an original story or one you already know.) Tell it to the class. The class writes a moral for your story.

**IDEAS**

This story / tale takes place in a town where . . .
It's set in a time when . . .
It's about a . . . who / to whom / for whom . . .
The moral of the story is . . .

**Step 3. Discussion.** Why do you think stories with morals exist in all cultures? What purpose do they serve?

# Writing: Describe an experience that taught you a lesson

## Punctuating adjective clauses

A **restrictive adjective clause** gives *essential* information: information that is needed to identify the noun or pronoun it modifies. It is not set off from the sentence by commas.

The person **who had cheated me** used to be my friend. (information needed to identify the person)

A **non-restrictive adjective clause** gives *additional* information: information that is not needed to identify the noun or pronoun it modifies. It requires commas before and after (except at the end of a sentence, when it ends with a period).

Lara Stevens, **who had cheated me**, used to be my friend. (information not needed to identify the person)

### ERROR CORRECTION

Correct the three errors in punctuating adjective clauses.

While working at my first job, which was at a clothing store, I had a co-worker who got me into a lot of trouble. She had stolen some money from the cash register and then blamed me. I insisted on my innocence, but my supervisor who did not believe me fired me that day.

Ten years later, I got an e-mail, that stunned me. It was from the woman who had gotten me fired. She was writing to tell me how sorry she was for what she had done! I now realize that the experience that cost me my job also taught me a valuable lesson. Sometimes people hurt themselves when they cheat or lie more than the people they lie to or about. This incident which I had almost forgotten still troubled my former co-worker, even after all these years.

**Step 1. Prewriting. Using information questions to generate ideas.** Think about an incident in your life that taught you a lesson. Then write questions about the incident to help generate ideas.

**Example:** Who *was involved?*

Who ............................................................................................

What ............................................................................................

When ............................................................................................

Where ............................................................................................

Why ............................................................................................

How ............................................................................................

Answer your questions on a separate sheet of paper. Read what you wrote and add other ideas.

### IDEAS

Forgiving someone
Helping out a person in need
Cheating or lying
Taking responsibility for a mistake
Other: ......................................

**Step 2. Writing.** On a separate sheet of paper, describe the experience that taught you a lesson, using the answers to your questions. Include details, using adjective clauses when possible.

**Step 3. Self-Check.**

☐ Did you include adjective clauses?

☐ Did you set off non-restrictive adjective clauses with commas?

☐ Were you able to add any more details, using adjective clauses?

**SUMMIT WEBSITE**
For Unit 2 online activities, visit the *Summit* Companion Website at www.longman.com/summit.

**A** 🎧 **Listening Comprehension.** Listen to the conversations. Then listen again and complete the chart after each conversation.

| | What is the person concerned about? | What will he or she do about it? |
|---|---|---|
| 1 | | |
| 2 | | |
| 3 | | |

**B** Complete the sentences with phrases from the box.

| | | |
|---|---|---|
| shift the blame | express regret | make up for it |
| tell the truth | make up an excuse | |

1. If Matt makes a mistake, he never admits it and instead tries to ........................ to other people in his office.

2. Dan forgot to prepare his report for the sales meeting. He didn't want to admit his mistake, so he decided to ........................ . He told his boss that his computer deleted the file.

3. After borrowing my umbrella, Alice forgot it on the train. She offered to buy me a new one to ........................ .

4. Jane has really poor manners. For example, she never thinks to ........................ when she does something wrong. I believe it's important to say that you're sorry when you make a mistake or cause problems for other people.

5. I really believe that in some situations it's better not to ........................ , especially when you are protecting someone's feelings. For example, if my grandmother spent all day cooking dinner, but it tasted terrible, I would still tell her it was delicious.

| | |
|---|---|
| who | whom |
| that | which |
| where | when |

**C** Complete the paragraph with words from the box.

Nora Richards, with ........(1)........ I worked for five years, was a person ........(2)........ could never get her work done on time. I still remember the time ........(3)........ she asked me to help her write a long report ........(4)........ was due the next day! The report, on ........(5)........ she had been working for an entire month, was needed for a business deal with a very important client. The deal, about ........(6)........ Nora talked all the time (instead of writing the report), fell through, and Nora was fired. There are situations in ........(7)........ you simply have to meet your deadlines. Nora was one of those persons ........(8)........ fails to understand that the office is a place ........(9)........, as the proverb says, "Actions speak louder than words."

**D** On a separate sheet of paper, give a personal example of each of the following and explain. Write one or two sentences for each one.

1. A favor I did for someone or that someone did for me
2. A person (or group of people) I feel sorry for
3. A person I look up to or feel proud of
4. An experience I found rewarding

PREVIEW

# Dealing with adversity

**UNIT GOALS**

1  Describe a dangerous or challenging experience
2  Express frustration, empathy, and encouragement
3  Describe how people confront adversity
4  Discuss the nature of heroism

**A** **Topic Preview.** Read the quotations. What attitude toward adversity do they express?

"I'm not afraid of storms for I'm learning to sail my ship. "

**Louisa May Alcott, writer**

"Obstacles don't have to stop you. If you run into a wall, don't turn around and give up. Figure out how to climb it, go through it, or work around it. "

**Michael Jordan, athlete**

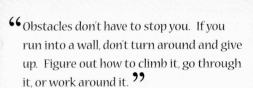

"When it gets dark enough, you can see the stars. "

**Lee Salk, psychologist**

**B** **Discussion.** Do you agree that adversity can be a positive experience? Do you find any of the quotations inspiring or relevant to your own life? Explain.

**C** 🎧 **Sound Bites.** Read and listen to a conversation between two friends about a scary experience.

**MATT:** Hey! You look a little shaky. Are you OK?
**ANNE:** I'm not sure. I was just stuck in the elevator.
**MATT:** Are you serious? You mean when the power went off? How long were you in there?
**ANNE:** Like twenty minutes. And it was pitch black, and I couldn't see a thing.
**MATT:** You must have been going out of your mind.
**ANNE:** Yeah. I was scared to death.

**D** **In Other Words.** Read the conversation again. Then say each of these statements another way.

1. "You look a little shaky."
2. "It was pitch black."
3. "You must have been going out of your mind."
4. "I was scared to death."

**E** **Discussion.** If you were stuck in an elevator, would you be scared, or would you keep your cool? Why does getting stuck in an elevator frighten some people?

## STARTING **POINT**

What scares *you*? Rate the following situations from 1 to 3, with 1 being very frightening, 2 being somewhat frightening, and 3 being not at all frightening.

| | | | |
|---|---|---|---|
| ◯ | getting stuck in an elevator | ◯ | being caught in a burning building |
| ◯ | being stung by a bee | ◯ | riding in a speeding car |
| ◯ | driving in very bad weather | ◯ | going to the dentist |
| ◯ | eating in a dirty restaurant | ◯ | walking down a dark street |
| ◯ | riding a horse | ◯ | experiencing turbulence during a flight |

**Pair Work.** Compare and explain your ratings.

# Describe a dangerous or challenging experience

**A** 🎧 GRAMMAR **SNAPSHOT.** Read the article and notice how past actions and events are described.

# Stranded climbers rescued by text message

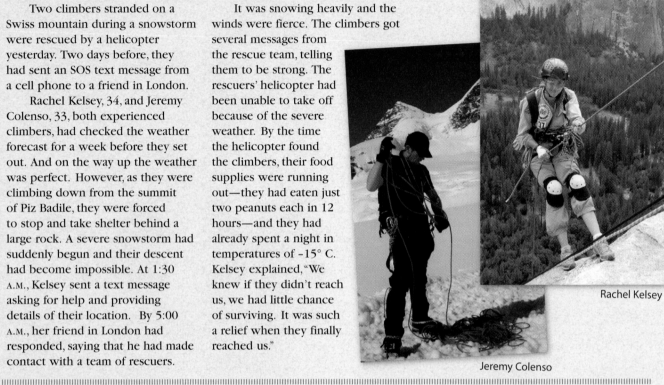

Two climbers stranded on a Swiss mountain during a snowstorm were rescued by a helicopter yesterday. Two days before, they had sent an SOS text message from a cell phone to a friend in London.

Rachel Kelsey, 34, and Jeremy Colenso, 33, both experienced climbers, had checked the weather forecast for a week before they set out. And on the way up the weather was perfect. However, as they were climbing down from the summit of Piz Badile, they were forced to stop and take shelter behind a large rock. A severe snowstorm had suddenly begun and their descent had become impossible. At 1:30 A.M., Kelsey sent a text message asking for help and providing details of their location. By 5:00 A.M., her friend in London had responded, saying that he had made contact with a team of rescuers.

It was snowing heavily and the winds were fierce. The climbers got several messages from the rescue team, telling them to be strong. The rescuers' helicopter had been unable to take off because of the severe weather. By the time the helicopter found the climbers, their food supplies were running out—they had eaten just two peanuts each in 12 hours—and they had already spent a night in temperatures of -15° C. Kelsey explained, "We knew if they didn't reach us, we had little chance of surviving. It was such a relief when they finally reached us."

Rachel Kelsey

Jeremy Colenso

Information source: www.guardian.co.uk

**B** **Discussion.** What problems did the climbers face while waiting for the rescuers? Why do you think they survived?

**C** **Grammar.** Describing the relationship of past events and actions to each other

The <u>simple past tense</u> can be used to describe a past event or action that occurred right after another past event or action.
> When they arrived, I **sent** an SOS message.
> (First they arrived. Then I sent the message.)

The <u>past perfect</u> can be used to describe an event or action that occurred before another past event or action.
> When they arrived, I **had** already **sent** an SOS message.
> (First I sent the message. Then they arrived.)

The <u>past continuous</u> can be used to describe an event or action that continued at the same time as another past event or action.
> When they arrived, I **was sending** an SOS message.
> (They arrived while I was sending the message.)

The <u>past perfect continuous</u> can be used to describe an event or action that had continued before another past event or action occurred.
> When they arrived, I **had been trying** to send an SOS message for an hour.
> (I was trying to send the message for an hour. Then they arrived.)

PAGES G4–G5
For more …

**D** Look at the order in which the events occurred and complete the sentences with the simple past tense, the past perfect, the past continuous, or the past perfect continuous.

1. (The plane took off. Then they arrived.)
   The plane _____ when they _____ at the airport.

2. (They left the airport. Then the plane took off.)
   They _____ the airport by the time the plane _____ .

3. (The plane took off at the same time they arrived.)
   When they _____ at the airport, the plane _____ .

4. (They canceled the expedition. Immediately the sky cleared.)
   When they _____ the expedition, the sky _____ .

5. (I locked all the doors. Then I went to bed.)
   I _____ all the doors by the time I _____ to bed.

6. (I lost my cell phone. That's why I didn't phone for help.)
   I _____ for help because I _____ my cell phone.

7. (They were walking for an hour. Then they realized they were lost.)
   When they _____ they were lost, they _____ for an hour.

8. (I was working hard all day. That's why I was exhausted.)
   I _____ hard all day, so I _____ exhausted when I went to bed.

**E** **Pair Work.** Read the article on page 28 again. Then close your books and retell the story about the climbers in sequence.

**EXPRESSING SEQUENCE**

One day . . .
Suddenly . . .
Then . . .
Afterwards . . .
By the time that . . .
When . . .
In the meantime . . .
Finally . . .

GRAMMAR **EXCHANGE** • *Now describe a dangerous or challenging experience.*

Have you (or has someone you know) ever been in a dangerous or frightening situation? Write notes about it on the notepad.

**Pair Work.** Tell each other your stories. Respond and ask questions as you listen. Use idioms from the box.

*"What did you do next? You must have been scared to death!"*

*"Actually, I tried to keep my cool."*

**IDIOMS**
be a little shaky
be going out of one's mind
be scared to death
keep one's cool

Location:

Time, date, season:

People involved:

The danger or fear:

The outcome:

# 2 Express frustration, empathy, and encouragement

## A 🎧 CONVERSATION **SNAPSHOT**

**A:** I give up!

**B:** What's the matter?

**A:** No matter how carefully I eat, my cholesterol just won't come down.

**B:** Well, maybe you just need to give it a little more time.

**A:** I've already given it six months! It's starting to get me down.

**B:** I know what you mean. I'd be frustrated, too.

🎧 **Frustration**

I give up!
I'm fed up!
I can't take it any more!
I've had it!
I'm at my wits' end!

🎧 **Rhythm and intonation practice**

🎧 **Empathy**

I know what you mean.

That must be { discouraging.
frustrating.
disappointing. }

## B Grammar. Clauses with no matter ...

**No matter** often introduces clauses in statements that express frustration or encouragement.

**No matter** is commonly combined with **who**, **what**, **when**, **why**, **where**, or the intensifier **how** + an adjective or adverb.

**No matter how** carefully I eat, my cholesterol won't come down.
**No matter who** makes the coffee, it's always too strong.
**No matter who(m)** they asked, the answer was always the same.
I can't seem to get it right, **no matter what** I do!
**No matter when** we call, it's always the wrong time.
**No matter where** she looked, she couldn't find what she needed.
You have to keep trying, **no matter how** tired you are.

*"No matter how much coffee I drink, I can't seem to stay awake."*

## C Pair Work. Take turns completing the following statements with your *own* experiences.

1. No matter how much coffee I drink, . . .
2. No matter what everyone says, . . .
3. No matter who(m) I talk to, . . .
4. No matter how much money you make, . . .
5. No matter how long you live, . . .
6. No matter what my parents think, . . .
7. . . . , no matter what you want.
8. . . . , no matter where my friends are.

**D** 🎧 **Vocabulary. Encouragement and discouragement.** Listen and practice.

**encourage someone** (to do something)
*My mother always encouraged me to become a dancer. When I was a child, she took me to dance classes and predicted that I would be a star one day.*

**cheer someone up / lift someone's spirits**
*It really cheered me up (OR lifted my spirits) when my friends visited me in the hospital. I smiled for the first time in weeks.*

**keep at it / stick with it / refuse to give up**
*At first, I could speak only a few words of French. I kept at it (OR stuck with it OR refused to give up), however, and after some hard work, I was finally able to speak with some fluency.*

**discourage someone** (from doing something) /
**talk someone out of** (something)
*I wanted to quit school, but my mother discouraged me from doing it (OR talked me out of it). She thought it was important for me to complete my studies.*

**let something get to you / let something get you down**
*My boss has been very critical of my work recently. I try not to let it get to me (OR let it get me down), but I am still upset by his comments.*

**feel like giving up / feel discouraged**
*I've been a car salesman for six months, but I haven't sold a single car. It just makes me feel like giving up (OR feel discouraged).*

**E** 🎧 **Listening Comprehension.** Listen to the people discussing problems. Then listen again and circle the statement that best characterizes each person's advice.

1. He's telling his friend ......... .
   a. not to let it get to her
   b. to cheer her son up

2. She's ......... .
   a. encouraging him to get the job done on time
   b. trying to talk him out of it

3. She thinks he ......... .
   a. shouldn't let it get him down
   b. should discourage his sister from doing it

4. She doesn't think her friend should ......... .
   a. talk her son out of it
   b. feel discouraged

Pronunciation Booster

**PAGE P4**
Vowel reduction

---

CONVERSATION **STARTER** • *Now empathize and give encouragement.*

**Pair Work.** On your notepad, discuss and list typical examples of each type of problem.

**Role Play.** Role-play a conversation in which you encourage your partner to overcome a difficulty. Use the Conversation Snapshot on page 30 and ideas from your notepad as a guide. Use clauses with <u>no matter</u>.

**Group Work.** What kinds of difficulties do *you* face or want to overcome? Give each other advice and encouragement.

Career problems: *a boss who doesn't give enough recognition for employees' achievements*

Career problems:

Academic problems:

Money problems:

Family problems:

Health problems:

31

# 3 Describe how people confront adversity

**A** **Reading Warm-up.** Are you familiar with Helen Keller's story? What do you know about her life?

**B** 🎧 **Reading.** Read the article. What obstacles did Helen Keller have to face in her life?

# TRIUMPH Out of TRAGEDY

For the first eighteen months of her life, Helen Keller was a normal infant who had learned to recognize the voices of her parents and take joy in looking at their faces. Then illness closed her eyes and ears and plunged her into a world of darkness and silence. The illness erased not only her vision and hearing but also, as a result, her power of speech.

Keller's life thereafter became a triumph over crushing adversity. In time, she overcame her disabilities and was a full and happy participant in life. She learned to see and hear in her own way, making use of her senses of touch and smell, and eventually she even learned to talk. She realized goals no similarly handicapped person had ever achieved — university study, success as a writer, worldwide recognition as a great humanitarian.

Although Keller was able to cope with some of her limitations, her early childhood was filled with frustration. She had to hold the hands of other people to learn what they were doing, and she was only able to recognize her parents and their friends by feeling their faces and clothes. She was able to communicate with her family, using signs she had invented to let them know what she wanted. For example, she would pretend to cut bread when she wanted to eat bread. However, communication with her family was one-sided. She wanted to communicate in the same way that her family did but was unable to talk. She expressed this frustration in outbursts of anger and bad behavior — "a wild, unruly child" who kicked, scratched, and screamed was how she later described herself.

Her parents were losing hope — until they found her a teacher. Anne Sullivan, partly blind

Helen Keller playing chess with her teacher, Anne Sullivan

herself, had learned to communicate with the deaf and blind through a hand alphabet. She came to live in the Keller home.

Keller's first lessons were far from encouraging. When Sullivan first arrived, Keller looked for candy in her bag. When she found none, she kicked and screamed. No matter how often Sullivan used the hand alphabet, Keller could not understand, which only made her frustrated and angry.

One day Sullivan had an idea. She took her student, who was not quite seven at the time, to the water pump and placed one of her hands under the spout while she spelled the word "water" into the other. Later Keller wrote about this experience, "Somehow the mystery of language was revealed to me. I knew then that

'w-a-t-e-r' meant the wonderful cool something that was flowing over my hand. That living word awakened my soul, gave it light, hope, joy, set it free. There were barriers still, it is true, but barriers that in time could be swept away."

Keller's progress from then on was amazing. She and Sullivan became lifelong companions, touring the world together. Keller worked tirelessly for the blind and inspired many other disabled people to similar accomplishments.

Keller once remarked, "I seldom think about my limitations, and they never make me sad. Perhaps there is just a touch of yearning* at times, but it is vague, like a breeze among flowers. The wind passes, and the flowers are content."

*yearning = a sad desire for something one can't have

Information source: Alden Whitman, "Triumph Out of Tragedy," *The New York Times*

**C** **Pair Work.** With a partner, complete the chart.

*All the world is full of suffering; it is also full of overcoming it.*
Helen Keller

| Obstacles Keller faced | Ways in which she overcame them |
| --- | --- |
|  |  |

**D** **Discussion.**

1. What do you think there was in Helen Keller's character or experience that enabled her to be successful in her life?
2. What does Keller's life teach us about confronting adversity?

## DISCUSSION **BUILDER** • *Now describe how people confront adversity.*

**Step 1.** Think of a person who faces (or has faced) adversity. On the notepad, write discussion notes about the person.

**IDEAS**
- Overcoming illness or a physical handicap
- Facing racial, ethnic, or sexual discrimination
- Coping with the effects of a natural disaster
- Experiencing political instability or war
- Lacking money, education, or support

Name:

Type of adversity:

Steps taken to overcome it:

The person's attitude:

What can be learned from this person's experience?

**Step 2. Group Work.** Tell each other about the people you took notes about. As you listen, ask questions to find out more.

**Step 3. Discussion.** How do people differ in the way they confront adversity in their lives? What do people who successfully overcome obstacles have in common?

# 4 *Discuss the nature of heroism*

**A** 🎧 **Word Skills.** Using parts of speech

| noun | adjective | adverb |
|---|---|---|
| bravery | brave | bravely |
| confidence | confident | confidently |
| courage | courageous | courageously |
| fearlessness | fearless | fearlessly |
| generosity | generous | generously |
| heroism | heroic | heroically |
| pride | proud | proudly |
| willingness | willing | willingly |

**B** 🎧 **Listening Comprehension.** Listen to the news report about a heroic act. Then listen again and write a summary of the report. Include as many details as possible.

...............................................................................
...............................................................................
...............................................................................
...............................................................................
...............................................................................

Seol Ik Soo after the crash

**C** Choose the correct word to complete each sentence.

1. Seol's decision to go back to the plane wreckage was very (courage / courageous / courageously).

2. Although aware that the airplane could explode at any moment, Seol (fearlessness / fearless / fearlessly) returned to the plane again and again to rescue wounded passengers.

3. Seol's boss was (pride / proud / proudly) of him for his (brave / bravery / bravely).

4. The story suggests that anyone, even an apparently ordinary person, is capable of (heroism / heroic / heroically) acts.

5. Seol's (willingness / willing / willingly) to risk his life to save others was extraordinary.

6. Frankly, I'm not (confidence / confident / confidently) that I could do what Seol Ik Soo did.

The plane wreckage

## DISCUSSION **BUILDER** • *Now discuss the nature of heroism.*

**Step 1. Pair Work.** On your notepad, discuss and write a definition of heroism. Use words from the chart in Exercise A.

Heroism is . . .

**Step 2. Discussion.** Read the three profiles. Would you call each of these people a hero? Why or why not?

Malden Mills, which makes fleece, a fabric used in sweaters and jackets, burned to the ground in 1995. Aaron Feuerstein, the owner of Malden Mills, spent millions of dollars of his own money to keep all 3,000 employees on the payroll with full benefits for three months until Malden Mills could be rebuilt. Feuerstein, a generous man who believes that his responsibility goes beyond just making money for investors in his company, said, "I have an equal responsibility to the community." He added, "I think it was a wise business decision, but that isn't why I did it. I did it because it was the right thing to do."

The 1995 fire that burned most of Malden Mills to the ground could have put 3,000 people out of work. But owner Aaron Feuerstein refused to let that happen.

Czech playwright and poet Václav Havel was a leader of the movement to establish a democratic Czechoslovakia. In 1968, after opposing the Soviet invasion of Czechoslovakia, Havel's plays were banned, his passport was taken away, and he was imprisoned three times — spending a total of almost five years in prison. In spite of this, Havel remained an activist, and when the Soviets left in 1989, he was elected president of the Czech Republic. Havel has spent his entire life speaking the truth, even at great personal risk.

Václav Havel opposed Soviet rule of Czechoslovakia and led the struggle for democracy.

60-year-old hero Alicia Sorohan rescued her friend from the jaws of a giant saltwater crocodile like this one.

On October 11, 2004, while camping in Queensland, Australia, Alicia Sorohan awoke to the sound of someone screaming. Rushing out of her tent, she came across her friend Mike Kerr in the mouth of a 14-foot (4.2 m) saltwater crocodile. The 60-year-old grandmother immediately jumped on the back of the giant crocodile, which dropped Kerr and attacked her, biting her in the face and arm. When shot and killed by another member of the group, the crocodile had Sorohan's arm in its mouth and was dragging her into the water. Sorohan and Kerr both survived the incident, though both had serious injuries. Family members of the victims, in shock after the horrible attack, said that Sorohan's bravery had been astonishing. "She deserves an award of some kind," said Wayne Clancy, her son-in-law.

**Step 3. Writing.** Choose one of the people in this lesson. Explain how the person's experiences and actions make him or her a hero.

# Writing: Narrate past events logically

## Time relationships

When narrating a story, it is important to clarify the order of events. One way to do this is with sequence words.

**First** she listened to my side of the story. **Then** she asked my brother to describe what he had seen. **Afterwards** she told us what she thought about the situation.

Prepositional time phrases and adverbial time clauses are two other effective tools to make sequences clear.

| Prepositional Time Phrases |
| --- |
| I used to volunteer at a soup kitchen **on Fridays**. |
| I graduated from college **in May**. |
| **At 8:00**, I was waiting for the train. |
| I worked there **from January to May**. |
| I lived there **until 2001**. |
| **By January**, I had sent out twenty job applications. |
| **During that time**, I got depressed often. |

| Adverbial Time Clauses |
| --- |
| **When I fell off my bike**, I hurt my back. |
| We saw a bear **while we were hiking**. |
| **Whenever someone tried to help me**, I refused. |
| **Before I left**, I gave my parents a letter. |
| **After I had shared my news**, I felt better. |
| Kyle and I were close friends **until he lied to me**. |
| I told her the plan **as soon as she arrived**. |

Punctuation note: When prepositional time phrases and adverbial time clauses appear at the beginning of a sentence, they are usually followed by a comma.

**Topics**
A dangerous, frightening, or exciting personal experience
An obstacle you or someone you know had to overcome

### Step 1. Prewriting. "Freewriting" to generate ideas.
- Choose a topic. On a separate sheet of paper, write, for five to ten minutes, all the details about the topic you can think of. Write quickly. Do not take time to correct spelling, punctuation, verb forms, time order, etc.
- Read what you wrote. Choose ideas you would like to develop and put them in logical order.

### Step 2. Writing. On a separate sheet of paper, tell your story. Use sequence words, prepositional time phrases, adverbial time clauses, and past verb forms to narrate the events logically.

### Step 3. Self-Check.
- ☐ Is the sequence of the events in your narrative clear and logical?
- ☐ Did you use time and sequence words?
- ☐ Did you use correct punctuation?
- ☐ Did you use correct past verb forms?

**WRITING MODEL**

While I was camping with my friend Eric last summer, we had some scary neighbors—bear cubs! In books and on TV, they are cute creatures. However, when they are steps away from you, it is a different story.

One morning, I was eating a snack by my tent when I heard a rustling noise behind me. I thought it was Eric until I turned around and saw a bear trying to open a garbage can. I tried to remember the different rules for scaring away bears. But before I could do anything, the bear noticed the apple I was holding in my hand . . .

# UNIT 3 CHECKPOINT

SUMMIT WEBSITE
For Unit 3 online activities, visit the *Summit* Companion Website at www.longman.com/summit.

**A** 🎧 **Listening Comprehension.** Listen to the descriptions of difficulties three people are having. Then listen again to each description and use a clause with <u>no matter</u> to write a sentence summarizing each person's frustration.

1.  Felix Tan

...........................................................

...........................................................

...........................................................

2.  Robert Reston

...........................................................

...........................................................

...........................................................

3. Eva Garcia

...........................................................

...........................................................

...........................................................

**B** Complete this excerpt from a biography of Helen Keller, using the simple past tense, the past continuous, the past perfect, or the past perfect continuous. In some cases, more than one answer is possible.

After Helen Keller's graduation with honors from Radcliffe College, she and Anne Sullivan ............................. (make) a good living from their lectures around the world. Keller ............................. (speak) of her experiences and beliefs, and Sullivan ............................. (interpret) what she said, sentence by sentence. However, by 1918, the demand for Keller's lectures ............................. (diminish) considerably, so they ............................. (start) a vaudeville show that demonstrated how Keller ............................. (understand) the word "water" for the first time. While Keller ............................. (perform) in this show, she was offered the chance to make a film about her life. Keller ............................. (accept), but the film was not the success she ............................. (hope) for.

While Keller and Sullivan ............................. (tour) the world with their vaudeville show, Sullivan ............................. (come down with)

an illness that ............................. (leave) her unable to speak above a whisper. After this, Polly Thompson, who ............................. (work) for Keller and Sullivan as a secretary since 1914, ............................. (take on) the role of explaining Keller to the theater public.

Sullivan ............................. (die) in 1936, but Keller ............................. (keep on) touring the world with Thompson, raising money for the blind. While Keller was abroad, she ............................. (learn) that a fire ............................. (destroy) her home as well as the latest book she ............................. (work) on. This book, which Keller ............................. (not finish) yet, was about Sullivan, and it was called *Teacher*. Once again, Keller showed her capacity to struggle against the odds. It was not long before she had rewritten the entire book.

(1) (2) (3) (4) (5) (6) (7) (8) (9) (10) (11) (12) (13) (14) (15) (16) (17) (18) (19) (20)

Information source: www.rnib.org.uk

**C** Write what you would say in each situation, using an expression of frustration, empathy, or encouragement.

1. You want to encourage someone to stick to a diet, for medical reasons.

   YOU ............................................................................

2. A friend is having marital difficulties, and you want to cheer him up.

   YOU ............................................................................

3. You want to express frustration to a classmate about a project you're having trouble with.

   YOU ............................................................................

4. A co-worker tells you about difficulties she's having at work, and you want to let her know you understand how she feels.

   YOU ............................................................................

PREVIEW

# Personality and life

**A**  **Topic Preview.** Look at the catalogue of self-help workshops. Which workshops seem the most or least interesting to you?

## THE LEARNING Center

Dedicated to helping you reach your goals

### UPCOMING EVENTS

*Get Organized Now* Discover how getting organized can help you increase your productivity many times over. Learn practical tips that will help you start putting your life in order today!
*May 4, 2:00–3:00 P.M.*

*Say Good-bye to Procrastination* Don't put off till tomorrow what you could do today! Eliminate time wasters. Easy-to-apply strategies that will get you using your time more efficiently than ever!
*May 4, 3:00–4:00 P.M.*

*Make It Happen* You've got big dreams, but you don't know how to get there? Discover how to achieve success by taking small, realistic steps that will help you reach your goals!
*May 5, 7:00–8:00 A.M.*

*Test Like a Champion* Find out how you can turn low scores into mega-scores! Tips from the experts will help you overcome test-taking jitters and achieve success.
*May 5, 8:00–9:00 A.M.*

*Boost Your Self-Esteem* Do you lack self-confidence? Discover the causes of low self-esteem and what you can do about them. Learn a simple and effective technique you can perform daily to turn your life around!
*May 6, 7:00–8:00 P.M.*

*Bite Your Tongue!* Hate your boss? Can't stand your co-workers? Learn how to get along with people and manage difficult relationships with six essential techniques for handling anger successfully.
*May 6, 8:00–9:00 P.M.*

*Sedentary No More* Are you a hopeless couch potato? Get out of that chair and get active today! Develop an exercise program that not only works but motivates you to stick with it!
*May 7, 8:00–9:00 A.M.*

*End to Insomnia* Having trouble sleeping? Finding it hard to get through the day with your eyes open? Identify the causes of your sleep problems and learn new techniques for coping with them.
*May 7, 7:00–8:00 P.M.*

### FEATURED SPEAKERS

**"Get Organized Now"**
**Carl Hernandez,** author, *Finding Your Efficiency Zone*

**"Make It Happen"**
**Karen Kringle, Ph.D.,** author, *Seven Essential Habits for Success*

**"Say Good-bye to Procrastination"**
**Bill Heiden,** CEO, Marcus Industries

**"Test Like a Champion"**
**Kate Yang,** Director, Harley Testing Center

**B**  **Pair Work.** Which workshops might be useful in the following situations? Explain your choices.

- You're thinking about applying for a new position, but you're not sure you're smart enough.
- You often get into arguments with people at work.
- You've always wanted to find a job overseas, but you're not sure where to begin looking.
- Because your desk is such a mess, you sometimes have difficulty finding important files and information.
- You have trouble getting started on big projects.

**C** 🎧 **Sound Bites.** Read and listen to a conversation between two colleagues.

**MEG:** What's all that racket?
**PAT:** Carla. Yelling at Phil. She's really ticked off at him.
**MEG:** Oh, Carla's always ticked off about something or other. She needs to get hold of herself. What's she so angry about now?
**PAT:** Well, it seems she confided in Phil, and …
**MEG:** Big mistake. Phil can't keep a secret. Everyone knows what a gossip he is … So what did she tell him?
**PAT:** Shame on you! Well, she told him she'd been offered a new job and that she was thinking of taking it.
**MEG:** No kidding. Where?
**PAT:** Hey, I don't feel comfortable talking behind her back. Now that it's out in the open, why don't you just ask her yourself?

"Carla's yelling at Phil. She's always ticked off about *something*."

**D** Answer the questions.

1. Why is Carla mad at Phil?
2. Why do you think Pat says, "Shame on you!" to Meg?
3. What was Carla's secret?
4. What do you think will happen next?

**E** **In Other Words.** Read the conversation again. Then say each of these statements another way.

1. "What's all that racket?"
2. "She's really ticked off at him."
3. "She needs to get hold of herself."
4. "Well, it seems she confided in Phil."
5. "Everyone knows what a gossip he is."
6. "I don't feel comfortable talking behind her back."

## STARTING **POINT**

**Pair Work.** Discuss the possible consequences of each of these problems in a person's life.

**Disorganization**     **Low self-esteem**     *Procrastination*

**The inability to follow through**     **Poor test-taking skills**

**Getting angry easily**     **Insomnia**

**A sedentary lifestyle**

# 1 Describe your shortcomings

## A ⌒ CONVERSATION **SNAPSHOT**

**A:** You know what my problem is?

**B:** What?

**A:** I'm a perfectionist. Nothing is ever good enough for me. It's a pretty negative attitude to have.

**B:** Really? I'm just the opposite. I don't think I'm critical enough!

**A:** Wouldn't it be nice if we could reach some kind of happy medium?

⌒ **Rhythm and intonation practice**

### ⌒ **Comparing oneself with others**

| | |
|---|---|
| That's my problem, too. | I'm just the opposite. |
| I'm like that myself. | I'm not like that. |
| Me too. | Not me. |

*Pronunciation Booster*

**PAGE P5**
Shifting emphatic
stress

## B ⌒ Vocabulary. Expressions for problematic attitudes and behaviors. Listen and practice.

**be a perfectionist** insist that things be done perfectly, whether by oneself or someone else

**be unable to say no** agree to requests for help too easily, even when one doesn't have the time to fulfill them

**have a negative attitude** never consider the good aspects of a situation, only the bad ones

**wait until the last minute** delay the things one needs to do because one finds them hard or unpleasant

**take on more than one can handle** accept more responsibility than one can realistically deal with

**overreact to things** respond too strongly or emotionally when there's a problem

## C ⌒ Listening Comprehension.
Listen to the radio advertisement for self-help workshops. Then listen again and determine which workshop is being described. Write the letter that matches the day it is being offered.

1. ........ *Afraid to say no?*
2. ........ *Why wait until the last minute?*
3. ........ *Drop your negative attitude*
4. ........ *Stop overreacting*
5. ........ *Being a perfectionist isn't easy*

    **a.** *Monday*
    **b.** *Tuesday*
    **c.** *Wednesday*
    **d.** *Thursday*
    **e.** *Friday*

**D** **Pair Work.** Use the vocabulary to describe each person's problematic attitude or behavior. Discuss the possible consequences in his or her life.

Simone Duval is a busy mother and housewife with three young children. Her neighbors often ask her to do errands for them or to watch their children when they go out. It's really too much for her! Lately, she's been losing her temper with her own kids.

"It sounds like she's unable to say no. I don't think that's so good—you can't just take care of everyone else's needs and ignore your own."

"I suppose. But if she agrees to help other people, they might be just as willing to do things for her in return. That can't be all bad."

Michael Novak is a manager in an advertising agency, and some of his employees find him a very difficult boss. No matter what they do, he always finds something to criticize. Over the last year, he's lost three of his staff to other agencies.

Ed Banks gets upset over every little thing. When he loses control, other people avoid being around him. It's interfering with his work, and his boss has had to speak with him about it.

Ana Ponte is a full-time college student. She usually begins working on projects the night before they're due. Then she goes into a panic worrying about whether or not she'll be able to finish them on time.

---

CONVERSATION **STARTER** • *Now describe your shortcomings.*

What are *your* most problematic attitudes and behaviors? Write specific examples of ways in which they have caused difficulties for you.

> 1. being a perfectionist
>    I don't invite friends to eat at my house because I don't think
>    I cook well enough. I'm also too critical of my children's behavior.

1.

2.

**Pair Work.** Discuss your shortcomings. Explain the consequences they have in your life. Use the Conversation Snapshot on page 40 as a guide and start like this: "You know what my problem is?"

# 2 Talk about ways to manage stress

**A** 🎧 GRAMMAR **SNAPSHOT.** Read the article and notice the use of the subjunctive.

## Easy ways to cope with STRESS

Everyone has stress. While it may not be possible to avoid stress entirely, it is important that you **be** aware of rising stress levels. And when you feel yourself getting tense, there are some simple techniques you can use to lower your stress level fast.

According to Dr. Robert Sharpe, the founder of the Lifeskills Stress Management Centre, the first step is to do nothing: "It's essential that one **begin** and **end** each day by taking a minute or two to consciously relax." He suggests that after the alarm clock wakes you up in the morning and again just before bedtime, you **spend** a few moments relaxing all the muscles of your body. And if you feel yourself getting stressed out during the day, slow your breathing down for five minutes by taking long, deep breaths. Dr. Sharpe

also suggests that you **think** about people and things you love. Just as thinking about someone you are angry with can cause stress, focusing your attention on a photo of a loved one can reduce it.

When counseling a patient facing a daunting task, psychologist Elise Labbe recommends that he or she **listen** to soothing music: "Anything from concertos to country music—whatever feels the most calming to you is the type of music most likely to help ease stress."

Laughter is another effective stress-buster. Health and medical writer Peter Jaret recommends that the stress sufferer **keep** something funny nearby. "It could be a favorite comic strip torn out of the newspaper or a funny card from a family member or a friend. Turn to this every so often during your day."

Not all of these techniques will work for everyone, but finding one or two that work for you can help you keep your cool when life starts to get out of control.

Information source: www.readersdigest.co.uk

**B** **Discussion.** Which tips sound the most useful? Have you tried any of these suggestions?

**C** **Grammar. The subjunctive**

The subjunctive form of a verb is used in noun clauses following verbs or adjectives of urgency, obligation, or advisability. The subjunctive form is always the same as the base form, no matter what the time frame.

The doctor suggested she **exercise** more and **not work** on weekends.
NOT The doctor suggested she ~~exercises~~ more and ~~doesn't work~~ on weekends.

It is important that you **be** aware of the sources of stress in your life.
NOT It is important that you ~~are~~ aware of the sources of stress in your life.

When the verb in the noun clause is in the passive voice, the subjunctive form is <u>be</u> + a past participle.
Psychologists recommend we **be trained** to cope with stress.
NOT Psychologists recommend we ~~are trained~~ to cope with stress.

| Urgency, obligation, and advisability | |
|---|---|
| **Verbs** | **Adjectives** |
| demand | critical |
| insist | crucial |
| propose | desirable |
| request | essential |
| recommend | important |
| suggest | necessary |

**REMEMBER**

Noun clauses following verbs and adjectives that *don't* express urgency, obligation, or advisability don't need the subjunctive.

Psychologists agree that too much conflict **is** harmful to relationships.

It's true that he **finds** his current position very demanding.

PAGE G5
For more…

**D** Decide whether to use the subjunctive and circle the correct form.

1. Sue thinks that Jack (overreact / overreacts) to problems.
2. It's essential that your father (avoid / avoids) taking on more than he can handle.
3. Everyone agrees that a certain amount of stress (be / is) unavoidable.
4. It's critical that Shelly (learn / learns) how to deal with pressure at work.
5. Bill's manager demanded that he (be / is) fired immediately.
6. It's crucial that she (doesn't accept / not accept) more projects than she can handle.
7. I really hope that this plan (be / is) successful.
8. John proposed that he (continue / continues) cooking dinner while we clean the house.
9. Our manager insisted that no one (be / is) late for the divisional meeting.
10. It's true that humor (help / helps) people handle major crises in their lives.
11. It's important that Bruce (try / tries) to exercise more.

## GRAMMAR **EXCHANGE** • *Now talk about ways to manage stress.*

I suggest . . .
I recommend . . .
I think it's important . . .
I believe it's essential . . .

**Pair Work.** Discuss each person's situation. Take turns giving advice, using the subjunctive.

Marie Klein has four exams to study for. She has to take care of her younger brother because her mother is away on a business trip.

Paul Nakamura is working on a huge project. He needs help to finish it, but he prefers working alone.

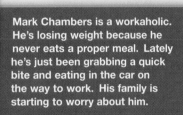

Mark Chambers is a workaholic. He's losing weight because he never eats a proper meal. Lately he's just been grabbing a quick bite and eating in the car on the way to work. His family is starting to worry about him.

Elaine Pace hasn't been sleeping well. She's tired all the time and finds it hard to function effectively during the day, probably the result of stress at work.

Jan Orlini thinks her co-workers are talking about her behind her back. It has her so worried that it's affecting her work.

**Interview.** Interview your partner about the greatest causes of stress in his or her life. List them on your notepad. Then write a tip for each one, using the subjunctive.

**IDEAS**
- too much pressure at work or school
- poor use of time
- conflicts between family members
- communication problems between family, friends, or co-workers

| Causes of stress | Your tips |
|---|---|
| deadlines at work | It's essential that you learn to organize your time better. |

| Causes of stress | Your tips |
|---|---|
| | |

## 3 Discuss how you handle anger

**A** 🎧 **Vocabulary.** **Expressions related to anger.** Listen and practice.

**hold it back** stop oneself from feeling a particular emotion
*Experts say that if you're upset about something, you shouldn't hold it back. Let people know how you feel.*

**keep it in** avoid expressing one's feelings
*I never like showing my anger. I prefer just to keep it in.*

**let it go / shrug it off** decide not to be bothered by something
*He said some pretty insulting things to me, but I just decided to let it go (OR shrug it off).*

**let off steam** get rid of one's anger in a way that does not harm anyone; for example, by doing something active
*Running after work really helps me let off steam. I always feel better afterwards.*

**lose one's temper** suddenly become so angry that one cannot control oneself
*I've never seen Maya lose her temper like that! I was really surprised.*

**make an issue out of something** argue about something others don't think is important
*I didn't like the way she was talking to me, but I didn't want to make an issue out of it.*

**say what's on one's mind** say what one is thinking about
*Look, I know you're angry with me. Why don't you just say what's on your mind?*

**take it out on someone** treat someone badly because one is angry or tired
*When my job is getting to me, I really try not to take it out on my kids.*

**tell someone off** talk angrily to a person who has done something wrong
*I was so mad at that rude waiter that I decided to tell him off. I mean, who does he think he is?*

**B** Which expressions in the vocabulary describe expressing anger? Which ones describe controlling anger?

**C** 🎧 **Listening Comprehension.** Listen to an interview with Michael Chen. Then listen again and check the correct statement, according to his point of view.

Michael Chen

| If Michael Chen were angry with . . . | he would . . . |
|---|---|
| his boss, | ☐ make an issue of it.<br>☐ say what's on his mind.<br>☑ hold his feelings back. |
| his friends or colleagues, | ☐ take it out on someone else.<br>☑ probably let things go for a while before reacting.<br>☐ probably lose his temper. |
| someone he didn't know, | ☑ let it go.<br>☐ possibly lose his temper.<br>☐ take it out on someone else. |

**44 UNIT 4**

**Step 1. Pair Work.** Discuss each situation. How similar is your behavior to your partner's? Use the vocabulary on page 44 to describe how you would handle each situation.

| | *What would you do?* | *How would you handle your anger?* |
|---|---|---|
| | **1.** If a friend were late for a date with me, . . . | |
| | **2.** If I told a friend or colleague something in confidence and he or she didn't keep it a secret, . . . | |
| | **3.** If a colleague talked about me behind my back, . . . | |
| | **4.** If someone lied to me about something that I thought was really important, . . . | |
| | **5.** If someone cut me off while I was driving, . . . | |
| | **6.** If someone borrowed something from me and didn't return it, . . . | |
| | **7.** If my next-door neighbor played very loud music and had late-night parties, . . . | |

**Step 2. Discussion.** Do you act the same way when you get angry with someone you know as you do with a stranger? Explain. Are there times when you don't express your anger? Why or why not?

**Step 3. Group Work.** Tell a true story about something that made you angry. What happened? What did you do about it?

# 4 *Identify what's important in your life*

**A**  **Reading Warm-up.**  What are the things in life that matter most to you?  Do you ever feel that you lack time for them?

**B**  🎧 **Reading.**  Read the article.  What radical changes did Donna Paxton make in her life?

## A Hectic Life Downsized

On paper, Donna Paxton lived a picture-perfect life. She was a successful executive at a large corporation. She lived in a beautiful, spacious home with her husband, also a busy professional, and their two children. Although Paxton was managing to juggle all of her responsibilities at home and at work, she increasingly felt that she was unable to give either her job or her family the time each deserved, and this made her very unhappy.

Paxton realized that she would have to make a choice between having more money and having more time—time to spend with her two daughters, to contribute to her community, and to relax. "I had to decide what was more important to me," she says, "making lots of money at a job that no longer inspired me or being part of my children's lives."

So Paxton made the decision to simplify her life. She quit her high-paying corporate job and took a less stressful job at a non-profit organization in her community. Because Paxton took a significant reduction in salary, her family learned to make do with less, shop more wisely, eat fewer dinners out (giving them more family time around the dinner table), and reduce spending on unnecessary items.

Paxton is still busy, but she is more satisfied and in control of her life. "Simplifying my life has made a big difference," she says. "I'm no longer stressed out and thinking about work when I should be having fun with my kids. I work fewer hours, so I can be involved in my children's school. I have time to exercise, and I'm healthier. Downsizing has brought our family closer together."

### Want To Downsize Your Life?

Donna Paxton simplified her life by making a huge change.  But there are many small changes you can make in your daily routine that will save money, time, and energy.

- **Make a list of the values that are really important to you.**  Is it time with your family?  Making money?  Being active in your community?  It makes sense to focus on doing a few things well instead of stretching yourself too thin.  Cut out activities that aren't consistent with your values.

- **Delegate when possible.**  If you routinely say, "It's faster to do this myself than to tell someone else what to do," try delegating anyway.  You may be surprised.

- **Guard your time as carefully as your money.**  You can always make more money, but time spent is gone forever.  Rather than struggling with a home repair yourself, hire someone to do the job for you.

- **Learn to say no.**  When faced with requests for your time, don't commit yourself when you would rather spend that time on something more important to you.  Make sure to say no politely but firmly.  For example, "I'm sorry, but I just don't have the time."

Information source: www.getmoredone.com

**C**  **Discussion.**

1.  In what ways did Donna Paxton's quality of life improve?

2.  Do you think that you would benefit from any of the suggestions made in the article?  Do you think that these suggestions would be effective for everybody?  Why or why not?

3.  Do you know anyone who has made an extreme change in his or her lifestyle?  What happened?

**D**  🎧 **Word Skills.  Distinguishing meaning.**  Use the context of the article to check the meaning of each of these expressions with <u>make</u>.

| make someone { happy / nervous / crazy | make a decision to (do something) | make a change |
|---|---|---|
| | make do with (something) | make sense to (do something) |
| make a choice between (two things) | make a difference | make sure to (do something) |

**E** Complete the paragraph by circling the correct expressions.

For most people, it doesn't <u>make sense / make a choice</u> to work long hours, live a hectic life, and
(1)
never be able to spend time with friends and family. Such a lifestyle doesn't bring happiness. On
the contrary, it can <u>make a change / make a person</u> miserable. Nevertheless, very few people
(2)
<u>make a decision / make sure</u> to quit their job and start a new life. This may be explained by the fact that
(3)
it isn't easy to <u>make a choice between / make do with</u> money and quality of life. If you quit your job, you'll
(4)
have to <u>make a choice between / make do with</u> fewer material possessions. Those who've decided to
(5)
<u>make a change / make a difference</u> like this don't seem to regret it. They say enjoying the pleasures of everyday
(6)
life—like going out for walks or sitting in the sun—<u>makes a choice / makes a difference</u> in their lives.
(7)

## DISCUSSION **BUILDER** • *Now identify what's important in your life.*

**Step 1. Pair Work.** Discuss and indicate your reaction to each statement with **a**, **b**, or **c**.

| a | b | c |
|---|---|---|
| "I'm just like that." | "I'm sort of like that." | "I'm just the opposite." |

| | My reaction | My partner's reaction |
|---|---|---|
| "If I have a few hours free, my favorite thing to do is just sit in a café and watch the world go by." | | |
| "I want to be able to afford the things that make life fun—stylish clothes, electronic gadgets, a new car, exotic vacations." | | |
| "I can hardly get through a day without some physical exercise—walking, running, working out. I just don't feel right if I can't fit that into my schedule." | | |
| "I could never live very far away from my family. It's important that they always be a big part of my life." | | |
| "I get bored really easily. If I don't have a full schedule with lots of activities planned, I go nuts!" | | |
| "Cooking is too much like work—I don't want to spend a lot of time in the kitchen. I prefer to eat out or just prepare something quick and simple." | | |
| "My friendships are the most important thing in my life. I need to call or get together with my best friends at least once a week, if not more." | | |
| "If I've got a school or work project that needs to get done, I finish it, even if it means getting home late or missing a chance to hang out with friends." | | |

**Step 2. Group Work.** Tell your class what you found out about your partner. What's important to your partner? Is your partner interested in making any changes in his or her life?

# Writing: Provide tips for solving a problem

## Supporting sentences

A paragraph consists of a series of sentences about one topic. A topic sentence introduces the topic and clarifies the focus of the paragraph. For example:

| topic | focus |
|---|---|
| A sedentary lifestyle | has many negative effects on your health. |

The supporting sentences in the paragraph must relate to that topic and focus—by providing details, examples, and other facts.

For one thing, studies show that lack of exercise leads to an increased risk of heart disease.
(a negative effect of a sedentary lifestyle)

Watching TV for long hours increases the chances that a person will snack on unhealthy fatty foods or sweets.
(a negative effect of a sedentary lifestyle)

To write an effective paragraph, avoid sentences that do not relate to the topic or focus of the topic sentence.

~~Most people think obesity is a serious problem only in Western countries.~~
(introduces a new topic unrelated to the topic sentence)

**ERROR CORRECTION**

Underline the topic sentence. Cross out three sentences that do not relate to the topic sentence.

A regular exercise routine can be an effective way to cope with the stresses of daily life. Many people also find listening to music helps them to relax. Exercise classes such as aerobics, yoga, and kick-boxing are a great way to work off tension. Increasing the amount of physical activity in your routine by even a small amount is usually enough to relieve everyday stresses. Joining a health club can be fun, and it is a great way to meet people. It is a well-known fact that regular exercise has a positive effect on the body's chemistry, and it reduces stress by increasing one's sense of well-being. Walking more and driving less is also good for the environment. No matter what activity you choose, exercising regularly will help you lower your stress level.

**Topics**
- A sedentary lifestyle
- Difficulty sleeping
- Lack of organization
- Poor time management
- Your own idea: .............

**Step 1. Prewriting. Outlining to generate ideas.** Choose one of the topics or think of a topic of your own. Write it on the line labeled "Problem" and then propose two or three solutions.

Problem: ............................................................
Solutions: 1. ......................................................
2. ......................................................
3. ......................................................

**Step 2. Writing.** Develop one solution you listed in Step 1 into a full paragraph. Start your paragraph with a topic sentence. Make sure the supporting sentences relate to that topic and focus.

**Step 3. Self-Check.**

☐ Does the paragraph have a topic sentence? Are the topic and focus clear?
☐ Do the supporting sentences in your paragraph all relate to the topic sentence?

# UNIT 4 CHECKPOINT

*SUMMIT* WEBSITE
For Unit 4 online activities, visit
the *Summit* Companion Website at
www.longman.com/summit.

**A** 🎧 **Listening Comprehension.** Listen to three people describe their problems. Then listen
again and complete the chart. Listen a third time if necessary to check your answers.

| Speaker | What is the problem? | What solution did the person find? | Did it work? |
|---|---|---|---|
| 1 | | | |
| 2 | | | |
| 3 | | | |

**B** Match each statement with one of the lettered phrases.
(You will not use all the phrases.)

1. ...... When someone asks Claire to help out, she always
agrees, even if she has too much to do. She . . .

2. ...... Instead of remaining calm, Bob panics when things
don't go as expected. He . . .

3. ...... Laura always misses her deadlines because she doesn't
get started on her assignments right away. She . . .

4. ...... Nick is always worrying about every little detail.
He hates making mistakes. He . . .

a. is a perfectionist.
b. has a negative attitude.
c. waits until the last minute.
d. overreacts to problems.
e. is unable to say no.

**C** Complete each statement about the situations in which you express or control your anger.

1. I hold my feelings back when

2. I tell someone off when he or she

3. I lose my temper when

**D** Use expressions with <u>make</u> to complete the sentences.

1. If your new job pays a significantly lower salary than your old one, you're going to have
to learn to ..................... with less money than before.

2. If you're not happy in your job, it ..................... to look for a new one.

3. ..................... to think carefully about your new responsibilities before you ..................... to take on that job.

4. He had to ..................... between staying in his job and working abroad.

**E** Complete each sentence with your own ideas and the subjunctive.

1. If you find that you never have enough time, I suggest .....................

2. To avoid burnout, it's essential .....................

3. If you can't sleep, I recommend .....................

4. In order to manage stress, it's important .....................

5. When you have a deadline, it's advisable .....................

6. If a person wants to be successful, it's critical .....................

# UNIT 5

## It's all in your mind

UNIT GOALS

1  Present views on superstitions
2  Evaluate suspicious claims
3  Identify fears and phobias
4  Describe and interpret a dream

**A** **Topic Preview.** Look at the website. Have you heard of any of these superstitions? Do you know others in the same categories?

Good Luck | Bad Luck | Animal | General | Baby | Death | Wedding | New Year's

# OldSuperstitions.com
## The Largest List of Superstitions on the Web

### Good Luck Superstitions
A frog brings good luck to the house it enters.

Seeing a spider spinning in the morning brings good luck.
Click here for more …

### Bad Luck Superstitions
Putting shoes on a table is bad luck.

Breaking a mirror brings seven years of bad luck.
Click here for more …

### Animal Superstitions
A dog eating grass brings rain.

Rats leaving a ship mean the ship will sink.
Click here for more …

### General Superstitions
An itchy nose means you will have a fight with someone.

A bed changed on a Friday will bring bad dreams.
Click here for more …

### Baby Superstitions
Babies born with teeth become extremely selfish.

It's unlucky to wash a baby's head for the first twelve months.
Click here for more …

### Death Superstitions
A bird flying through the window is a sign that someone has died.

A pregnant woman at a funeral brings bad luck.
Click here for more …

### Wedding Superstitions
If the groom drops the wedding ring during the ceremony, the marriage is doomed.

After the wedding, the spouse who goes to sleep first will be the first to die.
Click here for more …

### New Year's Superstitions
Empty pockets on New Year's Eve mean a year of financial trouble.

It's bad luck to let a fire go out on New Year's Eve.
Click here for more …

Good Luck | Bad Luck | Animal | General | Baby | Death | Wedding | New Year's

Source: www.OldSuperstitions.com

**B** **Discussion.** Why do you think people believe in superstitions? What purpose do superstitions serve?

**C** 🎧 **Sound Bites.** Read and listen to a conversation about a strange dream.

**CAROLYN:** You won't believe the dream I had last night!
**ANDREW:** Oh yeah?
**CAROLYN:** I was driving in the car and, as usual, it started shaking and making funny noises.
**ANDREW:** What's so weird about that?
**CAROLYN:** Well, listen to what happened next. There was this clap of thunder, and suddenly I was on the back of some giant bird.
**ANDREW:** OK. Then what happened?
**CAROLYN:** Nothing. The alarm went off, and I woke up.
**ANDREW:** Huh. Sounds like your unconscious is trying to tell you something.
**CAROLYN:** Like what?
**ANDREW:** Like maybe it's time to buy a new car?

**D** Answer the questions.

1. How does Carolyn's dream begin? How does it end?
2. What do you think Andrew means when he says, "Sounds like your unconscious is trying to tell you something"?
3. Does Andrew take the dream seriously?
4. What do you think Carolyn's dream means?

## STARTING **POINT**

**Pair Work.** What kinds of dreams do you usually have? Check all the items that apply. Compare and discuss your answers with a partner.

☐ I never dream.  ☐ I rarely remember my dreams.  ☐ My dreams are very pleasant.  ☐ I have scary nightmares.

My dreams are usually about . . .

☐ family
☐ friends
☐ strangers
☐ famous people

☐ food
☐ water
☐ fire
☐ animals

☐ flying
☐ falling
☐ being chased
☐ other: _____

**Discussion.** Do you think dreams have meanings? Why do you think people dream?

# Present views on superstitions

**A** 🎧 GRAMMAR **SNAPSHOT.** Read the responses and notice how non-count nouns are made countable.

## Are you superstitious?

**1**
"Me? No way. I don't believe in any of that silly stuff. But my grandparents did. They believed in the evil eye—that people can harm you just by looking at you. When I was a kid, my grandmother made me wear a lucky charm that looked like an eye—as **a kind of protection**. Truth is, I was always afraid of that charm!"

**2**
"Generally, no. But I have to admit that there are some things I'll always do—just in case. For example, they say it's bad luck if you accidentally spill salt. Well, I've also heard that it's good luck if you throw **a few grains of salt** over your shoulder. So I do that. I guess that makes me kind of superstitious, doesn't it?"

**3**
"Only when it comes to one thing—golf. Whenever I play golf, I wear my lucky socks. No matter how many **games of golf** I play, I never forget to wear them. Hey, you never know. Anything you do for good luck can't hurt. Right?"

**4**
"Well, I practice feng shui, which is a way of setting up your environment to attract good luck. According to feng shui, water holds positive energy that attracts good things, like money and love, into your life. So I always keep **a large bowl of water** filled with fish near my front door. Some people might call that superstition, but I don't agree. It's just a traditional way of doing things."

**B** **Discussion.** Which person are you most like? Why?

**C** **Grammar.** Non-count nouns made countable

**A non-count noun is neither singular nor plural. Except in certain circumstances, it is not preceded by an article. A non-count noun can be preceded by certain quantifiers such as** <u>much</u>, <u>a lot of</u>, <u>a little</u>, **and** <u>some</u>.

> Some people believe **a little** spilled salt is bad luck.
> NOT ~~A spilled salt~~ is bad luck. OR Spilled salt ~~are~~ bad luck.

**Many non-count nouns can be made countable by using a phrase to limit them or give them a form.**

> If you want to give someone some fruit, it's better to give **two pieces of fruit** instead of one. One piece might be unlucky.

> If you spill salt, you might have bad luck. You should throw **a few grains of salt** over your shoulder to make sure you don't.

> **A clap of thunder** after a funeral brings good luck.

**Some nouns can be used in both a countable and an uncountable sense.**

> According to popular **belief**, a lucky charm that looks like an eye can protect people against the evil eye. (Uncountable use)

> **The belief** in the evil eye is a superstition common to a number of different cultures. (Countable use, singular form)

> Superstitions are popular **beliefs** that are passed down from generation to generation. (Countable use, plural form)

**PAGES G5–G6**
**For more ...**

### Phrases that make non-count nouns countable

**a piece of** (fruit / paper / wood / metal / advice)
**a grain of** (sand / salt / rice / sugar)
**a game of** (tennis / soccer / chess)
**a type** (or **kind**) **of** (energy / behavior / courage)
**a symbol of** (love / companionship / eternity)
**an act of** (kindness / love / hatred / evil)
**an article of** (clothing)
**a bolt** (or **flash**) **of** (lightning)
**a clap of** (thunder)
**a drop of** (rain / coffee / water)
**a bowl of** (rice / soup / cereal)
**a loaf of** (bread)

### Nouns used in both a countable and an uncountable sense

| | |
|---|---|
| a fruit = a single piece of fruit | fruit = a type of food |
| a light = a light source, such as a light bulb, lamp, etc. | light = a type of energy |
| a metal = a specific substance, such as gold or steel | metal = a type of substance |
| a hair = a single hair | hair = all the hair on the head |
| a shampoo = a brand of shampoo | shampoo = soap for your hair |
| a chance = a possibility | chance = luck |

**D** Underline thirteen non-count nouns in the article. Circle four examples of non-count nouns made countable. Find three nouns that are used in both a countable and an uncountable sense.

At Western weddings, people perform some rituals that prove their unconscious belief in superstitions. There's a chance that misfortune will follow if the rituals are not observed, and no one seems to be willing to take such a risk. Throwing rice at the bride and groom is a ritual based on a superstition. So is wearing a plain gold wedding ring. Grains of rice are a symbol of fertility, and plain gold rings are a symbol of eternity.

My advice to those getting married and looking forward to a long-lasting relationship is that they leave nothing to chance. However, since there is no guarantee that happiness will follow, here is one more piece of advice—that they nurture their relationship by sharing companionship and love, which are far more important than good luck!

**E** On a separate sheet of paper, rewrite the superstitions, using a phrase to make each underlined non-count noun countable.

1. If you accidentally knock your hand against <u>wood</u>, you're going to have a love affair, but if you knock your hand against <u>metal</u>, it's a warning of danger.
2. <u>Lightning</u> will never strike a house where a fire is burning.
3. If you hear <u>thunder</u> and the sound comes on your right side, then you can expect good luck for the next twenty-four hours.
4. Letting the first <u>rain</u> in May touch your face brings you luck throughout the year.
5. If you sew or repair <u>clothing</u> while you are wearing it, bad luck will follow.
6. Turning <u>bread</u> upside down after a slice has been cut from it will bring bad luck.
7. Never stare at someone while you are eating <u>rice</u>, or you will slowly become ugly.

## GRAMMAR **EXCHANGE** • *Now present your views on superstitions.*

**Group Work.** Interview one to three classmates to find out if they are "superstitious." Write their superstitions on your notepad, using phrases to make non-count nouns countable when possible.

**IDEAS**
- practicing astrology
- practicing feng shui
- making wishes
- carrying lucky charms
- avoiding certain unlucky actions
- other: ........................

name: *Paul*
*believes spilling a drop of wine while proposing a toast brings good luck*

| name: | name: | name: |
|---|---|---|
| | | |
| | | |
| | | |
| | | |

**Discussion.** Write some of your classmates' superstitions on the board. Where do you think they originated? Is there reason to believe that any of them may in fact be worthwhile? Which ones do people practice without necessarily believing in them? Why is that?

## 2 Evaluate suspicious claims

CONVERSATION

### A 🎧 CONVERSATION **SNAPSHOT**

**A:** It says here they've figured out a way to make diamonds from garbage.

**B:** You don't believe that, do you?

**A:** Why not? They even give you a free 2-carat diamond if you invest in the company.

**B:** Sounds like a scam to me.

**A:** You're such a cynic! What if it's true?

**B:** It can't be true. You really shouldn't believe everything you read.

> 🎧 **Ways to express disbelief**
> You don't believe that, do you?
> Oh, come on!          That's too good to be true.
> That's impossible!    That can't be true!

🎧 **Rhythm and intonation practice**

**EXCEPTIONAL INVESTMENT OPPORTUNITY!**
Scientists at the International Gemstone Institute have unlocked one of the Earth's secrets. They've invented a unique process for creating diamonds—out of trash!

*Invest in IGI and Make Millions!*

*Act quickly! Invest now and you'll receive a free 2-carat diamond.*

### B Grammar. Indefiniteness and definiteness: article usage

**Indefiniteness**

A noun is indefinite when it doesn't refer to a specific person, place, or thing. Use the articles <u>a</u> / <u>an</u> with indefinite singular count nouns. Don't use articles with indefinite plural or non-count nouns.
>    You get **a diamond** if you invest in the company.
>    Are you sure **diamonds** can be made from **garbage**?

**Definiteness**

A noun is definite when it refers to a specific person, place, or thing; for example, when you mention something a second time. Use the article <u>the</u> with definite singular and plural count nouns and with definite non-count nouns.
>    You get a diamond made from garbage? Sounds like **the diamond** is a fake.
>    **The garbage** they use to make **the diamonds** is burned first.

**Uniqueness**

The article <u>the</u> can also be used with a noun to represent something unique.
>    **The president** has named two new foreign ministers. (There is only one president of a country.)
>    Now they're claiming that pollution has no effect on **the environment**. (The earth has only one environment.)

**Generic use**

To represent all members of a class or group of people, places, or things, a plural count noun or a singular count noun with a definite or an indefinite article may be used.
> Diamonds are
> The diamond is } the hardest naturally occurring substance on the earth.
> A diamond is

*Grammar Booster*
*Pronunciation Booster*
PAGES G7–G8          PAGES P5–P6
For more ...          Linking sounds

### C Read each statement and choose the description that more closely expresses its meaning.

1. Morning snow makes highways dangerous.
   ✓**a.** refers to morning snow in general
   **b.** refers to the snow that fell this morning

2. I think superstitions are ridiculous.
   **a.** refers to all superstitions
   **b.** refers to some superstitions

3. The diamond they sent me is a fake.
   **a.** refers to diamonds as a member of a class
   **b.** refers to a specific diamond we know about

4. Some cultures regard the shark as a sign of luck.
   **a.** refers to a specific shark we know about
   **b.** refers to sharks as a class or group

5. The queen will address Parliament this week.
   **a.** refers to a specific queen
   **b.** refers to queens generically

6. A queen can address Parliament.
   **a.** refers to a specific queen
   **b.** refers to queens generically

**D** Complete the statements about product claims. Insert <u>a</u>, <u>an</u>, or <u>the</u> before a noun or noun phrase where necessary. Write <u>X</u> if the noun should not have an article.

1. A British company claims to have invented ............ machine that allows ............ people to talk with their pets. ............ machine, called the PetCom, will be available this fall.

2. It's well known that ............ carrots are a good source of ............ vitamins. In fact, research has determined that drinking ............ glass of NutriPure carrot juice every day can add ............ years to your life.

3. The WeightAway diet plan promises to help you lose ............ weight fast. The company guarantees that people following ............ diet plan can lose up to 10 kg per week.

4. Last week, the news reported that thousands of people had sent ............ money to ............ organization advertising a shampoo that ............ organization claimed would grow ............ hair overnight.

5. Our Intellihat is guaranteed to make you smarter. Special mirrors on ............ hat use the power of ............ sun to increase brain activity.

---

## CONVERSATION **STARTER** • *Now evaluate some suspicious claims.*

**Group Work.** What suspicious claims have you seen on TV or in advertisements? Write the claims on the board and decide which ones you think are "believable," "unlikely," or "ridiculous." Explain your opinions.

**Pair Work.** Use the Conversation Snapshot on page 54 and these ads as a guide to talk about suspicious claims. Start like this: "It says here …"

New Audio CD Keeps Babies Asleep All Night!

New technology creates sounds that calm even the fussiest infant! You'll never have to wake up in the middle of the night again! Call 1-800-SHH-BABY now to order. As a bonus gift, the first 100 callers will receive a free portable CD player, perfect for car or stroller!

**AMAZING JUICE!!**

06:00  12:00  18:00  24:00

### Guarantees Weight Loss!

Eat anything you want. Just drink Miracle Juice <u>before</u> you eat and watch the weight melt away! We promise you'll see big results in just 24 hours! Buy now and get two bottles of Miracle Juice for the price of one!

**Attract your Soulmate!**

Put our amazing lucky charm in your pocket and you'll receive a marriage proposal in one week. Guaranteed! If you're not completely satisfied, we'll refund your money.

# 3 Identify fears and phobias

**A** **Reading Warm-up.** What are you most afraid of? Do your fears ever interfere with your life?

**B** 🎧 **Reading.** Read the article. Which phobias do you think would be the most difficult to live with?

**What are you afraid of?**

1 Are you so terrified of getting on a plane that you avoid traveling? Does seeing a spider in the sink make your blood run cold? When you go to the doctor for a shot, does the sight of the needle make you want to run the other way? If these situations—or the sight of blood, standing at great heights, going to the dentist, or being in open spaces—fill you with dread, then you may have a phobia.

2 Phobias are often laughed off as being totally irrational. People who don't have these fears find them difficult to understand. "It's all in your mind" is a common response. But it's believed that 10% of the population has some kind of phobia or overwhelming anxiety—and for them, it's no joke.

3 We all have a built-in defense system to protect ourselves from danger. Our heartbeat gets faster, our throat goes dry, sweating increases, and we do anything we can to remove ourselves from danger. This is normal. But phobias are exaggerated fears, usually unrelated to real dangers, and trying to avoid the cause only makes the phobias worse.

4 The list of recognized phobias is enormous, ranging from fear of spiders (arachnophobia) to fear of technology (technophobia). People can develop fears of almost anything. For some, being in social situations fills them with dread that others are looking at them critically or talking about them behind their backs. People with phobias often feel embarrassed or silly for having their fear. Although they know there's no actual danger, they're unable to make the fear go away.

5 If a phobia or an anxiety takes over your life, you may want to do something to try and help you deal with it—or even eventually overcome it. Let's say you're afraid of the dark. Try sleeping with a night light so that it's not so dark. The phobia won't necessarily go away, but you may be able to get a good night's sleep. There are a number of relaxation techniques you can try, such as meditation or deep breathing, which can help you control your anxiety.

6 And by all means, if you find the phobia getting in your way, interfering with doing what you want to do and being who you want to be, talk to your doctor. Chances are your phobia is not as weird as you may think it is. Keep in mind that you're not alone, and your doctor can probably help you.

**There are hundreds of phobias, and they each have a name—some you may have never heard of!**

acrophobia: heights
agoraphobia: open spaces
arithmophobia: numbers
aviophobia: flying
brontophobia: thunder and lightning
claustrophobia: enclosed spaces
dentophobia: dentists
hydrophobia: water
mechanophobia: machines
necrophobia: death
nyctophobia: the dark
oneirophobia: dreams
technophobia: technology
xenophobia: foreigners or strangers

Information sources: www.bbc.com and www.phobiaslist.com

**C** Scan the article and write the number of the paragraph that attempts to address each of these questions. (Do not use a number more than once.)

|  | How are phobias different from normal fears? |
|---|---|
|  | What can you do to deal with a phobia? |
|  | What different types of phobias are there? |
|  | What should you do if your phobia gets out of control? |
|  | How are phobias generally perceived? |
|  | How do you know if you have a phobia? |

**make up one's mind** If you make up your mind to do something, you decide to do it no matter what happens.

**change one's mind** If you change your mind, you change your opinion or decision about something.

**keep (something) in mind** If you keep something in mind, you pay attention to a piece of information because it may be important or helpful.

**put (something) out of one's mind** If you put something out of your mind, you try not to let it worry or bother you.

**be all in one's mind** If something is not real and a person is imagining it, you can tell the person, "it's all in your mind."

**be out of one's mind** If people believe you are out of your mind, they think you're behaving in a way that is crazy or foolish.

**E** Complete the paragraph with expressions with <u>mind</u>. Make any necessary changes.

Although Samantha had always had a fear of flying, she finally ................................... to travel by
(1)

plane. Her friends had told her she could overcome her fear if she ........................... that there
(2)

are very few plane accidents. However, just before boarding the plane, she ...........................
(3)

and decided not to take the flight. When she suddenly turned around and said, "I just can't

get on this plane," the other passengers thought she ........................... . She was afraid the plane
(4)

would crash, and she couldn't ........................... . She knew there was no real problem.
(5)

It ..........................., but she couldn't control her phobia.
(6)

## DISCUSSION **BUILDER** • *Now identify your fears and phobias.*

**Step 1. Pair Work.** Complete the survey. Discuss your answers with your partner.
What do you do to overcome your fears?

*RATE YOURSELF*
0 = not afraid at all
1 = a little uneasy
2 = somewhat fearful
3 = absolutely terrified

# HOW CHICKEN ARE YOU?
**Rate your response to each of the following situations.**

◯ The plane you're on takes off or lands.

◯ The plane you're on encounters turbulence.

◯ There's a spider on the wall.

◯ There's a spider on your shoulder.

◯ You're at a party where you don't know anyone.

◯ You have to give a speech in front of fifty people.

◯ You're about to be given an injection by your doctor.

◯ Your doctor tells you that you need surgery.

◯ You're driving in a bad rainstorm.

◯ You're a passenger in a car during a bad rainstorm.

◯ You're looking out the window from the top floor of a skyscraper.

◯ You're looking over the edge of a high cliff.

**INTERPRET YOUR SCORE:**
0–9 points = LIONHEARTED. Nothing seems to bother you.
10–18 points = CAUTIOUS. Hey, a little discomfort and anxiety never hurt anyone.
19–27 points = NAIL-BITER. Avoid too much excitement!
28–36 points = TOTAL CHICKEN. Doesn't take much to set you off, does it?

**Step 2. Discussion.** Which situations elicit the most fear among your classmates?
Why do you think so many people in the class found those situations frightening?
How rational are those fears? What could someone do to overcome them?

# Describe and interpret a dream

## A Word Skills. Using participial adjectives

> **REMEMBER**
>
> **A present participle can be used as an adjective to describe a noun or noun phrase.**
>    The dream I had last night was very **disturbing**. ("Disturbing" describes the dream.)
>
> **A past participle can be used as an adjective to describe a noun or noun phrase, but it has a passive meaning.**
>    After I woke up from the dream, I felt very **disturbed** by it. ("Disturbed" describes how the dream made me feel.)

| 🎧 Some participial adjectives | |
|---|---|
| confusing | confused |
| depressing | depressed |
| disappointing | disappointed |
| disturbing | disturbed |
| embarrassing | embarrassed |
| enlightening | enlightened 开明的 |
| exciting | excited |
| fascinating | fascinated 着迷的 |
| frightening | frightened |
| shocking | shocked |
| startling | startled 惊吓 |
| surprising | surprised |

## B Circle the correct participial adjective.

1. The violent images that appear in dreams can be very (shocking / shocked). But psychologists say we shouldn't be (shocking / shocked) by anything that appears in our dreams.

2. Mark found his frequent nightmares extremely (disturbing / disturbed).

3. I was (surprising / surprised) to learn that everyone has dreams, even if they don't remember them.

4. Researchers were (fascinating / fascinated) to discover that young children do not dream about themselves until the age of three or four.

5. Sometimes nightmares are so (startling / startled) that the brain reacts, causing some people to jerk their arms and legs suddenly while they sleep.

## C 🎧 Listening Comprehension. Listen to the radio call-in program. After each call, answer the questions about each dream.

| Margo's dream | Simon's dream |
|---|---|
| 1. How often has she had the dream? | 1. How often has he had the dream? |
| 2. How does she feel during the dream? | 2. How does he feel during the dream? |
| 3. What effect does the dream have on her afterward? | 3. What effect does the dream have on him afterward? |

## D 🎧 Pair Work. Read the questions below. Then listen to the program again. Discuss and answer the questions.

1. How does Margo interpret her own dream?
2. How does Dr. Walker interpret it?
3. How does Simon interpret his own dream?
4. How does Dr. Walker interpret it?

## E Discussion. Do you agree with what Dr. Walker says about dreams? If not, what purpose do you think dreams serve? Do you believe they predict the future?

## DISCUSSION **BUILDER** • *Now describe and interpret a dream.*

**Step 1. Pair Work.** If it is true that a dream can indicate the fears and wishes of the dreamer, how would *you* match the common dreams below with some possible meanings? If you don't find a meaning you agree with, write your own interpretation.

| Common dreams |
| --- |
| falling from a steep cliff |
| flying in a hot-air balloon |
| being chased by a terrible monster |
| climbing an endless flight of stairs |
| failing an important exam |
| winning a sports event or contest |

| Possible meanings |
| --- |
| desire to escape a responsibility or task |
| fear of failure |
| high self-esteem |
| pride in one's achievements |
| desire for success |
| lack of self-confidence |

**Step 2.** Write some notes on your notepad about a recurring dream—a dream you've had more than once—or a particularly memorable dream.

Who was in the dream?                    How often have you had this dream?


What was it about?                       What do you think it means?



**Step 3. Discussion.** Listen to your classmates describe their dreams.
Offer an interpretation of each dream's meaning.

# Writing: Describe a superstition

## Subject-verb agreement

In English, verbs and subjects must always agree in number.

**A belief** in superstitions **is** very common in different parts of the world.

**Remember these rules:**

1. When the subject and verb are separated by other words, the subject and verb must still agree.

   **The stories** that my grandmother tells me **are** fascinating.

2. When two subjects are connected with <u>and</u> in a sentence, the verb is plural.

   **A black cat** and **a broken mirror are** symbols of bad luck.

3. When verbs occur in a sequence, all the verbs must agree with the subject.

   My sister **believes** in ghosts, **avoids** the number 13, and **carries** a rabbit's foot in her pocket.

4. When the subject is an indefinite pronoun like <u>each</u>, <u>everyone</u>, <u>anyone</u>, <u>somebody</u>, or <u>no one</u>, use a singular verb.

   **Everyone worries** about the evil eye.

5. When the subject is <u>all</u>, <u>some</u>, or <u>none</u> and refers to a singular count noun or a non-count noun, use a singular verb. Otherwise, use a plural verb.

   If salt is spilled by accident, **some is** immediately thrown over the shoulder.

   **Some** superstitions **are** outdated, but **some are** not.

### ERROR CORRECTION

Identify and correct four errors in subject-verb agreement in the paragraph below.

One common superstition in Western countries concern the number thirteen. Because they are considered unlucky, many situations involving the number thirteen is frequently avoided. For example, in the past, the thirteenth floor of tall apartment buildings were often labeled "fourteen." While that is rare today, there are still many people who are uncomfortable renting an apartment on the thirteenth floor. In addition, there is a general belief that Friday the thirteenth brings bad luck, increases the chance of mishaps, and make it more difficult to get things done effectively.

## Step 1. Prewriting. "Freewriting" for ideas.

- Choose a superstition you're familiar with. On a separate sheet of paper, write, for five to ten minutes, any words, phrases, statements, or questions about the topic that come to mind. Write quickly. Do not take time to correct spelling, punctuation, organization, etc.

- Read what you wrote. Circle ideas that go together and add more details.

### Freewriting

the number 13

tall buildings

no 13th floor

Why won't people rent?

Friday the 13th

   unlucky day

   difficult to get

      things done

   people don't take trips,

      make appointments

## Step 2. Writing. On a separate sheet of paper, describe a superstition. Use your freewriting notes for ideas.

## Step 3. Self-Check.

☐ Does every sentence have a subject and a verb? Underline all the subjects and circle all the verbs.

☐ Do all the subjects and verbs agree? Correct errors in agreement.

SUMMIT WEBSITE
For Unit 5 online activities, visit the *Summit* Companion Website at www.longman.com/summit.

**A** 🎧 **Listening Comprehension.** Listen to the conversations. After each conversation, summarize the claim that the people are talking about. Then listen again. After each conversation, decide whether the people find the claim believable, unlikely, or ridiculous.

| | What is the claim? | believable | unlikely | ridiculous |
|---|---|---|---|---|
| **1.** | | ☐ | ☐ | ☑ |
| **2.** | | ☑ | ☐ | ☐ |
| **3.** | | ☐ | ☑ | ☐ |

**B** Correct eight errors in article usage.

A lucky charm is the object that some people carry because they think it will bring good luck. My lucky charm is a rabbit's foot that I received as gift on my birthday. I don't really know if it has ever brought me a good luck, but I always carry it in my pocket. Since medieval times, the rabbit's feet have been said to bring a good fortune because people believed that witches were capable of turning themselves into rabbits or hares when they were being chased. Both rabbit and hare are very fast animals, so witches stood a good chance of escaping if they turned into one of them. Since then, the people have believed that carrying a rabbit's foot will protect them.

**C** Choose the correct expression to complete each sentence.

1. If you have a fear of spiders, you should ............ that spiders are very easy to kill.
   **a.** make up your mind     **b.** keep in mind

2. Though he was hesitant at first, in the end he ............ to seek help for his problem.
   **a.** was out of his mind     **b.** made up his mind

3. She made the decision to get married, but a month before the wedding, she ............ .
   **a.** changed her mind     **b.** kept it in mind

4. People who have a phobia find it very difficult to ............ .
   **a.** make up their mind     **b.** put it out of their mind

**D** Circle the correct participial adjective.

1. When I was a child, a sudden bolt of lightning struck our house. I've been (frightened / frightening) by lightning ever since.

2. Some may find it (surprised / surprising) to learn that British statesman Winston Churchill liked to pet black cats for good luck.

3. John felt (enlightened / enlightening) by Dr. Howe's informative seminar on identifying and overcoming phobias.

4. Mary was (disturbed / disturbing) that her exam was scheduled for the 13th—a sure sign of bad luck.

5. The author's comparison of superstitions from around the world is absolutely (fascinated / fascinating).

# Travel hassles and experiences

**UNIT GOALS**

1 Express regret or relief
2 Ask someone for a favor
3 Describe a "travel nightmare"
4 Explain a life-changing event

**A** **Topic Preview.** Look at the travel supplies catalogue. Circle any products that seem useful to you.

## Travel Wise
### A New Concept in Travel Supplies

*"I could have avoided so many hassles on my last vacation if I'd bothered to read your catalogue first."*
—Joseph DeLeon, Montreal, Canada

*"If I had had some of these terrific products when I was traveling in Europe, my trip would have gone much more smoothly!"*
—Marta Chela-Flores, Caracas, Venezuela

## Featured Products

### The Point-O-Gram
Don't know the language? No problem! Point to the pictures on this foldable card and communicate with people in any culture.
Details on page 7
Item # 20027

### Cash Stash Key Ring
Run out of cash? Never! The Cash Stash Key Ring will hold your stash of cash for that unexpected emergency.
Details on page 22
Item # 20030

### The Docu-Pouch
Tired of fumbling around for your passport and boarding pass? Avoid unnecessary delays at airport security. Keep your most important travel documents close at hand.
Details on page 9
Item # 20028

### The Dry Pack
Don't let anything spoil your day at the beach. Our waterproof waist pack will let you keep your valuables with you while you swim.
Details on page 26
Item # 20031

### Conversion Wizard
Want to know how much that suit costs in *your* currency? Pesos, yen, dollars, won, reais, euros—you name it! Work out the price instantly with our handy currency converter.
Details on page 4
Item # 20026

### Luggage Spotters
Let's face it—too many suitcases look alike. Spot your bags from a distance with our practical fluorescent grips. Four per package.
Details on page 19
Item # 20029

3

**B** **Discussion.** Have you ever needed and wished you'd had one of these products? If you were to go on an overseas trip, which travel supplies from the catalogue would you consider taking?

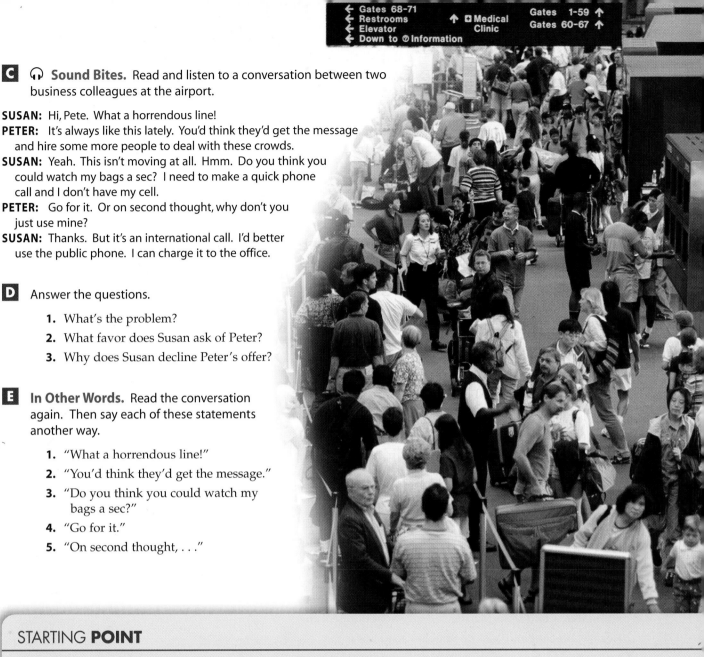

← Gates 68-71  
← Restrooms  
← Elevator  
← Down to ⓘ Information  

↑ ☒ Medical  
　 Clinic  

Gates 1-59 ↑  
Gates 60-67 ↑

**C** 🎧 **Sound Bites.** Read and listen to a conversation between two business colleagues at the airport.

**SUSAN:** Hi, Pete. What a horrendous line!

**PETER:** It's always like this lately. You'd think they'd get the message and hire some more people to deal with these crowds.

**SUSAN:** Yeah. This isn't moving at all. Hmm. Do you think you could watch my bags a sec? I need to make a quick phone call and I don't have my cell.

**PETER:** Go for it. Or on second thought, why don't you just use mine?

**SUSAN:** Thanks. But it's an international call. I'd better use the public phone. I can charge it to the office.

**D** Answer the questions.

1. What's the problem?
2. What favor does Susan ask of Peter?
3. Why does Susan decline Peter's offer?

**E** **In Other Words.** Read the conversation again. Then say each of these statements another way.

1. "What a horrendous line!"
2. "You'd think they'd get the message."
3. "Do you think you could watch my bags a sec?"
4. "Go for it."
5. "On second thought, . . ."

## STARTING **POINT**

**Pair Work.** Discuss and list some of the kinds of hassles that occur when people travel. Write the name of a product or idea that might help in dealing with each problem.

| | Hassle | Useful product or idea |
|---|---|---|
| at airports | | |
| in hotels | | |
| on planes | | |
| on trains | | |
| on buses | | |
| with language | | |
| with money | | |
| with food | | |

## Express regret or relief

**A** 🎧 GRAMMAR **SNAPSHOT.** Read the interviews and notice the conditional sentences.

This is Travel TV, and I'm Carolyn Savoy.

SAVOY: I'm here with Pietro Nasta, who just arrived in New York on a flight from Rome. He made the mistake of putting his film in his checked luggage, and it got damaged during screening. Isn't that right, Mr. Nasta?

NASTA: Unfortunately, yes. **If I'd put the film in my carry-on, it wouldn't have gotten damaged.** Good thing I brought along my digital, too!

SAVOY: We're at the lost baggage counter with Sonia Granger, who's filling out a claim form for two bags that disappeared on her flight from Buenos Aires. Ms. Granger, what happened?

GRANGER: I could just kick myself! **If only I'd put some of my essentials in my purse!** Everything I needed was in those bags. **If I'd taken a few simple precautions, I wouldn't be in this predicament now!**

SAVOY: I'm standing here with Kazu Kamamura. Mr. Kamamura, you just arrived from Tokyo. Did you have any problems with customs or immigration?

KAMAMURA: Actually, no. It was very easy. I only needed my passport. I'm lucky. **If I weren't Japanese, I probably would have needed a visa, too.**

**B** **Discussion.** Have you ever lost your luggage, forgotten your ID or passport, or taken something through security by mistake? What happened?

**C** **Grammar.** **Conditional sentences with mixed time frames**

PAGES P6–P7
Past participles;
Reduction

**Review: present and past conditional sentences**

Look at the sequence of tenses in the <u>if</u> clause and the result clause.

**The present factual conditional:** If you **check** the luggage limits, you { 'll avoid / 're going to avoid / may / might / can avoid } extra charges.

**The present unreal conditional:** If they **traveled** more often, they { wouldn't be / might not be } upset about all the delays.

**The past unreal conditional:** If I'd **looked** at the expiration date, I { would have renewed / could / might have renewed } my passport.

PAGES G8–G9
For more …

**Mixed time frames**

In some cases, the sequence of tenses in past conditional sentences changes to support specific meaning. Look at the following examples.

**A past unreal condition with a present result:**  If I'd **made** a hotel reservation, I **wouldn't be staying** with my relatives.
(I didn't make a hotel reservation, so I'm staying with my relatives.)

**A permanent unreal condition with a past result:**  If I **weren't** Japanese, I **might have needed** a visa to enter the country.
(I'm Japanese, so I didn't need a visa to enter the country.)

**D** Choose the sentence that best explains the meaning of each quotation.

1. "If my sister had watched her bags more carefully, her jewelry might not have gotten stolen."
   a. My sister doesn't watch her bags carefully, so her jewelry might get stolen.
   b. My sister didn't watch her bags carefully, so her jewelry got stolen.
   c. My sister watched her bags carefully, so her jewelry didn't get stolen.

2. "If the agent had printed the tickets correctly, I wouldn't be waiting around for new ones to arrive."
   a. The agent printed the tickets correctly, so I don't have to wait around for new ones to arrive.
   b. The agent didn't print the tickets correctly, so I have to wait around for new ones to arrive.
   c. The agent didn't print the tickets correctly, so I had to wait around for new ones to arrive.

3. "If my friend's luggage hadn't been stolen, he would go on the sightseeing tour."
   a. My friend's luggage was stolen, so he isn't going on the sightseeing tour.
   b. My friend's luggage wasn't stolen, so he's going on the sightseeing tour.
   c. My friend's luggage was stolen, so he didn't go on the sightseeing tour.

4. "If we hadn't remembered to bring our passports, we could have gotten into big trouble."
   a. We remembered to bring our passports, so we didn't get into big trouble.
   b. We didn't remember to bring our passports, so we got into big trouble.
   c. We didn't remember to bring our passports, but we didn't get into big trouble.

5. "If I were the kind of person who comes on time, I wouldn't have missed the plane."
   a. I'm not the kind of person who comes on time, so I missed the plane.
   b. I'm the kind of person who comes on time, but I missed the plane.
   c. I'm not the kind of person who comes on time, but I didn't miss the plane.

**E** Complete the statements. Use a negative if appropriate.

**Situation 1: Your friend is having trouble fitting some gifts in her luggage.**

1. If you _____ (check) the size of your suitcase, you wouldn't have this problem now.
2. Truth is, you _____ (be) worrying about this now if you had gotten a bigger suitcase to begin with.
3. If you _____ (have to) leave today, you could get a new suitcase.

**Situation 2: You and a friend are spending your first day visiting Athens.**

1. If we hadn't gotten up so late, we _____ (see) half of Athens already!
2. I'm sure we _____ (find) the Parthenon earlier if we'd brought a guidebook.
3. Do you think we might get better directions if we _____ (know) how to speak Greek?

## GRAMMAR EXCHANGE • *Now express regret or relief.*

On a separate sheet of paper, make a list of the kinds of things that can cause problems when you travel.

*1. Forgetting to pack things*
*2. Losing a ticket*

Then role-play a TV interview at an airport in another country. Use the conditional to express regret or relief. Use the Grammar Snapshot as a guide and your list for ideas.

**IDEAS**

**Problems with . . .**

luggage (carry-ons, security . . . )
documents (passports, visas, tickets . . . )
valuables (jewelry, money, cameras, laptops . . . )
people (passengers, flight attendants, family . . . )
reservations (hotels, flights, car rentals . . . )

*"If I hadn't forgotten to pack my aspirin, I might not have this headache now. Can you tell me if there's a drugstore at the airport?"*

# 2 Ask someone for a favor

## A 🎧 CONVERSATION **SNAPSHOT**

**A:** Paul? I wonder if you could do me a favor.

**B:** What's that?

**A:** I need to talk to the agent at the counter. Do you think you could keep an eye on my things for a few seconds?

**B:** Of course. I'd be happy to.

**A:** Thanks so much. I'll only be a moment.

🎧 **Rhythm and intonation practice**

## B 🎧 Vocabulary. Ways to ask for a favor. Listen and practice.

## Would you mind...

*keeping an eye on my things?*

*holding my place in line?*

*moving that bag?*

*turning the TV up a bit?*

## Could you please...

*let me know when my package arrives?*

FRONT DESK

*give me a hand with my bag?*

*get me a taxi?*

HOTEL

*point me in the right direction?*

## C 🎧 Listening Comprehension. Listen to the conversations and determine which favors the people are asking for. Then listen again and use the expressions from the vocabulary to complete each statement. Make changes as needed.

1. He wants him to ........................................ .

2. She would like her to ........................................ .

3. He needs her to ........................................ .

4. She's asking him to ........................................ .

5. He wants her to ........................................ .

6. She wants someone to ........................................ .

**Role Play.** Role-play all the possible opportunities in the illustration to ask for a favor. Use the Conversation Snapshot and the vocabulary as a guide. Start like this: "Excuse me ..."

# 3 Describe a "travel nightmare"

**A** **Reading Warm-up.** Have you ever had any serious problems while traveling? What happened?

**B** 🎧 **Reading.** Read the magazine article. Do you think the travel tips are useful?

SMART TRAVELER | TRIPFIX

# A Valuable Lesson

Dear Christopher:

My wife and I recently traveled to Portland with our children and stayed at the Fairview Hotel. While we were out, our rooms were burglarized. Two laptops, a digital video camera, and a PDA were stolen, among other items.

The loss was particularly devastating because one laptop contained data that enable me to operate my business. Hotel records indicated that a housekeeping key was used to enter the room. More than 24 hours passed before any employees were questioned, and then only after we insisted that the hotel investigate. In our opinion, the staff failed to provide my family with secure lodging. What's more, they made absolutely no attempt to recover or replace over $12,000 worth of stolen property. Can you help us?

—M. White, New York, NY

*Elliott's response:*

**The only thing** you and the Fairview can agree on is that your room was burglarized. Mark Rogers, the hotel's general manager, insists your complaint was handled properly.

As a "gesture of goodwill," the Fairview refunded your $645.12 room charge. Its insurance company also kicked in another $1,220. Does the hotel owe you more? I think so. After we intervened, the Fairview agreed to a settlement that covered your entire loss.

**Lessons learned:**

- Leaving $12,000 worth of property in a hotel room is always a bad idea. The most secure place for your valuables is the hotel manager's safe (though some in-room safes are now big enough to accommodate a laptop).

- If you back up important data before you leave home, your loss will be limited to hardware. Another tip: Take out travel insurance, which would cover a burglary. And check your homeowner's insurance: It might cover your losses.

- Consider traveling with less hardware. You might even be able to get away with leaving your laptop at home. Several online sites offer a service that allows you to connect with your home or work computer remotely from any Internet-connected computer.

- If I were you, on my next trip I wouldn't let my laptop—or any other valuables—out of my sight. That's the only way to make sure they aren't stolen.

—*Christopher Elliott*

**IN OUR NEXT ISSUE**
- Avoiding pickpockets
- Tipping
- Car rental information
- Exchanging currency for local cash
- Avoiding jet lag

Source: *National Geographic Traveler*

**C** Find the following information in the article.

1. What items were stolen?
2. What was the value of the stolen property?
3. How much did Mr. White pay for the rooms?
4. How much did the hotel offer to pay at first?
5. How much did the hotel finally pay in compensation?
6. What does Elliott suggest to protect business data?

**D** Discussion.

1. Besides the value of the stolen items, why was the loss such a problem? Why did Mr. White think the hotel was responsible? How was the problem resolved?
2. Do you think Mr. White had the right to claim $12,000 from the hotel?

**The past participle of a transitive verb can function as a noun modifier.**

| | |
|---|---|
| burglarized | *The room was burglarized by two men.  The **burglarized room** was searched by the police.* |
| broken | *Jim's new camera got broken.  The **broken camera** wasn't under warranty.* |
| soiled | *When my suitcase opened, all of my jackets got soiled.  I took the **soiled jackets** to a dry cleaner.* |
| crushed | *My laptop was crushed by the bus.  The bus company compensated me for the **crushed laptop**.* |
| stained | *My silk tie got stained.  The **stained tie** couldn't be cleaned.* |
| torn | *Her blouse was torn by the hotel laundry.  The hotel offered to repair or replace the **torn blouse**.* |
| damaged | *The luggage was damaged by the airline.  The airline claimed that it was not responsible for the **damaged luggage**.* |

**F** On a separate sheet of paper, rewrite each sentence containing an underlined object pronoun, using a participial adjective as a noun modifier.

**Example:** They canceled the tour of the museum.  When we complained, they offered to reschedule <u>it</u>.

*When we complained, the tour operator offered to reschedule the canceled tour.*

1. Julie's raincoat was stained.  She took <u>it</u> to the cleaners.
2. Someone stole the car we rented.  The police found <u>it</u> the next day.
3. The tailor ruined my shirts.  The owner of the store refused to compensate me for <u>them</u>.
4. While we were at the beach, I lost my sunglasses.  Fortunately, the lifeguard found <u>them</u>.
5. I tore my sleeve on the door of the taxi.  I'm sure <u>it</u> can be mended.
6. The mirror in our hotel room was cracked.  The hotel promised to replace <u>it</u> but never did.
7. The tablecloth got soiled when the customer spilled the coffee.  The manager said not to worry about <u>it</u>.
8. The chef burned my steak.  When I returned <u>it</u> to the kitchen, the chef became angry.
9. After walking up all those stairs, I noticed that the heel of my shoe was broken.  The guy in the shoe repair stand fixed <u>it</u> in less than ten minutes.

## DISCUSSION **BUILDER** • *Now describe a travel nightmare.*

**IDEAS**

You got bumped from a flight.
Your reservation e-mail wasn't received.
Your passport and wallet were stolen.
Your rental car broke down.
Your flight had a twelve-hour delay.
Other: ..............................................

**Step 1.** Choose a travel nightmare you or someone you know has had. On your notepad, write the facts to help structure a story.

**Step 2. Discussion.** With your classmates, role-play a radio call-in show in which a panel of editors like Christopher Elliott give advice in response to travel nightmares.

**Step 3. Writing.** Write a letter asking for advice about your travel problem.  Exchange letters with a partner and write advice in response to your partner's letter.

Who took the trip?

When was the trip taken?

Where did the traveler(s) go?

What problems occurred?

What did the traveler want done about the problem?

# Explain a life-changing event

**A** 🎧 **Listening Comprehension.** Listen to the conversation about what happened to two families on separate vacations during the tsunami of 2004. Then complete the chart with a partner.

|  | Tilly's family | Shira's family |
|---|---|---|
| Where were they? |  |  |
| What were they doing before the tsunami hit? |  |  |
| What was the outcome? |  |  |

**B** 🎧 **Pair Work.** Read the following false statements. Then listen again and discuss what's wrong with each statement.

1. The two families were in Thailand.
2. Tilly and her family are from the United States.
3. Tilly is a married woman with a ten-year-old daughter.
4. Tilly was having breakfast when the tsunami hit.
5. Tilly's family drove away in a van.
6. Shira was playing on the beach when the tsunami hit.
7. Shira's family was safe at the hotel.
8. Shira's van was filled with water.
9. Shira's family escaped by driving to a hotel several blocks away.

**C** **Group Work.** In small groups, choose Tilly's family's experience or Shira's family's experience. Recreate the events of the story in order. Listen again if necessary.

**D** **Discussion.**

1. Hundreds of thousands of people died in the tsunami of 2004. But the stories of Tilly's family and Shira's family were reported in many newspapers and on television. Why do you think these stories received so much attention?
2. Shira says that her experience was a "life-changing event." What do you think she means? How can events change our lives?

Cleaning up a flooded hotel lobby on Phuket Island, Thailand, after the tsunami of 2004

## DISCUSSION **BUILDER** • *Now explain a life-changing event.*

**Step 1. Group Story.** In small groups, create a "chain story" about a fictional life-changing vacation experience, with each student adding a sentence until the story is complete. Write the sentences on your notepads. The story can be serious or carefree and end well or badly. Include an explanation of why this experience changed someone's perspective on life in some way. Look at the pictures for ideas.

a beach vacation

a cruise

a visit to a big city

hiking in the woods

Vacation type and place: *camping in the woods*

Events (in order)

1. A friend got sick.
2. We had to get back to town quickly, so . . .

Vacation type and place:

Events (in order)

1.
2.
3.
4.
5.
6.
7.
8.

Continue on a separate sheet of paper if necessary.

a guided tour

**Step 2. Discussion.** Tell your stories to the class. Explain how the experience changed someone's life or taught someone something important. (Or if you have a story about a *real* life-changing experience, tell it to your class.)

*"Last year, I went camping in the woods with some friends. One night, one of my friends got very sick. We had to get back to town quickly, so we carried him all the way down the . . . "*

**Step 3. Writing.** Write the story on a separate sheet of paper. Use the events on your notepad and add sequence words (<u>first</u>, <u>then</u>, <u>next</u>, <u>suddenly</u>, <u>finally</u>, etc.) to clarify the order of events. Add adjectives and adverbs to develop your story more fully.

# Writing: Compare two cities

## Comparison and contrast

Expressions of comparison and contrast can help a writer examine the similarities (comparison) and differences (contrast) between two or more places, objects, people, ideas, etc. They also make a piece of writing clearer and more interesting. Note the punctuation used with these expressions.

| Comparison | Contrast |
|---|---|
| **like**<br>Like New York, Prague attracts a lot of tourists.<br><br>**similarly**<br>New York is known for its architecture. **Similarly,** Prague is famous for its historic buildings. OR:<br>New York is known for its architecture; **similarly,** Prague is famous for its historic buildings.<br><br>**both . . . and . . .**<br>Both New York and Prague have problems with pollution.<br><br>**also / too**<br>Prague has an exciting social scene, and New York **also** does. / and New York does, **too.** | **in contrast**<br>The cost of living in New York is very high. **In contrast,** Prague is affordable.<br><br>**nevertheless / however / yet**<br>Prague has fewer restaurants than New York. **Nevertheless,** the cuisine there is generally of high quality. OR:<br>Prague has fewer restaurants than New York; **nevertheless,** the cuisine there is generally of high quality.<br><br>**both . . . and . . . , but**<br>Both New York and Prague have many cultural attractions, **but** they are not always as affordable in New York as in Prague.<br><br>**On the one hand . . . On the other hand**<br>On the one hand, I would make less money in Prague. On the other hand, I would not work such long hours there. |

**Step 1. Prewriting. Planning ideas with a chart.** On the chart, write the name of the city where you live now (City 1) and the name of a city you have traveled to (City 2). List the similarities between the cities under BOTH and the differences under the city names.

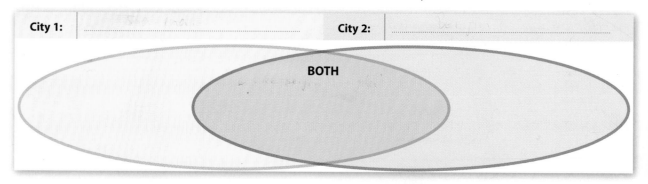

City 1: ......................................    City 2: ......................................

BOTH

**Step 2. Writing.** On a separate sheet of paper, compare and contrast the two cities in your chart. Explain which city you would prefer to live in. Use expressions of comparison and contrast and conditionals.

**Step 3. Self-Check.**

- ☐ Did you use expressions for comparison correctly?
- ☐ Did you use expressions for contrast correctly?
- ☐ Did you use conditionals to describe your preferences? Did you use them correctly?

### WRITING MODEL

If I had to choose to live in Prague or stay in New York City, I would choose Prague. **Both** New York **and** Prague are beautiful cities and have many great qualities, **but** Prague appeals to me more.

**On the one hand,** I love the fast pace of New York. It is exciting to live in one of the busiest cities in the world. **However,** I feel like I am always rushing somewhere. **In contrast,** the pace of life in Prague is much slower than in New York. I think that in a smaller city I would enjoy myself more and have a better . . .

SUMMIT WEBSITE
For Unit 6 online activities, visit the *Summit* Companion Website at www.longman.com/summit.

**A** 🎧 **Listening Comprehension.** Listen to the radio talk show host read two letters describing travel hassles. Summarize each travel problem in one sentence.

|  | summary of problem |
|---|---|
| Letter 1 | |
| Letter 2 | |

**B** 🎧 Now listen to the talk show host respond to the letters. Then listen again and write five travel tips based on his response.

1. .................................................................................
2. .................................................................................
3. .................................................................................
4. .................................................................................
5. .................................................................................

**C** A man has just arrived on an overseas flight. His luggage got lost. Complete the man's statements. Use a negative if appropriate.

1. If my luggage ........................... (turn up), I'm going to demand full compensation!

2. If I had known this would happen, I ........................... (put) my camera in my carry-on.

3. If my friends weren't with me, I ........................... (fly) right back home!

4. If this hadn't happened, I ........................... (be) on my way to the hotel.

5. If we ........................... (know) how long we had to wait, we could go get something to eat.

**D** Write a polite request using "Could you please" or "Would you mind" for each situation.

1. ........................... bring me a menu?
2. ........................... helping me with my bags?
3. ........................... turn the sound down a bit?
4. ........................... hold my place in line?
5. ........................... letting me know when my daughter arrives?
6. ........................... moving your bag out of the way?
7. ........................... point me in the right direction?

# UNIT 7

# Minds at work

## UNIT GOALS

1 Compare your strengths and weaknesses
2 Define intelligence
3 Explain how you produce your best work
4 Debate preferential treatment for the gifted

**A** **Topic Preview.** Take the self-assessment quiz to determine your strongest areas of intelligence.

## What kinds of intelligences do you have?

**According to the theory of multiple intelligences developed by Harvard psychologist Howard Gardner, there are several kinds of "intelligences" rather than a single intelligence. A person can have high-level abilities in some intelligences and low-level abilities in others.**

Rate your own intelligence for each type on a scale of 1 to 5, with 1 being "very low" and 5 being "very high."

☐ **Visual and Spatial**
 • Creating art
 • Understanding maps, charts, and diagrams

☐ **Mathematical**
 • Working with numbers and calculating amounts
 • Understanding and analyzing statistics

☐ **Linguistic**
 • Playing with words, such as doing puzzles and telling jokes
 • Learning foreign languages

☐ **Musical**
 • Playing a musical instrument
 • Having a natural sense of rhythm

☐ **Physical**
 • Playing sports
 • Assembling and repairing things, such as furniture or machines

☐ **Intuitive**
 • Creating or describing new ideas
 • Sensing opportunity or danger before others do

☐ **Interpersonal**
 • Cooperating with other people
 • Communicating ideas to others, such as by teaching or persuasion

☐ **Intrapersonal**
 • Completing tasks independently, without help from others
 • Knowing what your strengths and weaknesses are

Information source: www.ascd.org

**B** **Total Your Score.** Use a pencil to shade the bars to show your scores. Compare your scores with those of your classmates.

**Example:**

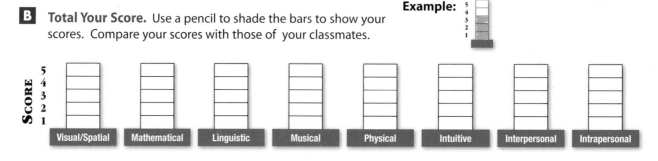

SCORE

5 4 3 2 1

| Visual/Spatial | Mathematical | Linguistic | Musical | Physical | Intuitive | Interpersonal | Intrapersonal |

**C** 🎧 **Sound Bites.** Read and listen to a conversation about someone who turned his life around.

**OLIVIA:** Do you remember Johnny Nolan?
**CHARLES:** I think so. Wasn't he the kid who was always failing in class and getting into trouble?
**OLIVIA:** That's the one. Well, he's apparently turned his life around. I just heard he's the CEO of MegaStar Foods.
**CHARLES:** Get out of here! Johnny Nolan? Head of a multimillion-dollar company?
**OLIVIA:** I guess he turned out to have a real head for business.
**CHARLES:** That's for sure. I didn't think he had it in him.
**OLIVIA:** It just goes to show you—you can't judge a book by its cover.

**D** **In Other Words.** Read the conversation again. Then say each of the statements another way.

1. "He's turned his life around."
2. "Get out of here!"
3. "He turned out to have a real head for business."
4. "That's for sure."
5. "I didn't think he had it in him."
6. "You can't judge a book by its cover."

**E** **Discussion.** What kinds of intelligences do you think Johnny Nolan might have? Why?

## STARTING **POINT**

**Pair Work.** Describe people you know or have heard of who . . .

| | |
|---|---|
| **turned their lives around.** | **did well in both school and life.** |
| **did well in school but not in life.** | **struggled in school or in life.** |
| **did poorly in school but well in life.** | **always got into trouble.** |

What kinds of intelligences do you think these people have (or had)?

# 1 Compare your strengths and weaknesses

## A ⌁ CONVERSATION **SNAPSHOT**

**A:** I wish I had a head for figures. I mean, I can't even balance my own checkbook.

**B:** Well, you can't be good at everything.

**A:** I guess that's true.

**B:** If you ask me, I'd say you've got a real knack for languages.

**A:** Do you think so? Thanks.

⌁ **Rhythm and intonation practice**

## B ⌁ **Vocabulary. Expressions to describe talents.** Listen and practice.

**have a head for figures** be good at mathematical calculations

**have an ear for music** be good at recognizing, remembering, and imitating musical sounds

**have an eye for detail** be good at seeing things that others don't notice

**have a way with words** be able to express your ideas and opinions well

**have a knack for languages** have a natural skill or ability to learn and speak foreign languages

**have a good intuitive sense** be able to draw conclusions based on feelings rather than facts

**have a way with people** be able to attract and influence people

**be good with one's hands** have the ability to use one's hands to make or do things

**be mechanically inclined** be able to understand how machines work

## C **Pair Work.** Use the expressions in the vocabulary to discuss the talents of the following people.

1. Irish writer James Joyce spoke thirteen languages.

2. The work of Chilean poet Gabriela Mistral, a Nobel Prize winner, conveyed profound feelings about common human experiences.

3. Indian genius Srinivasa Ramanujan astonished people by solving complex numerical problems instantly in his head.

4. U.S. industrialist Henry Ford built an early gasoline engine and one of the first automobiles.

5. Austrian physician Sigmund Freud, the founder of psychoanalysis, showed an immense capacity for understanding human behavior and feelings.

6. U.S. sculptor Louise Nevelson's abstract arrangements of wood, metal, and other materials demonstrated her artistic vision.

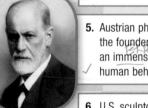

7. Joseph Dunninger was an American magician famous for reading people's minds and guessing their thoughts.

**D** Identify people you know or have heard about who have each of the following intelligences. Use the vocabulary on page 76 to describe their talents.

| Interpersonal | My older sister really has a way with people. |
|---|---|
| Visual/Spatial | |
| Mathematical | |
| Linguistic | |
| Musical | |
| Physical | |
| Intuitive | |
| Interpersonal | |
| Intrapersonal | |

**E** **Pair Work.** Tell a partner about the people you identified. Refer to the quiz on page 74 if necessary.

## CONVERSATION **STARTER** • *Now compare your strengths and weaknesses.*

On your notepad, list some things you're good at and some things you're not so good at.

| I'm good at … | I'm not so good at … |
|---|---|
| communicating my ideas. | making things with my hands. |

| I'm good at … | I'm not so good at … |
|---|---|
| | |
| | |
| | |
| | |

**Pair Work.** Compare and discuss your strengths and weaknesses. Use the Conversation Snapshot on page 76 as a guide. Start by using one of the phrases in the box.

**Group Work.** Tell your classmates about your partner. Use the vocabulary when you can.

**Discussing someone's abilities**
Would you say you're good at ………?
How are you at …………?
If you ask me, I'd say ………….

**Describing your own abilities**
I'm good / not so good at ………….
………… comes easy to me.
I have a knack for ………….
I wish I were / had ………….

# 2 *Define intelligence*

**A** 🎧 GRAMMAR **SNAPSHOT.** Read the article and notice the use of connecting words.

## IQ and EQ: Do they matter?

Our IQ (intelligence quotient) is a measure of general intelligence based on an IQ test score. An IQ test, **however**, can be an accurate measure of intelligence **only if** there is such a thing as "general intelligence"—intelligence that enables us to undertake a variety of everyday mental tasks. Some scientists believe that we have several different intelligences rather than one general intelligence and that IQ tests cannot provide a complete measure of intelligence.

**Although** the intelligence quotient has prevailed as a way to estimate intelligence, the concept of emotional intelligence, developed by psychologist Daniel Goleman, explains what the concept of general intelligence cannot. Emotional intelligence is the ability to motivate oneself, to focus on a goal, and to understand one's own emotions and those of others. According to Goleman, one's EQ (emotional intelligence quotient) can be high **even if** one's IQ is low, and it can also lead a person to success. A number of tests that measure EQ have been developed.

**Because** the science of investigating the brain is quite new, no theory of intelligence has yet been proved. **Nevertheless**, many institutions and private companies have accepted the idea that high IQs and EQs are crucial to success. **Consequently**, **unless** a new theory that is strong enough to take the place of the existing ones emerges, our abilities will continue to be measured with IQ and EQ tests.

Information source: www.bbc.co.uk

**B** **Discussion.** How do IQ and EQ differ? Do you think intelligence can truly be measured through tests? Why or why not?

> **REMEMBER**
>
> **If a dependent clause begins a sentence or shows contrast, use a comma.**
>
> **Even if** one's IQ is low, one's EQ can be high.
>
> Some people achieve success, **although** they don't have high IQs.

**C** **Grammar.** Subordinating conjunctions and transitions

**Use subordinating conjunctions to connect ideas within a sentence.**
**Use transitions to connect ideas between sentences or paragraphs.**

> **NOTE:** Use a comma after transitions.

| Meaning | Subordinating conjunctions | Transitions |
|---|---|---|
| one thing causes or is the result of another thing | **because / since**<br><br>**Since** the science of investigating the brain is quite new, no theory of intelligence has yet been proved. | **therefore / consequently**<br><br>Many companies believe high IQs and EQs are crucial to success. **Therefore,** they often require applicants to take IQ and EQ tests. |
| one thing contrasts with another thing | **(even) though / although**<br><br>Some people have achieved extraordinary successes, **even though** they don't have high IQs. | **however / nevertheless / nonetheless**<br><br>No theory of intelligence has yet been proved. **Nonetheless,** many institutions believe success depends on high IQs and EQs. |
| one thing will occur only if a specific condition exists | **unless**<br><br>**Unless** a new theory emerges, our abilities will continue to be measured with IQ and EQ tests. | **otherwise**<br><br>He must have a high IQ. **Otherwise,** he wouldn't have gotten that job. |
| one thing is a condition for another thing | **as long as / if / only if / provided that**<br><br>You will get that job **as long as** your score on the IQ test is very high. | |
| a condition doesn't matter | **even if**<br><br>One's EQ can be high **even if** one's IQ is low. | |

> **NOTE:** <u>However</u> and <u>therefore</u> are sometimes used between the subject and the verb. In that case, they are set off by commas.
>
> The IQ test, **however,** can be an accurate measure of intelligence only if there is a general intelligence. The IQ test, **therefore,** may not reflect a person's true intelligence.

**Pronunciation Booster**

**PAGES P7–P8**
Intonation with conjunctions and transitions

**Grammar Booster**

**PAGES G10–G11**
For more …

**D** Circle the correct subordinating conjunctions or transitions.

## Are people getting smarter?

IQ scores rise approximately twenty points with every generation. This increase is called the "Flynn Effect" because / therefore, it was discovered by New Zealand political scientist James Flynn. About fifty years ago, few people reached the scores most people get today. Otherwise, / Consequently, if people taking an IQ test today were scored with the norms used fifty years ago, more than 90 percent of them would be classified as geniuses. Nevertheless, / Even though we are not more intelligent than our ancestors; unless / otherwise, we would all excel at everything we do. The rise in IQ seems to be caused by a combination of factors such as better nutrition, more schooling, and exposure to more complex technologies. Researchers believe that if our grandparents were born today, they would get the same scores we get even if / as long as they were exposed to the same environment and education we are exposed to.

Information sources: www.psychologytoday.com and www.sciam.com

**E** On a separate sheet of paper, rewrite each statement two ways, once with the connecting word(s) in **a** and once with the connecting word in **b**. Change the wording as needed to retain meaning.

1. He has a high IQ, but he didn't get the job. (**a.** although **b.** nevertheless)
2. She achieved success, although she doesn't do well on EQ tests. (**a.** however **b.** though)
3. There isn't just one kind of intelligence, so intelligence is not easy to measure. (**a.** therefore **b.** since)
4. If you get a high score, you'll be given an interview. (**a.** as long as **b.** unless)
5. Intelligence can't be measured without considering the context in which a person lives, works, or studies. As a result, the same IQ test can't be used for people from different cultures. (**a.** because **b.** consequently)
6. IQ tests can predict success in low-stress conditions, but they often fail to predict performance in stressful situations. (**a.** even though **b.** nonetheless)
7. An IQ score will accurately measure a person's general intelligence if anxiety does not affect his or her performance during the test. (**a.** provided that **b.** unless)

## GRAMMAR **EXCHANGE** • *Now define intelligence.*

**Pair Work.** Circle the characteristics *you* think demonstrate intelligence. Discuss why you think some show intelligence and others do not. What would you add?

**capacity to learn**     artistic talent     problem-solving ability

**capacity to understand**     **good memory**     creativity

        common sense     practical ideas

ABILITY TO THINK LOGICALLY

ability to think abstractly     ability to see relationships

other: ................................

**Discussion.** How would you define intelligence? Describe and give examples of the characteristics that people with intelligence have. Use subordinating conjunctions and transitions.

*"In my opinion, a person is intelligent **only if** he or she has the capacity to learn. **Otherwise,** ..."*

*"**Although** good memory is important, it only shows one kind of intelligence. **However,** ..."*

# *3* *Explain how you produce your best work*

**A** **Reading Warm-up.** What do you do when you find it difficult to concentrate on what you're doing?

**B** 🎧 **Reading.** Read the article. What do you think the title "Stay on Target" means?

# STAY ON TARGET

You've got work to do, but you just can't seem to get your brain going. You stare at that blank piece of paper in front of you but can't get your thoughts organized. Your mind wanders to the argument you had with your spouse, the leftovers that are in the refrigerator . . . Then, just as your ideas finally start to come together, the phone rings, and you're back to square one.

Sound familiar? The ability to devote all of one's attention to a single task is the key to achievement in any occupation. On the other hand, being unable to concentrate can keep you from producing your best work. The following tips can help you to stay focused:

**Stay organized.** Let's face it — it's not easy to keep focused if your desk looks like it just got hit by a tornado. It pays to spend a few moments a day cleaning up your workspace and reducing the time you normally spend searching for mislaid files or your favorite pen.

**Develop a routine.** Studies show that following a systematic pattern of behavior can make it easier to devote your undivided attention to a task. For example, if you have trouble preparing for exams, try establishing a study ritual. Start and finish at the same time each day. Work at the same desk or favorite chair. If music helps you focus, choose a piece of music and play it during every study session.

**Make a list.** Each morning, write down all the tasks you need to accomplish that day and cross off each item as you complete it. This visual reminder will not only keep you focused on your goals but will also give you a sense of progress and achievement.

**Challenge yourself.** When faced with a boring, routine task that seems to drag on forever, it's easy to lose concentration and make careless mistakes. According to Mihaly Csikszentmihalyi, author of *Flow: The Psychology of Optimal Experience*, one of the best ways to engage your attention on a dull task is to make it harder. For example, turn the task into a game by giving yourself a time limit. The increased challenge stimulates blood flow and

activity in the brain, making it easier for you to focus on the job at hand.

**Reserve some "do not disturb" time.** If interruptions from family, friends, or co-workers prevent you from getting your work done, set aside a certain period of your schedule each day when you are unavailable. Let others know that they shouldn't disturb you during this time. Close the door to your office or find an area where you can work without being interrupted, such as a library or conference room.

**Go offline.** While the Internet is an invaluable tool for getting and sharing information, it can be a real concentration killer. If all those quick trips to the Net to "just check the news" are interfering with your productivity, make it a point to stay offline while you're working. And if you find your focus constantly broken by incoming e-mail and instant messages, resist the urge to read and reply to them as they arrive. Instead, set aside certain times of the day for reading and replying to them—and keep working.

**Take a breather.** Taking short breaks can help you to clear your mind and refocus on the next job. Stand up for a moment and take a short walk in the hallway or just close your eyes, relax your muscles, and breathe deeply.

The next time you have an important project that requires your full concentration, see if any of these strategies can make a difference for you.

Information sources: *Flow: The Psychology of Optimal Experience* by Mihaly Csikszentmihalyi; "Discover your Achievement Zone" by Edwin Kiester, Jr. and Sally Valente Kiester, *Reader's Digest;* and www.mumbai-central.com

**C** **Pair Work.** Match one of the seven tips in the article with each example below. Explain your choices.

1. A magazine writer is having trouble getting started on an article about a topic that doesn't inspire her. When someone suggests beginning every paragraph with a given letter of the alphabet, the words start flowing smoothly.

2. A university student has to study for two important exams that will be given the next day. She studies intensely but takes regular fifteen-minute breaks to relax. Before starting to study for the second exam, she takes a long walk in the park.

3. Just before every concert, an opera singer gets himself in the right frame of mind by drinking a full glass of water, reciting the first three lines of his favorite poem, and entering the stage by the same route.

4. An office worker decides to set up a separate e-mail account for friends and family and makes it a strict rule at the office to check it for messages only during lunch.

5. From 12:00 to 3:00 each day, a work-at-home mom keeps the door to her home office closed and turns her cell phone off. Her kids know that they are not to knock on the door or call unless it's an emergency.

6. A project manager responsible for five major projects deals with problems that come up on each of them daily. By the end of the day, his work area is in complete disarray, covered with memos and files related to the different projects. Before leaving the office each day, he takes five minutes to organize the papers on his desk.

**D** **Discussion.**

1. Describe a time when you were really able to concentrate, when your ideas flowed freely, and you completed a task at a fast pace. What was it like?

2. Do any of the tips in the article seem useful to you? Why or why not? Have you tried any of them before?

---

DISCUSSION **BUIILDER** • *Now explain how you produce your best work.*

**Step 1.** On your notepad, list the distractions that cause you to lose focus when you are working on a task. What strategies do you use to stay focused?

**Some distractions**
noise
phone calls
interruptions
worries
aches and pains
room temperature

| I lose focus when . . . | I stay focused by . . . |
|---|---|
| I'm interrupted by phone calls. | not answering calls. |

| I lose focus when . . . | I stay focused by . . . |
|---|---|
| | |
| | |
| | |
| | |

**Step 2. Discussion.** What conditions help you produce your best work? Compare how you and your classmates stay focused and how you overcome distractions.

*"I work best when it's very quiet. If I'm reading, I lose my focus when I get interrupted by people or phone calls. So I just close the door, and I never answer the phone while I'm reading."*

# Humor

## UNIT GOALS

1 Discuss the health benefits of laughter
2 Respond to a joke
3 Explain why something is funny
4 Explore the limits of humor

**A** **Topic Preview.** Look at the cartoons. Do you find any of them funny? Why or why not?

**1**

"No matter how busy I am, I'm never too busy to stop and complain about how busy I am."

**2**

"Richard, we need to talk. I'll e-mail you."

**3**

**"Would you mind talking to me for a while? I forgot my cell phone."**

**4**

"Don't you understand? This is _life_, this is what is happening. We _can't_ switch to another channel."

**B** **Pair Work.** Which of these topic(s) do you think each cartoon addresses? Complete the chart and explain your choices. Then discuss which you found the funniest and why.

| Topic | Cartoon number(s) | Topic | Cartoon number(s) |
|---|---|---|---|
| everyday frustrations | | generational differences | |
| technology in modern life | | relationships | |
| human nature | | other: | |

**C** 🎧 **Sound Bites.** Read and listen to a conversation between two colleagues at work.

**NORA:** So how did the meeting go?
**NICK:** Don't ask!
**NORA:** Uh-oh. What happened?
**NICK:** Well, first of all I was late, which was embarrassing enough.
**NORA:** Mm-hmm.
**NICK:** So, you know, I'm sneaking in, trying not to get noticed . . . and when I sit down, the chair leg breaks!
**NORA:** Right in front of everyone?! Sorry, . . . I didn't mean to laugh.
**NICK:** I have to admit, it *was* pretty funny.
**NORA:** You're a good sport. I would have died!

**D** **Pair Work.** With a partner, answer the following questions.

1. What happened to Nick?
2. Why does Nora laugh?
3. Do you think Nick laughed at the meeting?
4. How does Nick feel about the incident now?
5. What does Nora mean when she says, "You're a good sport"?
6. What does Nora mean when she says, "I would have died"?
7. In your opinion, can it ever be funny when someone falls down? Explain.

## STARTING POINT

**Pair Work.** Write a checkmark on the photos you find funny. Use one or more of the adjectives in your discussion of each photo.

amusing   hilarious   silly   childish   ridiculous   cruel   disgusting

1.

2.

3.

4.

5.

6.

# 1 Discuss the health benefits of laughter

**A** ⌒ **GRAMMAR SNAPSHOT.** Read the article and notice the verb forms in the indirect speech.

## Is Laughter the Best Medicine?

Norman Cousins's 1979 work *Anatomy of an Illness* recounts his recovery from a painful illness that doctors told him he **would never survive**. Cousins undertook an original program of self-healing, based on, among other things, laughter. The following explains how Cousins developed his theory and how laughter lessened his pain.

Cousins said that ten years earlier he **had read** Hans Selye's classic book *The Stress of Life*. According to Selye, negative emotions have negative effects on body chemistry. In addition, severe and life-threatening illnesses can be caused by emotional tension such as frustration or suppressed rage. Selye's

theory later caused Cousins to advise his doctors **never to tell** their patients that they **couldn't survive** an illness because it **might have** a negative effect on the patients' chances of survival.

As he continued thinking about what Selye had said, Cousins thought, "If negative emotions produce negative chemical changes in the body, wouldn't positive emotions produce positive chemical changes?" Cousins theorized that positive factors—such as love, hope, faith, laughter, confidence, and the will to live—**had to have** therapeutic value.

Cousins said that it **was** easy enough to have hope, love, and faith, but that laughter **was** more difficult to

achieve. He wrote that nothing **was** less funny than being flat on your back with every bone and joint in your body aching. Because two things he could do while lying in bed were watching TV and listening to jokes, Cousins began his self-healing program by watching funny movies and having people tell him jokes.

Almost immediately, Cousins reported that the "treatment" **had begun** to work. He discovered that ten minutes of genuine laughter had an anesthetic effect and would give him at least two hours of pain-free sleep. His book describes more profound effects of laughter on his condition, leading ultimately to his recovery.

Based on information from *Anatomy of an Illness,* 1979

**B** **Discussion.** Do you think it's possible Cousins was cured by laughter? Can you think of any other explanation for his recovery?

| Reporting Verbs | | |
|---|---|---|
| admitted | insisted | |
| advised | reported | |
| believed | said | **NOTE:** In indirect |
| claimed | thought | speech, don't use |
| continued | told | a comma after the |
| found | wrote | reporting verb. |

**C** **Grammar. Indirect speech: changes to preserve meaning**

Notice how verbs change from direct to indirect speech.

| direct speech | indirect speech |
|---|---|
| Selye wrote, "Negative emotions **are** dangerous and they **cause** illness." | Selye wrote (that) negative emotions **were** dangerous and (that) they **caused** illness. |
| Doctors said, "The studies **didn't prove** anything." | Doctors said (that) the studies **hadn't proved** anything. |
| Cousins wrote, "They **are telling** patients they **will die**." | Cousins wrote (that) they **were telling** patients they **would die**. |
| They claimed, "We **were telling** the truth." | They claimed (that) they **had been telling** the truth. |
| Many doctors admitted, "We**'ve learned** a lot from his book." | Many doctors admitted (that) they **had learned** a lot from his book. |
| She told him, "I**'ll check** to see how you**'re feeling** later." | She told him (that) she **would check** to see how he **was feeling** later. |
| He told us, "I **can't understand** that cartoon." | He told us (that) he **couldn't understand** that cartoon. |
| He said, "I **might not need** a doctor, but I **may need** a movie." | He said (that) he **might not need** a doctor but he **might need** a movie. |
| She told him, "You **have to see** this sitcom, and you **must rest**." | She told him (that) he **had to see** that sitcom and he **had to rest**. |
| Selye said, "**Never tell** patients about that." | Selye said **never to tell** patients about that. |

**BE CAREFUL!** Do not make changes to present and past unreal conditional sentences or to the modals <u>should</u>, <u>could</u>, <u>might</u>, and <u>ought to</u> when converting direct to indirect speech.

Expressions of time and place also change from direct to indirect speech.

| | | | | | | |
|---|---|---|---|---|---|---|
| now | → | **then** | this year | → | **that year** | |
| today | → | **that day** | last week | → | **the week before** | |
| tomorrow | → | **the next day** | next month | → | **the following month** | |
| yesterday | → | **the day before** | here | → | **there** | |

*Grammar Booster*

**PAGES G11–G12**
For more ...

Mark told me, "Judy was **here yesterday**." → Mark told me (that) Judy had been **there the day before**.

Claire told us, "Don't be late **tomorrow**." → Claire told us not to be late **the next day**.

**D** **Pair Work.** Take turns restating each of the following in indirect speech.

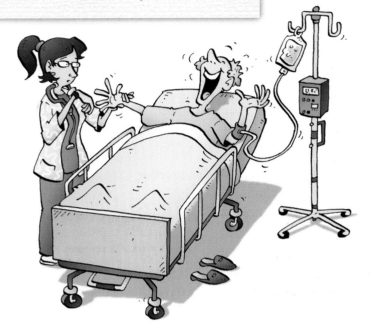

1. Pain researchers reported, "Laughter may help some patients."
2. They said, "Our new study will begin here next week."
3. Cousins's doctor said, "We've tried everything possible to cure his illness."
4. He insisted, "If I had known how effective humor could be, I would have recommended it to all my patients."
5. Cousins thought, "I've been cured."
6. The doctor advised his colleagues, "Try to make your patients laugh."

**E** On a separate sheet of paper, write what the people actually said, using direct speech.

1. They claimed that they had been misled by that book.
2. She told me that she had taken that book out of the library the day before.
3. Cousins said not to lose hope when a doctor says survival is impossible.
4. I said that if I hadn't read it in Cousins's book, I never would have believed that laughter could cure illness.
5. The nurses told me that they hadn't been surprised by Cousins's book.

## GRAMMAR **EXCHANGE** • *Now discuss the health benefits of laughter.*

**Pair Work.** With a partner, write a short summary of Cousins's ideas, as expressed in the article on page 88. Use indirect speech.

*Cousins said that . . .*

**Discussion.** Do you believe laughter can be good medicine? How could you apply Cousins's ideas to help heal a sick friend or family member? If you wanted to try laughter therapy, how might you do that?

# 2 *Respond to a joke*

## A 🎧 CONVERSATION **SNAPSHOT**

**A:** Did you hear the one about the penguin?

**B:** No. How does it go?

**A:** A man sees a penguin on his neighbor's lawn, so he calls his neighbor and says, "There's a penguin on your lawn. You should take him to the zoo."

**B:** So?

**A:** The next day, the penguin is still there. So he calls his neighbor and says, "Didn't you take that penguin to the zoo?" And the neighbor says, "I did. And we had such a good time that today I'm taking him to the movies."

**B:** What a riot!

🎧 **Rhythm and intonation practice**

## B 🎧 **Vocabulary.** Ways to respond to a joke. Listen and practice.

| | |
|---|---|
| **What a riot / a scream / a hoot!** <br> **That's hilarious / hysterical / too much!** <br> **That cracked me up!** <br> **That really tickled me.** | (It's really funny.) |
| **I don't get it.** <br> **That went over my head.** | (I don't understand why it's funny.) |
| [That's pretty good, but] **I've heard that one already.** | (That's why I'm not laughing.) |
| [I'm sorry, but] **That's pretty silly / lame* / ridiculous.*** | (I don't think it's very funny.) |
| [I'm sorry, but] **That's in poor taste.*** | (It's offensive.) |

**BE CAREFUL!** It would be impolite to use these expressions * directly to the person who told the joke.

**Pronunciation Booster**
**PAGES P8–P9**
Intonation of sarcasm

## C 🎧 **Listening Comprehension.** Listen to each joke and check if the listener liked it or not. Then listen again and write your own response to each joke, using the vocabulary.

| Did the listener like the joke? | | | |
|---|---|---|---|
| | **Yes** | **No** | **Your response to the joke** |
| joke 1 | ☐ | ☐ | |
| joke 2 | ☐ | ☐ | |
| joke 3 | ☐ | ☐ | |
| joke 4 | ☐ | ☐ | |
| joke 5 | ☐ | ☐ | |
| joke 6 | ☐ | ☐ | |

## D  Discussion.

1. In your opinion, what makes a joke funny? offensive? lame?
2. Do you enjoy telling jokes? Why or why not? What kind of person is good at telling jokes?

## E  🎧 Vocabulary.  Types of verbal humor.  Listen and practice.

| | |
|---|---|
| **a joke** | a funny story that ends with a "punch line" that makes one laugh |
| **a riddle** | a clever question with a funny answer |
| **an anecdote** | a funny, true story, often told to illustrate an idea |
| **a limerick** | a light, humorous five-line poem |
| **a blooper** | a clumsy verbal mistake, especially one made in public<br>**Example:** "Go and shake a tower," instead of "Go and take a shower." |
| **a pun** | a humorous use of a word or phrase that has two meanings, or of words with the same sound but different meanings<br>**Example:** "What's black and white and red all over? A newspaper." (The pun is on "read" and "red," which have the same sound.) |

### 🎧 Some joke types

**a dirty joke**  a joke about sex (often offensive)
**a clean joke**  a joke that isn't about sex
**an ethnic joke**  a joke about people of a certain ethnic background (often offensive)
**a political joke**  a joke about a political candidate, party, opinion, or government

## CONVERSATION **STARTER** • *Now respond to a joke.*

🎧 **Pair Work.**  Read and listen to the following examples of verbal humor. Classify each, according to the type of humor.

**1** What never gets any wetter, no matter how hard it rains?
Answer: the ocean

**3** A customer eating at Crewe
Found a very large bug in his stew.
Said the waiter, "Don't shout
And wave it about,
Or the rest will be wanting one too."

**2** A man goes to a psychiatrist and says, "Doctor, I'm worried about my brother. He thinks he's a chicken."
"That IS serious," says the doctor. "Why don't you put him in a mental hospital?"
So the man says, "I would, but I need the eggs."

**4** Puns are bad, but limericks are verse.

**5** "It's so meet to nice you . . . I mean, nice to meet you!"

- ○ joke
- ○ pun
- ○ limerick
- ○ riddle
- ○ blooper

**Joke.** Tell a favorite joke or retell the penguin joke on page 90 in your own words. Use the Conversation Snapshot on page 90 as a guide. Start like this: "Did you hear the one about …?"

**IDEAS**

Plan your joke on a piece of paper first before you tell it.

*"Uh, I don't get it."*

*"What a scream! I love it!"*

*"Sorry, I'm afraid I've heard that one already."*

# 3 Explain why something is funny

**A** **Reading Warm-up.** Who are your favorite comedians and actors? Why do they make you laugh?

**B** 🎧 **Reading.** Read the article about why people laugh. Can you think of any other explanations for why people laugh?

# What makes us laugh?

We all know that some things make us laugh, but it is hard to say *why* we laugh. There are three theories that explain what makes different situations and jokes funny.

## The Superiority Theory

The Superiority Theory states that we laugh at people who are at a disadvantage or suffer a small misfortune. This occurs, for instance, when a person gets a pie thrown in his or her face. We laugh, too, at mistakes people make. Mispronouncing a word or exchanging the first sounds of two words—for example, saying "I'll sew you to your sheet" instead of "I'll show you to your seat"—will often bring about laughter. According to this theory, the reason why we laugh at the misfortunes or mistakes of others is that they make us feel superior.

## The Incongruity Theory

The Incongruity Theory suggests that humor arises from unexpected, inappropriate, or illogical situations. For example, the child who places a toy cat in a basket and heads off to the vet may make us laugh. According to this theory, a joke becomes funny when we expect one thing to happen, but something else does. When someone starts telling a joke, our mind is already anticipating how it will end. When the joke goes in an unexpected direction, we experience two sets of incompatible thoughts and

emotions—the ones we had as we were listening and the ones that the punch line revealed at the end. This incongruity makes us laugh.

## The Relief Theory

According to the Relief Theory, humor is the feeling of relief that comes from the removal of restraint. When tension is high, we need a release, and laughter is the way of cleansing our system of the built-up tension. For example, people often laugh after a scary experience such as a roller-coaster ride or a rough airplane landing. This theory explains why humor can help people cope with stressful situations.

Regardless of the theory, in order to be able to appreciate a situation or joke as funny, some detachment is always necessary; that is, we have to feel uninvolved with the situation. For example, we can often laugh at our own past mistakes because, with the passage of time, we have become detached. Conversely, if the joke or situation is too familiar or realistic, it may evoke feelings of sadness and concern instead of ones of cheerfulness. To understand a joke—to "get it"—we might also need some knowledge of cultural, economic, political, and social issues, without which some jokes are impossible to understand. Although humor is universal, there is no universal joke.

Information sources: www.howstuffworks.com and http://library.thinkquest.org

**C** **Pair Work.** Check the theory *you* think best explains why some people laugh in response to each of the following situations and explain your answers. (You may choose more than one.) On a separate sheet of paper, give examples of some other situations that make people laugh and use the three theories to explain why.

| People often laugh when they . . . | The Superiority Theory | The Incongruity Theory | The Relief Theory |
|---|---|---|---|
| discover the strange noise they heard downstairs was only the cat. | ◯ | ◯ | ◯ |
| see someone slip and fall down. | ◯ | ◯ | ◯ |
| see someone wearing inappropriate clothes to an event. | ◯ | ◯ | ◯ |
| arrive at a party where someone is wearing the same outfit. | ◯ | ◯ | ◯ |
| see a little girl wearing her mother's high heels. | ◯ | ◯ | ◯ |
| see someone make an embarrassing social mistake. | ◯ | ◯ | ◯ |

# DISCUSSION **BUILDER** • *Now explain why something is funny.*

**Step 1.** 🎧 **Group Work.** Read and listen to each joke and discuss what you think of each one. Decide which theory from the reading best explains the intended humor of each joke and why.

## Joke 1

"How much do you charge?" a woman asks a lawyer.
"I get $50 for three questions," the lawyer answers.
"That's awfully steep, isn't it?" says the woman.
"Yes, it is," replies the lawyer. "Now what's your final question?"

## Joke 2

A couple of dog owners are arguing about whose dog is smarter.
"My dog is so smart," says the first owner, "that every morning he waits for the paperboy to come around. He tips the kid and then brings the newspaper to me, along with my morning coffee."
"I know," says the second owner.
"How do you know?"
"My dog told me."

## Joke 3

A man is hitting golf balls at a driving range with his nine-year-old son. Each time he hits the ball, his son cheers him on. "Great shot, Dad!" "Perfect!" "Way to go!"

A woman hitting balls next to them watches as each of the man's shots flies farther and farther away.

After a few minutes, the woman walks over and asks, "Do you think I could borrow your son for a few minutes?"

**Step 2. Class Survey.** Poll the class. Which joke do most students think is the funniest? Which was the most popular among the men? Which among the women? What conclusions can you draw based on the poll?

**Step 3. Discussion.** Take turns telling the class about something funny that happened to you or someone you know. Discuss why you think the experience was funny.

# 4  Explore the limits of humor

**A** 🎧 **Vocabulary. Discussing practical jokes.** Listen and practice.

**play a joke on someone** trick someone, in order to make that person appear silly, stupid, or ridiculous

**be the butt of a joke** be the person on whom the practical joke is played; be the object of ridicule

**can take a joke** be able to laugh at oneself, even when one is the butt of the joke (Often said to someone upset by being the butt of the joke: "Can't you take a joke?")

**be a good sport** be able to take a joke without getting hurt or insulted

**be in bad** (or **poor**) **taste** be offensive or extremely cruel

**cross the line** go beyond funny into something offensive or cruel

**B** 🎧 **Listening Comprehension.** Listen to a description of a practical joke a doctor played on another doctor. Then listen again and work with a partner to summarize the story in your own words, using indirect speech.

"The woman described a practical joke her father had once played on someone. One day, …"

**C** Complete each statement, according to the listening.

1. Dr. Adams ............ .
   a. played a practical joke on another doctor
   b. was the butt of another doctor's joke

2. The woman thinks her father's joke ............ .
   a. was in pretty good taste
   b. may have crossed the line

3. In the end, the younger doctor proved that ............ .
   a. he could take being the butt of a practical joke
   b. the joke was in pretty poor taste

4. The man thinks that ............ .
   a. the joke crossed the line
   b. the younger doctor was a pretty good sport

**D** 🎧 **Listening Comprehension.** Listen to three people who had practical jokes played on them. Then listen again and take notes on the chart. Use your notes to discuss whether you think each joke crossed the line. How would *you* have reacted?

| Speaker | What was the joke? | How did the person react? |
|---|---|---|
| 1 | *friends put note on car, pretending car was damaged* | |
| 2 | | |
| 3 | | |

DISCUSSION **BUILDER** • *Now explore the limits of humor.*

**Step 1. Pair Work.** Take turns reading the practical jokes aloud. Rate each one according to how funny you think it is. If you were the butt of the joke, how would you respond? Would you be a good sport about it, or would you be offended?

> X = don't get it
> 1 = lame
> 2 = kind of funny
> 3 = hilarious
> 4 = crosses the line

**A** ○
Someone leaves a very real-looking toy snake in a drawer with your clothes. You open the drawer and are about to put your hand in when you suddenly see the snake.

**D** ○
Someone offers you a cup of coffee or tea. When you take the first sip, it tastes so bad you can hardly swallow it. You realize it has salt in it instead of sugar.

**C** ○
A colleague tells you that another colleague is going to get married. When you see her, you congratulate her happily. She has no idea what you're talking about.

**B** ○
A friend puts an ad in the paper offering your house for sale at a very good price—with your phone number as a contact. You start getting lots of calls inquiring about your house.

**E** ○
You're invited to a costume party. When you arrive at the party, everyone is nicely dressed, and you are the only one wearing a costume.

**Step 2. Discussion.**

1. When do you think a practical joke crosses the line? Can you generally take a joke, or are you easily offended?

2. Have you ever played a practical joke on someone? Have you ever been the butt of a joke? What happened?

# Writing: Write a story that includes dialogue

## Punctuation of dialogue

When writing a story that includes dialogue, you can use a combination of direct and indirect speech. Review the punctuation rules for writing direct speech.

**When the reporting verb comes before a quotation,**
- put a comma after the reporting verb.
- put the end punctuation inside the quotation marks.

    Mr. King said, "Please turn off the lights."

**When the reporting verb comes after a quotation,**
- put a comma, question mark, or an exclamation point at the end of the quoted sentence, inside the quotation marks.
- put the speaker's name before or after the reporting verb.

    "Please turn off the lights," Mr. King said.
    "Did anyone turn off the lights?" asked Mr. King.

**When the reporting verb comes within a quotation, put quotation marks around each part of the quotation.**

    "Mark and Jan," Mr. King said, "please turn off the lights."

**If the reporting verb comes between complete sentences, put a period after the reporting verb.**

    "Mark and Jan, please turn off the lights," Mr. King said. "I'm going to show the video."

**NOTE: When writing indirect speech, don't use a comma after the reporting verb.**

    NOT  Mr. King said, not to turn off the lights.

About a year ago, my grandmother was walking down the street, stopping from time to time to look in shop windows. At one store, she stopped to admire a dress in the window. Just as she turned to enter the store, a businessman walking very fast and, not looking where he was going, bumped into her, knocking her down.

"Oh, I'm so sorry!" said the man. "Are you OK?"

My grandmother was too stunned to reply. But then after a moment she said she was fine.

"Look!" she heard someone say from across the street. "An old woman just fell down!"

She quickly sat up and looked around with great concern and said, "Where?"

When she told us this story, we all laughed.

---

**Step 1. Prewriting. Ordering events.** Think about an anecdote—a funny story—you can tell. It can be something you've experienced, or it can be something you've heard about, read, or seen in a movie or on television. Write a summary of the events in the order in which they happened.

1. ................................................................................
2. ................................................................................
3. ................................................................................
4. ................................................................................
5. ................................................................................

**Step 2. Writing.** On a separate sheet of paper, write the story, telling what happened and what people said, using a combination of direct and indirect speech. Each time you use the direct speech of a new speaker, begin a new paragraph.

**Step 3. Self-Check.**

☐ Did you use both direct and indirect speech in your story?

☐ Did you punctuate direct and indirect speech correctly?

☐ Did you make appropriate shifts in tense, pronouns, and expressions of time and place in indirect speech when needed?

SUMMIT WEBSITE
For Unit 8 online activities, visit the *Summit* Companion Website at www.longman.com/summit.

**A** 🎧 **Listening Comprehension.** Listen to three examples of humor and write the type of humor that each example represents. Listen again if necessary.

1. ......................................... 2. ......................................... 3. .........................................

**B** Write the response you would give in each situation. Use the vocabulary.

1. Someone tells you a joke you don't find very funny. YOU .........................................

2. You hear a joke that insults an ethnic group. YOU .........................................

3. Someone tells you a joke that uses complicated words or facts you don't understand.
   YOU .........................................

4. You hear a joke that you find very funny. YOU .........................................

5. Someone tells you the same joke that you heard last week. YOU .........................................

**C** Change each of the following to indirect speech.

1. Mary admitted, "I didn't get the joke." .........................................

2. The students insisted, "We weren't telling dirty jokes at lunch yesterday." .........................................
   .........................................

3. My father admitted, "Twenty-five years of practicing medicine have taught
   me that laughter can be the best medicine." .........................................
   .........................................

4. Jeff told his friends, "I'll tell you about a blooper I made at my job interview
   yesterday if you promise not to laugh." .........................................
   .........................................

5. "I can't understand British humor," said Anne. .........................................
   .........................................

6. She said, "I may not have enough knowledge of British culture to understand
   all the pop culture references." .........................................
   .........................................

7. John insisted, "If I had known the joke was offensive, I wouldn't have told it." .........................................
   .........................................

**D** On a separate sheet of paper, write what the people actually said, using direct speech.

1. Jane said I was a good sport for not getting angry about the practical joke
   she had played on me.

2. He admitted that he hadn't gotten my joke about the penguin.

3. The host told his guests not to tell any political jokes at the party.

4. He promised that he would explain the joke to me later.

# UNIT 9

# What lies ahead?

**UNIT GOALS**

1 Discuss the feasibility of future technologies
2 Describe applications of innovative technologies
3 Discuss future trends
4 Consider ways to protect the environment

**A** **Topic Preview.** Read these two quotations from the past. How were they wrong?

"There is no reason for any individual to have a computer in his home."

Kenneth Olsen, President of Digital Equipment, 1977

"Everything that can be invented has been invented."

Charles H. Duell, Commissioner of the U.S. Patent Office, 1899

**B** **Discussion.** Why do you think Duell and Olsen, who were specialists in their fields, were unable to foresee the future? If you had to make a statement in one sentence about the future, what would it be?

**C** 🎧 **Sound Bites.** Read and listen as two women discuss the future.

**OLGA:** Wouldn't it be great if there were some way to be flown to another planet? I mean comfortably. Like a tourist.

**KATE:** Forget about it. That's not happening in our lifetime.

**OLGA:** Don't be so sure. There was this piece on the news about someone trying to get investors to start up a space tourism company. There are even a couple of space tourism websites. It's not as far off as you think.

**KATE:** Yeah, right! Who would invest in that? The cost would be astronomical. And then, to top it off, no one would go.

**OLGA:** I think you're wrong. Lots of people would. I would. I think it would be a great investment.

**KATE:** Well, I think it's pretty far-fetched.

**OLGA:** Hey, fifty years ago, who would have thought we'd be able to do all the things we do today?

**D** **Discussion.** Why does Olga think space tourism may not be so far off? Why does Kate think the possibility is far-fetched?

**E** **What About You?** In your opinion, when might the following future events occur: in the next decade, by the end of the century, or never?

- space tourism
- the widespread use of non-petroleum-dependent technology
- the elimination of cancer as a health threat
- the widespread use of flying automobiles

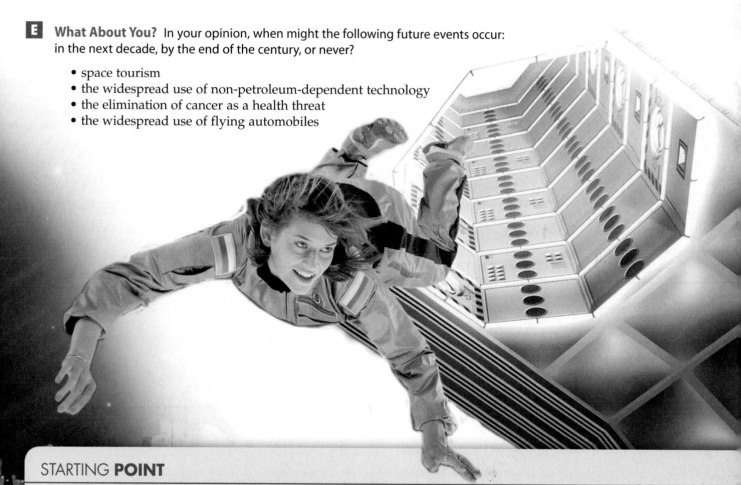

## STARTING **POINT**

**Pair Work.** Make a list of one modern innovation or technology in each of the following categories that would have surprised a person who lived 100 years ago. Explain why.

| | innovation or technology |
|---|---|
| the home | |
| the workplace | |
| transportation | |
| leisure | |
| education | |

# 1 Discuss the feasibility of future technologies

## A ⌒ GRAMMAR **SNAPSHOT.** Read the article and notice the passive forms.

# JULES VERNE

(1828–1905) was internationally renowned for his science fiction and adventure stories, many of which dealt with exploration of the sea, the interior of the Earth, and outer space. The 19th century in Europe was a time of great interest in developing science and technology, and Jules Verne was among the first writers to explore in fiction how people **would be affected** by technology in the future. Verne's great writings deal with contemporary scientific innovation and its potential for human benefit or destruction.

Three of Verne's early novels, *Twenty Thousand Leagues Under the Sea*, *Journey to the Center of the Earth*, and *From the Earth to the Moon*, expressed optimism that nature **would be understood** and **controlled** by humans through new technologies. In these books, Verne's heroes are scientists who travel to unknown places to gain knowledge that will benefit humanity.

In his later works, Verne is less optimistic about the future. In *The Eternal Adam*, for example, Verne is extremely pessimistic, portraying scientists as unscrupulous and willing to allow others to use their scientific discoveries and inventions for war and destruction.

Although a beloved storyteller, Verne **will** always **be credited** with having foreseen the invention of many modern machines and technologies.

**Predicted by Verne:**
- **Long-distance travel by balloon** • **Interplanetary travel** • **A moon landing** • **The electric engine**
- **The tank** • **The picture telephone** • **Scuba-diving gear** • **The helicopter** • **The satellite**

## B Discussion. How do you think Jules Verne was able to envision so many future technologies? What future technologies are being predicted today?

## C Grammar. The passive voice: the future, the future as seen from the past, and the future perfect

**The future**
Use <u>will be</u> or <u>be going to be</u> + a past participle to make predictions and statements about the future in the passive voice.

In the future, appliances **will be linked** to each other and to the Internet as well.
In coming years, our lives **are going to be made** easier by new home technologies.

**The future as seen from the past**
Use <u>would be</u> or <u>was / were going to be</u> + a past participle to make statements about the future as seen from the past in the passive voice.

Verne predicted that spaceships **would be taken** into outer space.
He thought that one day nature **was going to be controlled** by humans.

**The future perfect**
Use <u>will have been</u> + a past participle to make statements in the future perfect in the passive voice.

By 2025, commercial space travel **will have been started**.
Cities **will have been built** on the moon by the end of the century.

> NOTE: The passive voice is often used when discussing science and technology. Use a by phrase when it's important to name the agent (the performer of the action).
>
> Our lives will be improved **by technology**.

**Grammar Booster**

PAGE G13
For more ...

## D Look at the ad for the "home of the future." Then, on a separate sheet of paper, change the four statements in the ad from active to passive voice.

### Build your home of the future today with our complete kit.

**In your home:**

- **robots will do household chores.**
- **computers will turn heating and air-conditioning on and off.**
- **space-age wiring will link appliances to the Internet.**
- **solar energy will fully power your home.**

**E** **Pair Work.** Read about some failed predictions from the past. With a partner, create an advertisement for one prediction. Use the passive voice, explaining the future benefit of the technology.

> "Run, don't walk, to see Smell-O-Vision at your local theater. You'll be surrounded by the smells of the scenes on the screen!"

## "It sounded like a good idea at the time."

**Smell-O-Vision.** In 1960, the movie *Scent of Mystery* combined visual images with releases of odors into the theater. The movie-maker predicted this technology would be used in all movies of the future.

*(Smell-O-Vision was a flop.)*

**The flying car.** On November 17, 1947, the New York Times reported that a prototype of a flying car, the ConvAIRCAR, had circled San Diego, California, for one hour and eighteen minutes. The maker of the car predicted that the flying car would be a commercial success.

*(The flying car never caught on.)*

**Rocket-delivered mail.** On June 8, 1959, a rocket carrying 3,000 letters was launched from a submarine in the ocean and delivered to a U.S. naval station in Florida. Some people believed the age of rocket-delivered mail had begun.

*(But rocket-delivered mail was a bust.)*

**Cryonics for immortality.** In the 1960s, Robert Ettinger's book *The Prospect of Immortality* argued that people with fatal illnesses could have their bodies frozen before death and, once a cure for the illness was found, could then be thawed and cured. This would permit us to live beyond our natural life.

*(This technology never took off.)*

Information source: http://retrofuture.com

Pronunciation Booster

**PAGE P9**
Formal pronunciation, rhythm, and intonation

**F** **Discussion.** Why do you think each of these ideas failed to catch on?

---

GRAMMAR **EXCHANGE** • *Now discuss the feasibility of future technologies.*

**Pair Work.** First, restate each Jules Verne "quotation," using the future as seen from the past. Next, on a separate sheet of paper, rewrite each sentence, using the passive voice. Then, with a partner, make three wild predictions about the future.

Verne thought . . .
Verne believed . . .
Verne claimed . . .
Verne was sure that . . .
Verne theorized that . . .

- "Ordinary people will one day purchase picture telephones."
- "People are going to take trips to outer space some day."
- "The military will use tanks in the future."
- "Scuba-diving gear will protect divers searching for undersea treasures."

**Discussion.** What future technologies do you think will catch on? Are you optimistic or pessimistic about the use of science and technology in the future? Why?

## 2 Describe applications of innovative technologies

### A 🎧 CONVERSATION **SNAPSHOT**

**A:** You know, they say that with cloning, couples who haven't been able to have kids will be able to.

**B:** If you ask me, I think that's pretty scary.

**A:** Really? How come?

**B:** Well, it's like opening a can of worms. I mean, even if cloning were permitted for a good purpose, who's to say it wouldn't then be used for something bad?

**A:** True. But people have always said that about new things.

> 🎧 **Ways to express a fear of consequences**
> It's like opening a can of worms.
> It's like playing with fire.
> It's like opening Pandora's box.
> It's a slippery slope.

🎧 **Rhythm and intonation practice**

### B 🎧 **Vocabulary. Innovative technologies.** Listen and practice.

**remote surgery** an operation performed by a robot controlled by a surgeon at a distant location

**artificial intelligence** a computer designed to do things that the human brain can do, such as think and make decisions

**computer chip implants** electronic chips placed under the skin in order to make identification easy and foolproof

**human cloning** taking a cell from the human body and developing it artificially in order to make an exact living copy of that body

**genetic engineering** changing the structure of the genes of animals or plants for specific purposes

### C 🎧 **Listening Comprehension.** Listen to five conversations in which people discuss the applications of innovative technologies. After each conversation, write the type of technology they're discussing. Then listen again and, with a partner, write a description of the application they mention.

| | Technology | Application |
|---|---|---|
| 1 | | |
| 2 | | |
| 3 | | |
| 4 | | |
| 5 | | |

### D 🎧 **Pair Work.** Listen to the conversations again. Circle the correct words to indicate whether the speakers are for or against each technology. Explain your answer, citing information in the conversations.

1. He's (for it / against it).
2. She's (for it / against it).
3. She's (for it / against it).
4. They're (for it / against it).
5. He's (for it / against it).

**E** **Grammar.** The passive voice in unreal conditional sentences

The passive voice can appear in one clause, or both clauses, of unreal conditional sentences.

**The present unreal conditional**

If lots of effective cancer-fighting drugs **were developed** through genetic engineering, that technology **might be** more widely **accepted**.

If they implanted chips in all credit card users, signatures **would not be required**.

If artificial intelligence **were applied** to kitchen inventions, we wouldn't have to spend so much time in the kitchen.

**The past unreal conditional**

If antibiotics **had been discovered** in the 19th century, the death toll of the 1918 influenza epidemic might have been lower.

If gunpowder **had not been invented**, other tools of war **would have been developed**.

PAGE G13
For more ...

**F** Read the untrue statements. Then write conditional statements with your own opinions, using <u>if</u> clauses in the passive voice.

**Example:** Operations are always performed by robots.

*If operations were always performed by robots, there would never be any surgical errors.*

1. Chips are implanted in our bodies at birth.

2. Genetic engineering is prohibited.

3. Human cloning is permitted.

4. The airplane wasn't invented.

5. The dinosaur was not made extinct.

6. Written language was never developed.

7. Electricity wasn't discovered.

## CONVERSATION **STARTER** • *Now describe some applications of future technologies.*

On your notepad, write an innovative technology that exists in the present and one you'd like to see in the future. Write one important possible application or use of each technology.

Present technology
*genetic engineering*
Application
*create disease-resistant seeds*

| Present technology | Future technology |
|---|---|
| Application | Application |
| | |

**Pair Work.** Discuss the innovative technologies of the present and future that you wrote on your notepad. Use the Conversation Snapshot on page 102 as a guide. Start like this: "You know, they say that ..."

# 3 Discuss future trends

**A** 🎧 **Vocabulary. Demographics.** Listen and practice.

**sta·tis·tic** /stə'tɪstɪk/ *n.* **statistics** [plural] a collection of numbers which represents facts or measurements: *Government crime statistics indicate that the murder rate is falling.*

**dem·o·graph·ic** /ˌdɛmə'græfɪk◂/ *n.* **demographics** [plural] information about the people who live in a particular area, such as how many people there are or what types of people there are: *the changing demographics of Southern California*

**rate** /reɪt/ *n.* [C] the number of times something happens, or the number of examples of something within a certain period: *Prisoners escaped from the center at the rate of one every five days.*

**trend** /trɛnd/ *n.* [C] a general tendency in the way a situation is changing or developing: *If current trends continue, tourism in the state will increase by 10%.* | [+ **in**] *The agency monitors trends in drug use among teenagers.* | [+ **toward**] *There is a recent trend toward more parental involvement in schools.* | *Davis is hoping to* **reverse the trend** (=make a trend go in the opposite direction) *of rising taxes.*

Excerpted from *Longman Advanced American Dictionary* © 2005

**B** 🎧 **Listening Comprehension.** Listen to people discussing social trends. After each conversation, write the number of the conversation next to the rate or rates they are discussing. Then circle the word to indicate if the rate is rising or falling. Listen again to check your work. (In one conversation, the speakers are discussing two rates.)

|  |  |  |
|---|---|---|
| ☐ | crime rate | (rising / falling) |
| ☐ | birthrate | (rising / falling) |
| ☐ | literacy rate | (rising / falling) |
| ☐ | fertility rate | (rising / falling) |
| ☐ | divorce rate | (rising / falling) |

**literacy** = ability to read and write
**fertility** = ability to reproduce
**mortality** = death

**C** 🎧 **Listening Comprehension.** Listen to a lecture predicting world population trends. Read the list of subjects. Then listen again and check the subjects that were discussed.

|  |  |  |  |
|---|---|---|---|
| ☐ | population growth | ☐ | divorce rates |
| ☐ | life expectancy | ☐ | mortality rates |
| ☐ | marriage trends | ☐ | unemployment rates |
| ☐ | birthrates | ☐ | literacy rates |

**D** 🎧 Read the statements. Then listen to the lecture again. Circle the word or phrase that best completes each statement, according to the information presented in the lecture.

In comparison with the year 2000, . . .

1. the world's population in 2015 will be (higher / lower / the same).
2. birthrates in developed countries will be (higher / lower / the same).
3. populations in India and Pakistan will be (higher / lower / the same).
4. the population in African countries with high birthrates and high AIDS mortality will be (higher / lower / the same).
5. populations in Russia and Eastern Europe will be (higher / lower / the same).
6. populations in Japan and Western Europe will be (higher / lower / the same).
7. the rate of population growth in North America, Australia, and New Zealand will continue to be (higher than / lower than / the same as) in other developed countries.

**E** **Discussion.** Do any of the statistics about future world demographics concern you? Why or why not?

---

## DISCUSSON **BUILDER** • *Now discuss future trends.*

**Step 1. Pair Work.** On your notepad, write some social trends in *your* country that concern you. Do you and your partner have similar concerns?

> Marriage and divorce: *Fewer and fewer people are getting married.*

| |
|---|
| Government and politics: |
| The news media: |
| Education: |
| Marriage and divorce: |
| Family life: |
| Other: |

**Step 2. Group Work.** On the board, write the trends that students discussed. Choose one topic you're concerned about and meet in small groups with others who have chosen that topic. Discuss your concerns and predict at least three consequences if the trend continues.

**Step 3. Writing.** On a separate sheet of paper, write two paragraphs about the trend you discussed. In the first paragraph, explain the problem and give examples. In the second paragraph, explain what will happen as a result of the trend.

> *In this country, there has been a trend toward getting married at an older age . . .*

# 4 Consider ways to protect the environment

**A** **Reading Warm-up.** What are some ways we can save energy and water?

**B** 🎧 **Reading.** Read the article. What do you think about the steps the dealership took?

## World's First "Green" Dealership

GreenZone, believed to be the world's first "green" dealer facility, was opened in Umeå in northern Sweden. It is expected to pave the way for other green facilities worldwide. The project was developed by Ford dealer Per Carstedt, in conjunction with Ford, McDonald's, and Statoil. It includes three different buildings—a car dealership, a restaurant, and a gas station.

GreenZone uses solar collectors to absorb energy from the sun.

The GreenZone project has two very challenging goals: to conserve resources by using only renewable energy sources to meet energy demands and to reduce energy consumption by 60–70% by using green technologies.

The car showroom building is heated by a geothermal system that collects heat energy from within the earth and from solar collectors that absorb the energy from the sun. In addition, the dealership, restaurant, and gas station are all linked by pipes. Water in the pipes carries heat from one building to another. For example, excess heat from the restaurant kitchen is used to heat the car showroom.

The energy used for lighting is provided by augmenting electricity from the national power company with power generated by a local wind generator. This cuts down on the amount of power that needs to be purchased. And to reduce the need for lighting, skylights have been installed in the roofs to give better light during the day.

Fresh water from the public water supply is needed only for the kitchen and the restaurant. Rainwater is collected for other uses within the facility, and used water is always filtered and reused. In this way, the demand for fresh water is reduced by 90%.

All the materials used in the construction of the facility were either reused or recycled, cutting down on waste and pollution. Living plants, known as "green filters," are used to purify air that circulates in the ventilation system in the buildings.

The entire staff has been educated in environmental matters so that they are also committed to the dealership's environmental goals.

### GLOSSARY

**renewable** can be replaced so it is never used up

**energy** power that is used to produce heat and make machines work

**consumption** amount used

**pipes** tubes through which gas or liquid can travel

**generator** a machine that produces electricity

**recycle** to process used objects so they can be used again

**waste** unwanted materials that are left after something has been used or consumed

Source: Ford Motor Company

**C** Complete each statement about the GreenZone project.

1. Reducing ............ demands is the purpose of green technologies.
   a. pollution     b. energy     c. renewable

2. At GreenZone, a decision was made to avoid using ............ energy sources.
   a. nonrenewable     b. renewable     c. power

3. Waste and pollution are reduced by ............ materials at the dealership.
   a. using     b. recycling     c. linking

4. Employees know that one way to protect the environment is to protect its ............ .
   a. wastes     b. solar power     c. resources

5. The GreenZone project uses a variety of ............ sources: electric, wind, geothermal, and solar.
   a. pollution     b. waste     c. power

**D** **Pair Work.** Complete the chart about the systems at GreenZone, according to the reading. Write the sources of energy for each system and describe the process.

| System | Source of energy | Process |
|---|---|---|
| Heating | geothermal and solar | Heat is transported from one building to another. |
| Lighting | | |
| Water | | |
| Ventilation | | |

**E** Answer the questions, based on what you learned in the reading and from your own general knowledge.

1. What are some renewable energy sources?
2. What are some nonrenewable energy sources?
3. How do solar collectors work?
4. What are the benefits of using recycled materials?

**F** **Discussion.** Why do you think a car company, a gas station, or a fast-food restaurant would be interested in a green dealership? What might motivate a company to create a project such as this?

---

DISCUSSION **BUILDER** • *Now discuss ways to protect the environment.*

**Step 1. Pair Work.** Complete and discuss the self-test. How differently did you respond? Who seems to be more environmentally conscious, according to the self-test?

**How environmentally conscious are you? Here are some ways you can protect the environment with the decisions you make at home.**

**Check off those that you do.**

**In the Kitchen**
- ☐ Cover pots when boiling water.
- ☐ Use microwave ovens and pressure cookers when you can.
- ☐ Use energy-efficient appliances.

**In the Bathroom**
- ☐ Place a brick or a closed container filled with water in the reservoir tank of your toilet.
- ☐ Take showers instead of baths.
- ☐ Turn off the water when you brush your teeth or shave.

**In the Laundry**
- ☐ Use cold water in the washing machine.
- ☐ Always wash full loads instead of small ones. Presoak heavily soiled items.
- ☐ Hang your clothes to dry outside instead of using a dryer.

**General**
- ☐ Turn off your computer when not using it.
- ☐ Use fluorescent light bulbs instead of incandescent bulbs.
- ☐ Walk as often as you can or take public transportation instead of driving.

**Step 2. Discussion.** What do you think of the tips in the self-test? Do you think any of them are practical ideas or are they just a waste of time? Why? Do you think it's important to protect the environment for the future? Why or why not?

*"I think it's silly to worry about how much water you use at home. I don't think it makes a bit of difference to the environment."*

*"I totally disagree. I think protecting the environment starts at home."*

# Writing: Predict life in the future

## The essay

When writing an essay, present your personal view on a topic and give reasons, facts, or examples to support that view. The outline on the left and the sample essay on the right indicate an effective way to organize an essay.

I. **Introduction:**
- Include a thesis statement—a sentence that presents the topic and focus of the entire essay.
- Write general statements about your topic that suggest what the body paragraphs will be about.

II. **Body paragraphs:** Develop the idea presented in the thesis statement in two or more paragraphs. Each paragraph should have a topic sentence, followed by supporting examples.

III. **Conclusion:** Summarize the main points and restate the thesis.

thesis statement

**WRITING MODEL**

**In twenty years, cars will be very different from today's cars.** The car of the future will probably be powered by an alternative energy source, and it will be equipped with new technologies brought about by advances in computing.

Experts predict the car of the future will be powered by electricity. This will benefit the environment in several ways. First of all, [other details] . . . In addition, [other details] . . .

Advances in computing will also bring a lot of changes in car design. The car of the future will have many advanced technological features. For example, [other details] . . .

Although we cannot predict exactly what the car of the future will be like, we can make some educated guesses based on the direction the car industry is heading in. In twenty years, we will probably not remember . . .

**Step 1. Prewriting. Planning ideas.** Choose a topic and write a thesis statement.

**Topics**
- Transportation in the future
- Communication in the future
- The classroom of the future
- Your own topic: ...............

**Thesis statement:** _____

On a separate sheet of paper, plan the body paragraphs of your essay. Write a topic sentence for each paragraph you plan to write. Follow each topic sentence with a list of supporting examples.

**Body paragraph 1:**
topic sentence
supporting example
supporting example

**Body paragraph 2:**
topic sentence
supporting example
supporting example

**Step 2. Writing.** On a separate sheet of paper, write an essay about your topic. Use your thesis statement and your topic sentences and develop your supporting examples.

**Step 3. Self-Check.**

☐ Does your thesis statement announce what the essay will be about?
☐ Does the body of the essay give sufficient support for your point of view?
☐ Does your conclusion summarize the main points of your essay and restate its thesis?

**SUMMIT WEBSITE**
For Unit 9 online activities, visit the *Summit* Companion Website at www.longman.com/summit.

**A** 🎧 **Listening Comprehension.** Listen to the conversations. Write the technologies the people are referring to.

1. ................................ 2. ................................ 3. ................................ 4. ................................

**B** 🎧 Read the following idioms from the conversations. Then listen again and infer their meanings from the context.

1. "I find that a little sketchy." ................................
2. "I think it's just pie in the sky." ................................
3. "I'm still on the fence." ................................
4. "You know—you buy everything hook, line, and sinker!" ................................

**C** Complete the paragraph with words and phrases from the box. Make any necessary changes.

| trend   life expectancy   mortality rate   population growth   statistics   birthrate |
|---|

................................ indicate that there are over 6 billion people in the world, with an increase of
(1)
76,570,430 people each year. This ................................ is not a result of an increased ................................. In fact,
(2) (3)
there is actually a worldwide ................................ for women to have fewer children. This increase in
(4)
population is mainly the result of a decrease in the child ................................, with more children living
(5)
to adulthood. People are living much longer lives. When the first humans walked the earth, the
average person lived only to the age of twenty. Today, the worldwide ................................ is 77.1.
(6)

**D** Rewrite each of the following sentences in the passive voice. Include a <u>by</u> phrase only if that information is necessary.

1. In two years, engineers will have designed a new factory. ................................

2. Engineers are going to equip the factory with filters. ................................

3. Workers will recycle paper, metal, and plastic. ................................

4. They're going to treat waste before they dump it into rivers. ................................

5. New technologies are going to reduce energy demands by 50 percent. ................................

6. Pipes will collect rainwater, and they will transport it to tanks. Pipes will also carry excess heat from one building to another. ................................

7. If engineers hadn't designed the factory to use solar energy, the national grid couldn't have met its demand for electricity. ................................

# An interconnected world

### UNIT GOALS

1 Describe the cultural impact of foreign imports
2 React to news about global issues
3 Discuss the economic impact of globalization
4 Discuss the role of English in international communication

**A** **Topic Preview.** Read what these people say about globalization. Who seems enthusiastic about it? Who seems to be critical? Who seems neutral?

**glob·al·i·za·tion** /ˌgloʊbələˈzeɪʃən/ *n.* [U] the process of making something such as a business international, or the result of this: *the globalization of world markets* —**globalize** /ˈgloʊbəˌlaɪz/ *v.* [I,T]

*Longman Advanced American Dictionary* © 2005

"This is a very exciting time in the world of information . . . The whole pace of business is moving faster. Globalization is forcing companies to do things in new ways."

**Bill Gates, USA**
**CEO Microsoft**

"Globalization has changed us into a company that searches the world, not just to sell or to source, but to find intellectual capital—the world's best talents and best ideas."

**Jack Welch, USA**
**former CEO General Electric**

"[Globalization] increases to breakneck pace the speed of our transactions, financial or informational, but it also facilitates the spread of global plagues such as AIDS, social and ecological devastation, drugs, and international trafficking in arms or human beings."

**Queen Noor, Jordan**

"When protesters shout about the evils of globalization, most are not calling for a return to narrow nationalism but for the borders of globalization to be expanded, for trade to be linked to labor rights, environmental protection, and democracy."

**Naomi Klein, Canada**
**activist and writer**

"Across the world, as the 'free market' brazenly protects Western markets and forces developing countries to lift their trade barriers, the poor are getting poorer, and the rich richer."

**Arundhati Roy, India**
**author and activist**

"If we cannot make globalization work for all, in the end it will work for no one."

**Kofi Annan, Ghana**
**Secretary-General of the United Nations**

"Globalization is not something we can hold off or turn off . . . It is the economic equivalent of a force of nature . . . like wind or water."

**Bill Clinton, USA**
**former president**

**B** **Discussion.** Which of the quotations come closest to *your* own views?

**C** 🎧 **Sound Bites.** Read and listen to a conversation about globalization.

**EVA:** You may want to head home soon. They're closing off the streets for that antiglobalization demonstration.

**CRAIG:** Another one? What is it with these people? What's the big deal about globalization, anyway?

**EVA:** There are a lot of reasons to be against it. I think they have a point.

**CRAIG:** No offense, Eva, but don't you think you're talking out of both sides of your mouth? I mean, you've got your Brazilian shoes, your Chilean wine, your German car. How can you be against globalization?

**EVA:** OK, maybe I'm being a bit hypocritical. But not everyone benefits like we do. I still think we've got to stand up for what's right.

**D** Answer the questions.

1. Why does Craig think Eva is being hypocritical?

2. What benefits of globalization is Eva referring to?

3. Why does Eva think the demonstrators have a point?

## STARTING **POINT**

**Discussion.** According to the dictionary definition on page 110, which of the following do you think are *not* examples of globalization? Explain your answers.

**a** Every year, New York City hosts a flamenco festival featuring artists from around the world who sing and dance in this traditional Spanish gypsy style.

**b** At an international meeting in Porto Alegre, Brazil, participants from more than forty countries use English to communicate.

**c** Nike, the U.S. sports apparel company, calls a news conference to answer further charges that workers in their factories in Southeast Asia are being paid poverty wages.

**d** Canada charges that French and Russian fishing ships have violated its waters by fishing within the two-hundred-mile limit it claims along its Pacific and Atlantic coasts.

**e** Unemployed communications workers in Italy complain that their jobs are being taken by lower-paid workers in Sri Lanka.

**f** Mexico, the United States, and Canada agree to eliminate trade barriers and permit sales of products from one country to the other without taxes.

# *1* *Describe the cultural impact of foreign imports*

**A** 🎧 GRAMMAR **SNAPSHOT.** Read the people's opinions and notice the use of phrasal verbs.

**Sanjita Kalyani, India**

"Go anywhere young people shop and you'll **come across** foreign brand names everywhere you look. **Try** a shirt **on**, and it's probably made in China. **Check** those new CDs **out** at the local music store, and they may be from Brazil or Spain. Or **try** some new product **out** at the electronics store and you can bet it's imported. I know a lot of people here see all this as a threat to our culture. But the way I see it, we can enjoy foreign things and still value and appreciate our own traditions."

**Daniel Odunje, Nigeria**

"When I **turn** my television **on**, it's great having the choice of so many movies and shows from all over the world. But I have to admit, I'm concerned about the influence of Hollywood movies on my children. I really don't care for the values they teach. But my kids are crazy about those films. If I were to ask my kids to **give** them **up**, I'm sure I'd never hear the end of it! I've been trying to **talk** them **into** watching other things, but it's a bit of a losing battle, I'm afraid."

**Claire Hamilton, Canada**

"It's amazing to see all the foreign things that we take for granted now. If you have an interest in martial arts, you can **take up** karate from Japan, kung fu from China, tae kwon do from Korea, or capoeira from Brazil. When it comes to food, you can always **count on** finding someplace that serves Indian, Thai, Mexican, Japanese, Korean—all foods that would have been hard to find here a generation ago. If you like karaoke, you can **try** it **out** almost anywhere now. People are a whole lot more sophisticated about these things than they were in my parents' time."

**B** **Discussion.** Are any of the opinions in the Grammar Snapshot ones that might be heard in your country? Explain.

**C** **Grammar. Separability of transitive phrasal verbs**

**REMEMBER:** Transitive* phrasal verbs can be separable or inseparable.

**Separable phrasal verbs**

**A direct object noun can generally come before or after the particle.**
  Let's **check out** those new CDs. OR Let's **check** those new CDs **out**.

**BE CAREFUL!** A direct object pronoun must come before the particle.
  Let's **check** them **out**. NOT Let's ~~check out them~~.

**Some separable verbs are** *always* **separated: the direct object always comes before the particle.**
  I've been trying to **talk** my kids **into** watching other things.
  NOT I've been trying to ~~talk into my kids~~ watching other things.

**Inseparable phrasal verbs**

**With inseparable phrasal verbs, all direct objects always come AFTER the particle.**
  Those kinds of companies **cater to** younger customers.
  NOT Those kinds of companies ~~cater younger customers to~~.

| Separable | Always separated | Inseparable |
|---|---|---|
| check out | keep (something) on | carry on |
| figure out | see (something) through | cater to |
| find out | start (something) over | come across |
| give up | talk (someone) into | count on |
| hand out | | do without |
| pick up | | go after |
| put off | | run into |
| take up | | |
| throw away | | |
| try on | | |
| try out | | |
| turn on / off | | |

For a complete list and definitions, see the Appendices, pages A4–A6.

PAGE G14
For more ...

*Transitive verbs are verbs that take direct objects.

**D**  Complete each statement, using a form of the phrasal verb with the pronoun _it_ or _them_.
Pay attention to whether or not the phrasal verb is separable.

1. Although only a small minority of the population can read English, English words are visible everywhere. You often (come across) _____ on signs, product advertisements, and even clothing.

2. Tai chi has become really popular in this country. Even my eighty-year-old great-grandmother has (take up) _____!

3. For the governments of some countries, the benefits of globalization are not so clear. It may not be easy to (talk into) _____ dropping trade tariffs.

4. Because many young adults have tremendous economic power, many fashion companies develop marketing campaigns that (go after) _____ exclusively.

5. A common marketing technique is to hand out free samples of new products at international trade fairs so people can (try out) _____.

6. Many parents feel that certain songs express a negative social attitude and worry that their children will (pick up) _____ just by listening to the songs.

## GRAMMAR **EXCHANGE** • _Now describe the cultural impact of imports._

On your notepad, list examples of things from foreign countries or cultures that you come across often.

Foods you eat:

Music you listen to:

Home furnishings:

Clothes and accessories you buy:

TV programs or movies you watch:

Other:

**Pair Work.** Discuss whether the items you listed have had a positive or negative impact in your country. Of the things that are a part of your life, are there any that you would be willing to give up? Which products or traditions from _your_ country do you think would have a positive impact on other countries?

**Discussion.** Do you agree with any of these statements about the future cultural impact of globalization? Explain. Try to use phrasal verbs when you can.

"Globalization will lead to the creation of one global culture as people **give up** local traditions."

"Because of globalization, people will imitate the shallow, negative values they **pick up** from foreign movies, TV shows, and ads."

"Thanks to globalization, people around the world will **take up** the best aspects of each other's cultures while still retaining their own."

# 2 *React to news about global issues*

## A ∩ CONVERSATION **SNAPSHOT**

**To react positively**

**A:** Can you believe how much money was donated for hunger relief?

**B:** It really makes you feel good, doesn't it?

**A:** I guess it just goes to show you what people can do when they put their minds to it.

**To react negatively**

**A:** Can you believe that no one's doing anything about global warming?

**B:** It's really mind-boggling, isn't it?

**A:** Yeah. You'd think in this day and age they could come up with a way to slow it down.

∩ **Rhythm and intonation practice**

∩ **Ways to react to world issues and news**

It's really (mind-boggling / shocking / appalling), isn't it?
It really makes you feel (angry / depressed / helpless), doesn't it?
It's really (wonderful / heartwarming), isn't it?
It really makes you feel (great / teary-eyed / fantastic), doesn't it?
It's not really surprising, is it?
It makes you feel kind of guilty, doesn't it?
It really makes you stop and think, doesn't it?

*Pronunciation Booster*

**PAGES P9–P10**
Intonation in tag questions

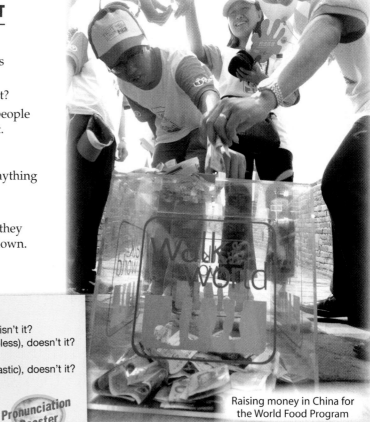

Raising money in China for the World Food Program

## B ∩ Vocabulary. Phrasal verbs to discuss global issues. Listen and practice.

**lay off** to stop employing a worker, especially for a period of time in which there is not much work to do
*The company announced they were laying off two hundred employees.*

**put up with** to accept a bad situation or person without complaining
*For many years, the people in that village have put up with inadequate roads.*

**run out of** use all of something and not have any left
*If we're not careful, we'll run out of oil before alternative sources of energy have been found.*

**go without** to live without something you need or usually have
*No one should have to go without clean water to drink.*

**wipe out** to remove or destroy
*Illiteracy has been nearly wiped out there.*

**come up with** to think of an idea, plan, reply, etc.
*They need to come up with a new plan to shelter the homeless.*

**come down with** to become sick with a particular illness
*Since the flood, hundreds have come down with malaria.*

**carry out** to do something that needs to be organized and planned
*It's time the president carried out her plan to vaccinate all school-age children.*

**bring about** to make something happen
*We need to tell management our ideas if we expect to bring about any policy changes.*

**C** There are seven errors with phrasal verbs in the article. Make corrections.

# UN HUNGER RELIEF

In order to assist local hospitals in their battle against acute malnutrition, the UN World Food Program is carrying through operations in the southern region, where thousands of children have been going with proper food or sanitary conditions. The terrible hardship these children have had to put on with is the result of extreme poverty brought to by ongoing drought conditions and the increasing number of people who have been recently laid away in the region because of factory closings. The poorest and most isolated families have run away of money to buy the staples they need to feed their children. The program has come down with a plan to provide emergency rations to these families.

**D** Fill in the blanks with appropriate forms of phrasal verbs from the vocabulary on page 114.

## Drug Discovery Plan to Tap and Help Rain Forests

In Madagascar, off the coast of Africa, as farmers ............... usable land,
(1)
they burn and destroy the rain forests to make more room for farming. If action is not taken, Madagascar's rain forests will soon be ............... .
(2)

A team of international scientists have ............... an interesting idea to
(3)
help save the forests. Led by researcher Patricia Wright, they are currently negotiating agreements with local government officials to ............... research
(4)
in the area through a program called "The Drug Discovery and Biodiversity Program." The program will study local traditional healing methods from a scientific point of view. Researchers believe the rain forests of Madagascar may be home to sources of new drugs that will fight the numerous illnesses that millions of people ............... each year, such as malaria, AIDS, and even
(5)
the common cold. They are confident their plan will ............... much needed
(6)
economic growth in the area.

Information source: http://news.nationalgeographic.com

## CONVERSATION STARTER • *Now react to news about global issues.*

**Pair Work.** Read and react to each newspaper clipping about global problems. Use the Conversation Snapshot on page 114 as a guide. Start like this: "Can you believe ...?"

### Study Warns of Global Warming Threat
By 2050, more than a million species of animals and plants will have been wiped out because of rising temperatures caused by greenhouse emissions, according to a new study carried out by conservation biologist Chris Thomas.

### Philippine Authorities Concerned about New Outbreaks
Hundreds of people have come down with malaria in Mindanao, causing authorities to increase their recent mosquito eradication campaign and further restrict travel there.

### Scientists Concerned about South Asia Smog
A vast blanket of pollution stretching across South Asia, brought about by breakneck economic growth, is modifying rainfall patterns and putting the health of hundreds of thousands of people at risk.

### Leaders Agree to Do More to Fight Poverty
World leaders gathered in Malta this week to come up with a plan to stamp out poverty by the end of the decade, while protesters fought with police outside.

### Famine Sends Thousands into Refugee Camps
A catastrophic drought that has forced more than four million people to go without adequate food is filling United Nations refugee camps to capacity.

**Discussion.** What do you think could be done to address some of the following world problems? Use phrasal verbs if you can.

| | | | |
|---|---|---|---|
| hunger | pollution | war | destruction of the rain forests |
| poverty | illiteracy | disease | global warming |

## 3  Discuss the economic impact of globalization

**A** **Reading Warm-up.** Are people in your country generally advocates or critics of globalization? Why is that?

**B** 🎧 **Reading.** Read the article about economic globalization. Which view do you agree with?

# GLOBALIZATION
## Experts Debate Pros and Cons

### The People Weigh In

The Pew Global Attitudes Project surveyed more than 38,000 people in forty-four countries. Majorities in all countries took a favorable view of growing international trade and business ties. Faster communication and travel, the growing availability of foreign culture, and the wide variety of products were cited as benefits.

Over the past few decades, more and more countries have opened up their markets, increasingly transforming the world economy into one free-flowing global market. The question is: Is economic globalization good for all?

According to the World Bank, one of its chief proponents, economic globalization has helped reduce poverty in a large number of developing countries. It cites one study that shows increased prosperity contributing to improved education and longer life expectancies in twenty-four developing countries as a result of integration of local economies into the world economy. Home to some three billion people, these twenty-four countries have seen incomes increase at an average rate of five percent—compared to two percent in developed countries.

Globalization advocates claim economies in developing countries will benefit from new opportunities for small and home-based businesses. For example, small farmers in Brazil who produce cashew nuts that would previously have sold only in local open-air markets can now promote their goods worldwide via the Internet.

Critics take a different view, believing that economic globalization is actually widening the gap between the rich and poor. A study carried out by the U.N.-sponsored World Commission on the Social Dimension of Globalization shows that only a few developing countries have actually benefited from integration into the world economy and that the poor, the illiterate, unskilled workers, and indigenous peoples have been left behind. Furthermore, they maintain that globalization may ultimately threaten emerging businesses. For example, Indian artisans who currently seem to benefit from globalization because they are able to export their products may soon face stiff competition that could put them out of business. When large-scale manufacturers start to produce the same goods, or when superstores like Wal-Mart move in, these small businesses will not be able to keep up and will be crowded out.

One thing is certain about globalization—there is no turning back. Advances in technology combined with more open policies have already created an interconnected world. The challenge now is finding a way to create a kind of globalization that works for the benefit of all.

Information sources: http://econ.worldbank.org and http://news.bbc.co.uk

### Growing Trade and Business Ties

| | SEE IT HAPPENING | THINK IT'S GOOD FOR THE COUNTRY |
|---|---|---|
| | % | % |
| Angola | 79 | 89 |
| Argentina | 28 | 60 |
| Bangladesh | 31 | 84 |
| Bolivia | 65 | 77 |
| Brazil | 70 | 73 |
| Bulgaria | 42 | 89 |
| Canada | 59 | 85 |
| China | 53 | 90 |
| Czech Republic | 60 | 84 |
| Egypt | 55 | 67 |
| France | 50 | 88 |
| Germany | 58 | 91 |
| Ghana | 70 | 85 |
| Great Britain | 61 | 87 |
| Guatemala | 59 | 83 |
| Honduras | 70 | 93 |
| India | 65 | 69 |
| Indonesia | 73 | 87 |
| Italy | 71 | 79 |
| Ivory Coast | 48 | 96 |
| Japan | 74 | 72 |
| Jordan | 50 | 52 |
| Kenya | 67 | 90 |
| Lebanon | 74 | 83 |
| Mali | 79 | 95 |
| Mexico | 77 | 79 |
| Nigeria | 82 | 95 |
| Pakistan | 63 | 78 |
| Peru | 45 | 83 |
| Philippines | 78 | 83 |
| Poland | 76 | 78 |
| Russia | 75 | 88 |
| Senegal | 74 | 98 |
| Slovak Republic | 51 | 86 |
| South Africa | 69 | 88 |
| South Korea | 77 | 90 |
| Tanzania | 52 | 82 |
| Turkey | 51 | 82 |
| Uganda | 69 | 95 |
| Ukraine | 79 | 93 |
| United States | 67 | 78 |
| Uzbekistan | 84 | 97 |
| Venezuela | 45 | 86 |
| Vietnam | 92 | 98 |

Pew Research Center revises its country list each year.

**C** **Discussion.**

1. According to the article, what are the two opposing views of globalization? What examples are given to illustrate each view? Can you give other examples?

2. According to the survey, in which countries were people the most and least enthusiastic about globalization? What are the main reasons people felt positive about globalization in the survey?

**D** **Group Work.** Take the survey and compare the responses in your class. What percentage of the students checked each box? Share your opinions and support your ideas with specific examples.

| Do you see the following effects of globalization occurring in your country? Do you think they're beneficial? | I see it occurring. | I think it's beneficial. |
|---|---|---|
| 1. Growing trade and business ties | ☐ | ☐ |
| 2. Faster communication and travel | ☐ | ☐ |
| 3. Growing availability of foreign culture | ☐ | ☐ |
| 4. Wide variety of products from different parts of the world | ☐ | ☐ |

**E** 🎧 **Vocabulary. Economic terms.** Listen and practice.

**standard of living** level of wealth, comfort, and access to goods
> *Many hope globalization will raise the standard of living in developing countries.*

**investment** money put into a company or business in order to make a profit and make a business successful
> *The World Bank believes that foreign investment will benefit local economies.*

**employment rate** the percentage of people who have jobs

**unemployment rate** the percentage of people who don't have jobs
> *Advocates of globalization cite an increased employment rate in countries that have been integrated into the world economy. Critics, however, worry that the unemployment rate will, in fact, increase.*

**income** money earned from work or investments

**wages** money paid according to the number of hours worked
> *The World Bank reports that on average, incomes have improved in developing countries, but critics complain that inadequate wages are keeping the poorest people stuck in poverty.*

**imports** products brought to one country from another to be sold

**exports** products sent from one country to another to be sold
> *The promise of globalization is that old protective barriers against trade will give way to a freer flow of imports and exports.*

**F** 🎧 **Listening Comprehension.** Listen to the conversations. After each conversation, determine which economic term from the vocabulary best describes the topic of the conversation. Listen again if necessary.

**Conversation 1:** ............................................
**Conversation 2:** ............................................
**Conversation 3:** ............................................
**Conversation 4:** ............................................

## DISCUSSION **BUILDER** • *Now discuss the economic impact of globalization.*

**Step 1. Pair Work.** On your notepad, write the names of at least three foreign companies that do business in your country. What is the general response of the public to these companies or their products: positive, negative, or neutral?

| Name of business / Product | General response of public |
| --- | --- |
|  |  |
|  |  |
|  |  |
|  |  |

Some well-known international companies
BP (British Petroleum)
Coca-Cola
Daewoo
IKEA
Nestle
Sony
Starbucks
The Gap
Volkswagen

**Step 2. Discussion.** What benefits or problems have these businesses and products brought to your country? Overall, do you think globalization is good or bad for your economy? Explain. Use the terms from the vocabulary in your discussion to clarify your ideas.

> "In my opinion, Starbucks hasn't had a particularly strong impact. The stores are small, so they haven't really reduced **unemployment**."

> "Volkswagen's **investment** in local factories has been good for the country. It's provided **employment** for thousands, and it pays good **wages**. Its products are reliable and affordable, raising the **standard of living** for a lot of people."

117

# Discuss the role of English in international communication

**A** 🎧 **Listening Comprehension.** Listen to four people talking about their views on using English for international communication. Summarize each speaker's opinion.

| | |
|---|---|
| Speaker 1 | |
| Speaker 2 | |
| Speaker 3 | |
| Speaker 4 | |

**B** 🎧 Now listen again. Write the number of the speaker you think would be most likely to make each statement. Explain why.

☐ "I'm willing to learn whatever language is needed for international communication."

☐ "English makes international communication really fair."

☐ "I really don't mind if I have an accent or make a few mistakes in English."

☐ "There's no other language I'd rather learn than English."

**C** **Word Skills. Using a dictionary.** Use the key to answer the following questions.

- Which of the verbs can be intransitive?
- Which entries indicate that the word can be used as a part of speech other than a verb?
- Which two verbs are appropriate for formal use?
- Which entry includes an antonym (a word that means the opposite)?

| KEY |
|---|
| **Grammar Codes** |
| [C]   countable |
| [U]   uncountable |
| [I]    intransitive |
| [T]   transitive |
| [I,T]  intransitive or |
|        transitive |
| **Parts of Speech** |
| *adj.*   adjective |
| *adv.*   adverb |
| *n.*     noun |
| *v.*     verb |

**dom·i·nate** /ˈdɑmə,neɪt/ *v.* **1** [I,T] to control someone or something, or to have more power or importance than them: *Movie directing is a profession dominated by men.* | *New Orleans dominated throughout the game.* **2** [I,T] to be the most important feature of something: *The murder trial has dominated the news this week.* **3** [T] to be larger or more noticeable than anything else in a place or situation: *A pair of red-and-gold boots dominated the display.* —**dominating** /ˈdɑmə,neɪtɪŋ/ *adj.* —**domination** /,dɑmə'neɪʃən/ *n.* [U]

**max·i·mize** /ˈmæksə,maɪz/ *v.* [T] **1** to increase something as much as possible: *We need to look at how to maximize our cash flow.* | *Diamonds are cut to maximize the stone's beauty.* **2** to CLICK on a special part of a WINDOW on a computer screen so that it becomes as big as the screen —**maximization** /,mæksəmə'zeɪʃən/ *n.* [U] —compare MINIMIZE

**neu·tral·ize** /ˈnutrə,laɪz/ *v.* [T] **1** to prevent something from having any effect: *The Oilers managed to neutralize the other team's defenses.* **2** TECHNICAL to make a substance chemically NEUTRAL: *This fertilizer neutralizes the salts in the soil.* **3** a word meaning to kill someone, especially an enemy in a war, used when you do not want to say "kill" directly: *Government forces neutralized the rebels.* **4** to make a country or population NEUTRAL in war —**neutralization** /,nutrələ'zeɪʃən/ *n.* [U]

**sur·pass** /sɚ'pæs/ *v.* [T] **1** to be even better or greater than someone or something else: *In 15 years, China will likely surpass the U.S. as the world's largest market.* | **surpass expectations/hopes/dreams** (=be better than you had expected, hoped etc.) **2 surpass yourself** FORMAL to do something even better than you have ever done before: *Stewart has surpassed himself with his latest novel.*

**u·til·ize** /ˈyutl,aɪz/ *v.* [T] FORMAL to use something for a particular purpose: *The old fire station could be utilized as a theater.* —**utilizable** *adj.* —**utilization** /,yutl-ə'zeɪʃən/ *n.* [U]

Excerpted from *Longman Advanced American Dictionary* © 2005

**D** Use the dictionary entries to find words to complete each sentence. Use the context of the sentence to determine the appropriate meaning and the correct part of speech.

1. The import-export company enrolls all new employees in an intensive English program designed to ................... the amount of time they are exposed to written and spoken English.

2. Some have argued that the ................... of world communication by the English language has reduced the use of other languages.

3. Language experts point out that students of English are more likely to ................... their English skills to speak with other non-native speakers than with native speakers.

4. With approximately 100 million Chinese Internet users, it's not surprising that six of the world's top 20 most popular websites are in Chinese and that the number of websites in Chinese will soon ................... the number in English.

5. In some countries with populations who speak different languages, English is used to ................... any arguments about which language to use in government and business transactions.

---

## DISCUSSION **BUILDER** • *Now discuss the role of English in international communication.*

**Step 1. Pair Work.** Complete the survey. Rate how important each English skill is to you, with 1 being very important, 2 somewhat important, and 3 not important. Then compare and explain your answers with a partner.

| English Skills | Importance | | |
|---|---|---|---|
| 1. understanding the customs of the U.S., Britain, Australia, or other English-speaking countries | 1 | 2 | 3 |
| 2. sounding like a native speaker | 1 | 2 | 3 |
| 3. watching movies or TV without subtitles in one's own language | 1 | 2 | 3 |
| 4. being able to participate in business meetings and other business communication | 1 | 2 | 3 |
| 5. reading academic journals and writing papers | 1 | 2 | 3 |
| 6. functioning socially, such as meeting people or knowing how to be polite | 1 | 2 | 3 |
| 7. expressing opinions precisely | 1 | 2 | 3 |
| 8. being able to travel easily in English-speaking countries | 1 | 2 | 3 |
| 9. teaching English to others | 1 | 2 | 3 |
| 10. other | 1 | 2 | 3 |

**Step 2. Discussion.** Do you agree with any of the statements below? How do you think the use of English as an international language will change over the next fifty years?

*"English will soon be surpassed by another language as the number one international language in the world."*

*"The use of English as an international language is a reflection of how the United States and Britain dominate the world economically and culturally. If that changes, English will decline as an international language."*

*"Using English is actually an excellent way to neutralize any difficulties in international communication."*

**Step 3. Writing.** Write about the importance of learning English in your life. What role do you hope English will play in your life? What are your goals in studying English? What do you plan to do to achieve them?

# Writing: Make a complaint

## A formal letter of complaint

- Begin with a formal salutation and end with a formal complimentary close.

| Salutations | Complimentary Closes |
|---|---|
| Dear [title + last name], | Sincerely, |
| To whom it may concern: | Yours truly, |
| Dear Sir or Madam, | Respectfully yours, |

- In your opening, summarize the purpose of the letter. This can be a sentence saying "I am writing to tell you about . . ." or "I am writing to let you know that . . ."
- Then explain the problem in more detail in the body of the letter.
- In your conclusion, finish with a thank you or an invitation for the person to get in touch with you.
- Keep the tone formal. Use standard language as well as regular spelling and capitalization rules.

**WRITING MODEL**

Ul. Topolowa 16 } your address
31-506 Krakow
March 2, 2006 } date

Customer Representative
McDonald's } recipient's address
Ul. Florianska 55,
31-444 Krakow

To whom it may concern: } salutation

   I am writing to voice concern over the new McDonald's that has opened in our town's Old Square. } opening

   I understand that you have leased the space and that you have a right to decorate it as you wish. However, I am concerned that the golden arches at the top of this historic building clash with the surrounding architecture and interfere with the feel of the city. I would be most grateful if you would consider using a more discreet design for your symbol. } body

   I look forward to hearing from you and thank you for your consideration of this matter. } conclusion

        Respectfully yours, } complimentary close

*Anna Stawicka*
Anna Stawicka } signature

### Step 1. Prewriting. Generating ideas.

- Think about three situations you might like to complain about. They can be problems in the community, at work, at a local store or business, or at school.
- List the problems and write possible solutions.

### Step 2. Writing. Choose one of the problems to write about. Find the recipient's address for your letter. On a separate sheet of paper, write a formal letter of complaint to the appropriate person. Follow the formal letter format in the model.

### Step 3. Self-Check.

- ☐ Does the letter follow the format for addresses and dates?
- ☐ Does the letter start with a salutation and end with a complimentary close?
- ☐ Does the letter have an opening and a conclusion?
- ☐ Did you explain the problem in detail?
- ☐ Is the tone of the letter formal?

**IDEAS**

- a public building that needs repairs
- unfriendly staff in a store
- a dangerous traffic light at an intersection

Problem 1:

   Solution:

Problem 2:

   Solution:

Problem 3:

   Solution:

*SUMMIT* WEBSITE
For Unit 10 online activities, visit the *Summit* Companion Website at www.longman.com/summit.

**A** 🎧 **Listening Comprehension.** Listen to three news reports on globalization-related topics. After each report, complete each statement so that it is true, according to the information presented in the report. Listen again if necessary.

**Report 1:** WorldWatch is concerned that improving living standards in developing countries ............ .
   a. will cause natural resources to run out
   b. will bring about an increase in prices for luxury goods

**Report 2:** According to the report, most people think that globalization ............ .
   a. is causing social and economic problems
   b. is not causing social and economic problems

**Report 3:** The chairman of Starbucks believes that his customers appreciate ............ .
   a. the convenience of having Starbucks stores in so many locations
   b. both the coffee and the experience of being in the store

**B** Complete each phrasal verb with the correct particle.

   1. The island voted to carry ............ a plan to find foreign investors to develop the island into a tourist resort.
   2. Technological advances such as cell phones and the Internet have brought ............ great changes in the way people communicate.
   3. The government is determined to figure ............ how to increase trade with other countries without causing a rise in unemployment.
   4. Clerks were handing ............ free cups of Colombian coffee at the supermarket in the hopes that it would catch on with local shoppers.
   5. I picked ............ a little French when I visited my uncle in Paris last summer, but I wouldn't say that I'm fluent.
   6. A lot of families have been putting ............ large purchases because they're afraid they may soon be out of work if the economy doesn't improve.
   7. To be honest, I'm worried that the culture of rich nations will one day wipe ............ the traditional culture of poorer nations.
   8. Asian martial arts have become really popular recently. I know so many people who have taken ............ tae kwon do, karate, or judo.

**C** On a separate sheet of paper, rewrite each sentence, replacing the underlined phrase with the pronoun <u>it</u> or <u>them</u>.

   1. We should check out <u>that new French film</u>.
   2. We're trying to do without <u>imported products</u>.
   3. They voted to give up <u>protections against imports</u>.
   4. Falling profits forced the factory owner to lay off <u>the workers</u>.
   5. Just turn on <u>your TV</u> and you'll see news and films from all over the world.

# Irregular verbs

| base form | simple past | past participle | base form | simple past | past participle |
|---|---|---|---|---|---|
| be | was / were | been | mean | meant | meant |
| beat | beat | beaten | meet | met | met |
| become | became | become | mistake | mistook | mistaken |
| begin | began | begun | pay | paid | paid |
| bend | bent | bent | put | put | put |
| bet | bet | bet | quit | quit | quit |
| bite | bit | bitten | read /rid/ | read /rɛd/ | read /rɛd/ |
| bleed | bled | bled | ride | rode | ridden |
| blow | blew | blown | ring | rang | rung |
| break | broke | broken | rise | rose | risen |
| bring | brought | brought | run | ran | run |
| build | built | built | say | said | said |
| burn | burned / burnt | burned / burnt | see | saw | seen |
| burst | burst | burst | sell | sold | sold |
| buy | bought | bought | send | sent | sent |
| catch | caught | caught | set | set | set |
| choose | chose | chosen | shake | shook | shaken |
| come | came | come | shed | shed | shed |
| cost | cost | cost | shine | shone | shone |
| creep | crept | crept | shoot | shot | shot |
| cut | cut | cut | show | showed | shown |
| deal | dealt | dealt | shrink | shrank | shrunk |
| dig | dug | dug | shut | shut | shut |
| do | did | done | sing | sang | sung |
| draw | drew | drawn | sink | sank | sunk |
| dream | dreamed / dreamt | dreamed / dreamt | sit | sat | sat |
| drink | drank | drunk | sleep | slept | slept |
| drive | drove | driven | slide | slid | slid |
| eat | ate | eaten | smell | smelled / smelt | smelled / smelt |
| fall | fell | fallen | speak | spoke | spoken |
| feed | fed | fed | speed | sped / speeded | sped / speeded |
| feel | felt | felt | spell | spelled / spelt | spelled / spelt |
| fight | fought | fought | spend | spent | spent |
| find | found | found | spill | spilled / spilt | spilled / spilt |
| fit | fit | fit | spin | spun | spun |
| fly | flew | flown | spit | spit / spat | spit / spat |
| forbid | forbade | forbidden | spoil | spoiled / spoilt | spoiled / spoilt |
| forget | forgot | forgotten | spread | spread | spread |
| forgive | forgave | forgiven | spring | sprang / sprung | sprang / sprung |
| freeze | froze | frozen | stand | stood | stood |
| get | got | gotten | steal | stole | stolen |
| give | gave | given | stick | stuck | stuck |
| go | went | gone | sting | stung | stung |
| grow | grew | grown | stink | stank / stunk | stunk |
| hang | hung | hung | strike | struck | struck / stricken |
| have | had | had | swear | swore | sworn |
| hear | heard | heard | sweep | swept | swept |
| hide | hid | hidden | swim | swam | swum |
| hit | hit | hit | swing | swung | swung |
| hold | held | held | take | took | taken |
| hurt | hurt | hurt | teach | taught | taught |
| keep | kept | kept | tear | tore | torn |
| know | knew | known | tell | told | told |
| lay | laid | laid | think | thought | thought |
| lead | led | led | throw | threw | thrown |
| leap | leaped / leapt | leaped / leapt | understand | understood | understood |
| learn | learned / learnt | learned / learnt | upset | upset | upset |
| leave | left | left | wake | woke / waked | woken / waked |
| lend | lent | lent | wear | wore | worn |
| let | let | let | weave | wove | woven |
| lie | lay | lain | weep | wept | wept |
| light | lit | lit | win | won | won |
| lose | lost | lost | wind | wound | wound |
| make | made | made | write | wrote | written |

## Verbs that can be followed by a gerund

| | | | | | |
|---|---|---|---|---|---|
| admit | complete | enjoy | mind (as in *object to*) | quit | risk |
| advise | consider | finish | miss | recall | suggest |
| appreciate | discuss | keep (as in *continue*) | postpone | recommend | tolerate |
| avoid | dislike | mention | practice | resent | understand |
| can't help | don't mind | | | resist | |

## Expressions that can be followed by a gerund

| | | | |
|---|---|---|---|
| be excited about | be opposed to | believe in | blame [someone or something] for |
| be worried about | be used to | participate in | forgive [someone or something] for |
| be responsible for | complain about | succeed in | thank [someone or something] for |
| be interested in | dream about / of | take advantage of | keep [someone or something] from |
| be accused of | talk about / of | take care of | prevent [someone or something] from |
| be capable of | think about / of | insist on | stop [someone or something] from |
| be tired of | apologize for | look forward to | |
| be accustomed to | make an excuse for | | |
| be committed to | have a reason for | | |

## Verbs that can be followed directly by an infinitive

| | | | | | |
|---|---|---|---|---|---|
| afford | claim | hesitate | offer | regret | wait |
| agree | decide | hope | plan | seem | want |
| appear | demand | intend | prepare | struggle | wish |
| arrange | deserve | learn | pretend | swear | would like |
| ask | expect | mean | promise | threaten | |
| care | fail | need | refuse | volunteer | |

## Verbs that must be followed by an object before an infinitive

| | | | | | |
|---|---|---|---|---|---|
| advise | challenge | force | need | remind | want |
| allow | convince | help | order | require | warn |
| ask | encourage | hire | permit | teach | would like |
| beg | expect | instruct | persuade | tell | |
| cause | forbid | invite | promise | urge | |

## Verbs that can be followed by a gerund or an infinitive

**with a change in meaning**

| | |
|---|---|
| forget | remember |
| regret | stop |

**without a change in meaning**

| | | | | |
|---|---|---|---|---|
| begin | continue | like | prefer | try |
| can't stand | hate | love | start | |

## Adjectives that can be followed by an infinitive

| | | | | |
|---|---|---|---|---|
| anxious | delighted | glad | prepared | sad |
| ashamed | depressed | happy | proud | sorry |
| certain | disappointed | lucky | ready | upset |
| content | fortunate | pleased | relieved | |

## Participial adjectives

| | | | | | | | |
|---|---|---|---|---|---|---|---|
| alarming | – | alarmed | embarrassing | – | embarrassed | paralyzing | – | paralyzed |
| amazing | – | amazed | enlightening | – | enlightened | pleasing | – | pleased |
| amusing | – | amused | entertaining | – | entertained | relaxing | – | relaxed |
| annoying | – | annoyed | exciting | – | excited | satisfying | – | satisfied |
| astonishing | – | astonished | exhausting | – | exhausted | shocking | – | shocked |
| boring | – | bored | fascinating | – | fascinated | soothing | – | soothed |
| confusing | – | confused | frightening | – | frightened | startling | – | startled |
| depressing | – | depressed | horrifying | – | horrified | stimulating | – | stimulated |
| disappointing | – | disappointed | inspiring | – | inspired | surprising | – | surprised |
| disgusting | – | disgusted | interesting | – | interested | terrifying | – | terrified |
| distressing | – | distressed | irritating | – | irritated | tiring | – | tired |
| disturbing | – | disturbed | moving | – | moved | touching | – | touched |

# Stative verbs

| | | | | | |
|---|---|---|---|---|---|
| amaze | contain | feel* | look* | please | smell* |
| appear* | cost | forget | look like | possess | sound |
| appreciate | desire | hate | love | prefer | suppose |
| astonish | dislike | have* | matter | realize | surprise |
| be* | doubt* | hear | mean | recognize | taste* |
| believe | envy | imagine | mind | remember* | think* |
| belong | equal | include* | need | resemble | understand |
| care | exist | know | owe | see* | want * |
| consist of | fear | like | own | seem | weigh* |

\* These verbs also have action meanings. Example: *I see a tree.* (non-action) *I'm seeing her tomorrow.* (action)

# Transitive phrasal verbs

**Some transitive phrasal verbs have more than one meaning. Not all are included here.**

**Abbreviations**
s.o. = someone
sth. = something
e.g. = for example
inf. = informal

## SEPARABLE

**blow** sth. **out**    stop a flame by blowing on it
**blow** sth. **up**    1 make sth. explode  2 fill sth. with air, e.g., a balloon  3 make sth. larger, e.g., a photo
**bring** sth. **about**    make sth. happen
**bring** sth. **back**    1 return sth. to a store  2 revive or renew sth., e.g., a custom or tradition
**bring** sth. **out**    1 introduce a new product  2 make a quality more noticeable
**bring** s.o. **up**    raise a child
**bring** sth. **up**    start to talk about an issue
**burn** sth. **down**    burn a structure completely
**call** s.o. **back**    return a phone call
**call** sth. **off**    cancel sth.
**call** s.o. **up**    call s.o. on the phone
**carry** sth. **out**    conduct a plan
**check** s.o./sth. **out**    look at s.o. or sth. more closely
**cheer** s.o. **up**    make s.o. feel happier
**clean** s.o./sth. **up**    clean s.o. or sth. completely
**clear** sth. **up**    clarify sth.
**close** sth. **down**    force a business or institution to close
**cover** sth. **up**    1 cover sth. completely  2 change facts to avoid responsibility
**cross** sth. **out**    draw a line through sth.
**cut** sth. **down**    make sth. fall by cutting, e.g., a tree
**cut** sth. **off**    1 remove sth. by cutting  2 stop the supply of sth.
**cut** s.o. **off**    interrupt s.o who is speaking
**dream** sth. **up**    invent or think of a new idea
**drink** sth. **up**    drink a beverage completely
**drop** s.o./sth. **off**    leave s.o. or sth. somewhere
**empty** sth. **out**    empty sth. completely
**figure** s.o./sth. **out**    understand s.o. or sth. after some thought
**fill** s.o. **in**    tell s.o. about recent events
**fill** sth. **out**    complete a form
**fill** sth. **up**    fill a container completely
**find** sth. **out**    learn new information
**follow** sth. **through**    do everything to complete a task
**get** sth. **across**    help s.o. understand an idea
**give** sth. **away**    give sth. you do not need or want
**give** sth. **back**    return sth. to its owner
**give** sth. **out**    distribute sth.
**give** sth. **up**    quit doing sth.
**hand** sth. **in**    submit work, e.g., to a boss or a teacher
**hand** sth. **out**    distribute sth.
**hang** sth. **up**    put sth. on a hanger or hook, e.g., clothes
**help** s.o. **out**    assist s.o.
**keep** s.o./sth. **away**    cause s.o. or sth. to stay at a distance
**lay** s.o. **off**    fire s.o. because of economic conditions
**leave** sth. **on**    1 not turn sth. off, e.g., an appliance  2 not remove sth. such as clothing or jewelry

**leave** sth. **out**    omit sth.
**let** s.o. **down**    disappoint s.o.
**let** s.o./sth. **in**    allow s.o. or sth. to enter
**let** s.o. **off**    allow s.o. to leave a bus, car, taxi, etc.
**let** s.o./sth. **out**    allow s.o. or sth. to leave
**light** sth. **up**    illuminate sth.
**look** s.o./sth. **over**    examine s.o. or sth.
**look** s.o./sth. **up**    1 try to find s.o.  2 try to find sth. in a book, the Internet, etc.
**make** sth. **up**    create a fictional story
**pass** sth. **out**    distribute sth.
**pass** sth. **up**    decide not to take an opportunity
**pay** s.o. **off**    bribe s.o.
**pay** sth. **off**    pay back money one owes
**pick** s.o./sth. **out**    identify or choose s.o. or sth.
**pick** s.o. **up**    stop a vehicle so s.o. can get in
**pick** s.o./sth. **up**    lift s.o. or sth.
**pick** sth. **up**    1 get or buy sth. from somewhere  2 learn sth. new  3 get an infectious disease
**point** s.o./sth. **out**    show s.o or sth. to another person
**put** sth. **away**    put sth. in its appropriate place
**put** sth. **back**    return sth. to its original place
**put** s.o./sth. **down**    1 stop holding or lifting s.o. or sth.  2 insult s.o.
**put** sth. **off**    delay or postpone sth.
**put** sth. **on**    get dressed or place sth. on one's body
**put** sth. **together**    1 put sth. on a wall  2 build sth.
**put** sth. **up**    build or erect sth.
**set** sth. **off**    cause sth. to explode
**set** sth. **up**    1 establish a new business, organization, etc.  2 prepare equipment for use
**show** s.o./sth. **off**    display the best qualities of s.o. or sth.
**shut** sth. **off**    stop a machine or supply
**straighten** sth. **up**    make sth. neat
**switch** sth. **on**    start a machine, turn on a light, etc.
**take** sth. **away**    remove sth.
**take** sth. **back**    1 return sth. to a store  2 accept sth. returned by another person
**take** sth. **down**    remove sth. that is hanging
**take** sth. **in**    1 notice and remember sth.  2 make a clothing item smaller
**take** sth. **off**    remove clothing, jewelry, etc.
**take** s.o. **on**    hire s.o.
**take** s.o. **on**    agree to do a task
**take** s.o. **out**    invite s.o. somewhere and pay for his/her meal, show, etc.
**take** sth. **up**    start doing an activity habitually
**talk** sth. **over**    discuss sth.
**tear** sth. **down**    destroy sth.

A4

| | |
|---|---|
| **tear** sth. **up**    tear sth. into small pieces | **turn** sth. **in**    submit a paper, application, etc. |
| **think** sth. **over**    consider sth. | **turn** sth. **off**    stop a machine, light, etc. |
| **think** sth. **up**    invent or think of a new idea | **turn** s.o. **off**    cause s.o. to lose interest (inf.) |
| **throw** sth. **away**    put sth. in the garbage | **turn** sth. **on**    start a machine, light, etc. |
| **throw** sth. **out**    put sth. in the garbage | **turn** sth. **out**    make or manufacture sth. |
| **touch** sth. **up**    improve sth. with very small changes | **turn** sth. **over**    turn sth. so the bottom is at the top |
| **try** sth. **on**    try clothing to see if it fits | **turn** sth. **up**    raise the volume, heat, etc. |
| **try** sth. **out**    use sth. to see if one likes it or if it works | **use** sth. **up**    use sth. completely |
| **turn** sth. **around**    **1** turn so the front is at the back  **2** cause | **wake** s.o. **up**    cause s.o. to stop sleeping |
|   things to get better | **wipe** sth. **out**    remove or destroy sth. |
| **turn** s.o./sth. **down**    reject s.o. or sth. | **work** sth. **out**    **1** resolve a problem  **2** calculate a math problem |
| **turn** sth. **down**    lower the volume, heat, etc. | **write** sth. **down**    write sth. to have a record of it |

## ALWAYS SEPARATED

| | |
|---|---|
| **ask** s.o. **over**    invite s.o. to one's home | **see** sth. **through**    complete a task |
| **bring** s.o./sth. **down**    remove a ruler or government from power | **start** sth. **over**    begin sth. again |
| **do** sth. **over**    do sth. again | **talk** s.o. **into** sth.    persuade s.o. to do sth. |
| **keep** sth. **on**    not remove sth. such as clothing or jewelry | |

## INSEPARABLE

| | |
|---|---|
| **cater to** s.o.    provide what s.o. wants or needs | **go over** sth.    examine sth. carefully |
| **carry on** sth.    continue sth. another person has started | **go without** sth.    live without sth. one needs or wants |
| **come across** s.o./sth.    find s.o. or sth. unexpectedly | **run into** s.o.    meet s.o. unexpectedly |
| **count on** s.o./sth.    depend on s.o. or sth. | **run into** sth.    accidentally hit or crash into sth. |
| **do without** s.o./sth.    live without s.o. or sth. one needs or wants | **stick with** s.o.    stay close to s.o. |
| **go after** s.o./sth.    pursue s.o. or sth. | **stick with** sth.    continue doing sth. as before |

## Intransitive phrasal verbs

**Some intransitive phrasal verbs have more than one meaning. Not all are included here.**

| | |
|---|---|
| **blow up**    **1** explode  **2** suddenly become very angry | **go off**    explode; make a sudden noise |
| **break down**    stop functioning | **go on**    continue to talk about or describe sth. |
| **break out**    start suddenly, e.g., a war, disease, or fire | **go out**    **1** leave a building  **2** leave one's home to meet people, |
| **burn down**    burn completely |   enjoy entertainment, etc. |
| **call back**    return a phone call | **go up**    be built |
| **carry on**    **1** continue doing sth.  **2** behave in a silly or emotional way | **grow up**    become an adult |
| **catch on**    become popular | **help out**    do sth. helpful |
| **check in**    report one's arrival at an airport or hotel | **hang up**    end a phone call |
| **check out**    pay one's bill and leave a hotel | **hold on**    wait during a phone call |
| **cheer up**    become happier | **keep away**    stay at a distance |
| **clear up**    become better, e.g., a rash or the weather | **keep on**    continue |
| **close down**    stop operating, e.g., a factory or a school | **keep up**    go or think as fast as another person |
| **come along**    accompany s.o. | **lie down**    rest on a bed |
| **come back**    return | **light up**    **1** begin to shine brightly  **2** look pleased or happy |
| **come in**    enter | **make up**    end an argument and reestablish a friendly relationship |
| **come off**    become unattached | **pass out**    become unconscious |
| **come out**    **1** appear, e.g., the sun  **2** be removed, e.g., a stain | **pay off**    be worthwhile |
| **dress up**    wear more formal clothes or a costume | **pick up**    improve, e.g., the economy |
| **drop in**    visit unexpectedly | **play around**    have fun or not be serious |
| **drop out**    quit a class, school, or program | **run out**    no longer in supply |
| **eat out**    eat in a restaurant | **show up**    appear |
| **empty out**    empty completely | **sign up**    register |
| **fall off**    become unattached | **sit down**    sit |
| **fill out**    become bigger | **slip up**    make a mistake |
| **fill up**    become completely full | **stand up**    rise to one's feet |
| **find out**    learn new information | **start over**    begin again |
| **follow through**    continue working on sth. until it is completed | **stay up**    not go to bed |
| **fool around**    have fun or not be serious | **straighten up**    make neat |
| **get ahead**    make progress or succeed | **take off**    depart by plane |
| **get along**    to not argue | **turn in**    go to bed (inf.) |
| **get back**    return from a place | **turn out**    have a particular result |
| **get together**    meet somewhere with a friend or acquaintance | **turn up**    appear |
| **get up**    get out of bed | **wake up**    stop sleeping |
| **give up**    quit | **watch out**    be careful |
| **go along**    **1** accompany s.o.  **2** agree | **work out**    **1** exercise  **2** be resolved; end successfully |
| **go back**    return | |

## Three-word phrasal verbs

Some three-word phrasal verbs have more than one meaning. Not all are included here.

catch up on sth.    **1** do sth. one didn't have time to do earlier
                    **2** get the most recent information
catch up with s.o.    exchange information about recent activities
check up on s.o.    make sure s.o. is OK
come away with sth.    learn sth. useful from s.o. or sth.
come down to sth.    be the most important point or idea
come down with sth.    get an illness
come up against s.o./sth.    be faced with a difficult person or situation
come up with sth.    think of an idea, plan, or solution
face up to sth.    accept an unpleasant truth
fall back on sth.    use an old idea because new ideas have failed
follow through on sth.    continue doing sth. until it is completed
get around to sth.    finally do sth.
get away with sth.    avoid the consequences of a wrong act
get back at s.o.    harm s.o. because he / she harmed you
give up on s.o.    stop hoping that s.o. will change

give up on sth.    stop trying to make sth. happen
go along with sth.    agree to do sth.
go through with sth.    do sth. difficult or painful
grow out of sth.    stop doing sth. as one becomes an adult
keep up with s.o.    stay in regular contact
look down on s.o.    think one is better than another person
look out for s.o.    protect s.o.
look up to s.o.    admire or respect s.o.
make up for sth.    do sth. to apologize
put up with s.o./sth.    accept s.o. or sth. without complaining
run out of sth.    no longer have enough of sth.
stand up for sth.    support an idea or a principle
stand up to s.o.    refuse to let s.o. treat anyone badly
team up with s.o.    do a task together
think back on s.o./sth.    think about and remember s.o. or sth.
walk out on s.o.    end a relationship with a wife, boyfriend, etc.
watch out for s.o./sth.    protect s.o. or sth.

# *Verb forms: overview*

## Summary of verb forms

|  | Present time | Past time | Future time |
|---|---|---|---|
| **Simple** | **Simple present** walk / walks | **Simple past** walked | **Simple future** will walk |
| **Continuous** | **Present continuous** am walking / is walking / are walking | **Past continuous** was walking / were walking | **Future continuous** will be walking |
| **Perfect** | **Present perfect** have walked / has walked | **Past perfect** had walked | **Future perfect** will have walked |
| **Perfect continuous** | **Present perfect continuous** have been walking / has been walking | **Past perfect continuous** had been walking | **Future perfect continuous** will have been walking |

## Simple verb forms: usage

|  | Present time | Past time | Future time |
|---|---|---|---|
| **Simple verb forms** describe habitual actions or events that occur at a definite time. | **Simple present**[1] **Habitual action** *The department **meets** once a month to review the status of projects.* | **Simple past** **Completed action that occurred at a definite time in the past** *Last year researchers **discovered** a new cancer treatment.* | **Simple future**[3] **Action that will occur at a definite time in the future** *Next year they **will offer** a course on global trade.* |
|  | **Facts and generalizations** *The Earth **rotates** around the sun every 365 days.* | **Habitual action in the past**[2] *When I was young we **visited** my grandparents every week.* | **Habitual action in the future** *Next month I'll **go** to the gym three times a week.* |

[1] The simple present can also express a future action: *Her flight arrives this evening at eight.*

[2] <u>Used to</u> and <u>would</u> also express habitual actions in the past: *When I was a child, we used to spend the summer in the mountains. In the mornings we would go hiking and in the afternoons we would swim in a nearby lake.*

[3] <u>Be going to</u> can also express a future action: *Next year they are going to offer a course on global trade.*

## Continuous verb forms:  usage

|  | Present time | Past time | Future time |
|---|---|---|---|
| **Continuous verb forms** describe continuous actions or events that occur at a definite time. | **Present continuous\*** **Action in progress now** *The business managers are discussing next year's budget right now.* | **Past continuous** **Action in progress at a definite time in the past** *None of the computers were working when I came in this morning.* | **Future continuous** **Action that will be in progress during a definite time in the future** *We'll be listening to the speech when you arrive.* |

\* The present continuous can also express a future plan: *They're getting married next month.*

## Perfect verb forms:  usage

|  | Present time | Past time | Future time |
|---|---|---|---|
| **Perfect verb forms** describe actions or events in relation to other time frames. | **Present perfect\*** **Completed action that occurred at an indefinite time before the present** *She has made many contributions to the field.* **Recently completed action** *He has just published an article about his findings.* **Uncompleted action (action that began in the past, continues into the present, and may continue into the future)** *They have studied ancient cultures for many years.* | **Past perfect** **Action that occurred at some point before a definite time in the past** *By 2002, he had started a new business.* **Action that occurred before another past action** *They had already finished medical school when the war broke out.* | **Future perfect** **Action that will be completed by some point at a definite time in the future** *By this time next year, I will have completed my research.* |

\* Many statements in the present perfect can also be stated correctly using the simple past, depending on the speaker's perspective: *She made many contributions to the field.*

## Perfect continuous verb forms:  usage

|  | Present time | Past time | Future time |
|---|---|---|---|
| **Perfect continuous verb forms** describe continuous actions or events in relation to other time frames. | **Present perfect continuous** **Uncompleted continuous action (action that began in the past, continues into the present, and may continue into the future)** *She has been lecturing about that topic since 2001.* **Very recently completed action** *The workers have been protesting. They're finished now.* | **Past perfect continuous** **Continuous action that occurred before another past action or time** *By 2005, researchers had been seeking a cure for AIDS for more than twenty years.* | **Future perfect continuous** **Continuous action that occurred before another action or time in the future** *When the new director takes over, I will have been working at this company for ten years.* |

# Pronunciation table

These are the pronunciation symbols used in *Summit 2*.

| | Vowels | | | | Consonants | | | |
|---|---|---|---|---|---|---|---|---|
| **symbol** | **key word** | **symbol** | **key word** | | **symbol** | **key word** | **symbol** | **key word** |
| i | beat, feed | ə | banana, among | | p | pack, happy | z | zip, please, goes |
| ɪ | bit, did | ɚ | shirt, murder | | b | back, rubber | ʃ | ship, machine, |
| eɪ | date, paid | aɪ | bite, cry, buy, eye | | t | tie | | station, special, |
| ɛ | bet, bed | aʊ | about, how | | d | die | | discussion |
| æ | bat, bad | ɔɪ | voice, boy | | k | came, key, quick | ʒ | measure, vision |
| ɑ | box, odd, father | ɪr | beer | | g | game, guest | h | hot, who |
| ɔ | bought, dog | ɛr | bare | | ʧ | church, nature, | m | men, some |
| oʊ | boat, road | ɑr | bar | | | watch | n | sun, know, |
| ʊ | book, good | ɔr | door | | ʤ | judge, general, | | pneumonia |
| u | boot, food, student | ʊr | tour | | | major | ŋ | sung, ringing |
| ʌ | but, mud, mother | | | | f | fan, photograph | w | wet, white |
| | | | | | v | van | l | light, long |
| | | | | | θ | thing, breath | r | right, wrong |
| | | | | | ð | then, breathe | y | yes, use, music |
| | | | | | s | sip, city, | t̬ | butter, bottle |
| | | | | | | psychology | t˺ | button |

# *Pronunciation Booster*

The *Pronunciation Booster* is optional. It provides more information about pronunciation as well as additional practice. The exercises can be found on both the Class Audio Program and the Student's Take-Home Audio CD.

## Unit 1

### Sentence stress and intonation: review

**Sentence stress**
**Remember: Content words are generally stressed in a sentence.**
> I've **ALWAYS DREAMED** about **BEING** a **PHOTOGRAPHER**.
> You've been **TALKING** about **DOING** that for **YEARS**!
> Have you **EVER THOUGHT** about a **CAREER** in **LAW**?

| Content words | |
|---|---|
| nouns | photographer, Robert, career |
| verbs | think, study, discuss |
| adjectives | important, young, successful |
| adverbs | carefully, ever, recently |
| possessive pronouns | ours, yours, theirs |
| demonstrative pronouns | this, that, these |
| reflexive pronouns | myself, yourself, ourselves |
| interrogative pronouns | who, what, why |

**In compound nouns, stress only the first word.**

She has just been accepted to a top **BUSINESS** school.

Have you made any progress with your **JOB** search?

**Intonation**
**Lower pitch after the stressed syllable in the last stressed word in statements, commands, and information questions. Raise pitch after the last stressed syllable in yes/no questions.**

I love the outdoors, so I've decided to become a naturalist.

What's stopping you?

Tell me something about your experience.

Have you made plans to get married?

**If the last syllable in the sentence is stressed, lengthen the vowel and lower pitch. In yes/no questions, lengthen the vowel and raise pitch.**

I just gave notice at the bank.

Have you decided on a career?

**A** 🎧 Listen and practice.

1. I've always dreamed about being a photographer.
2. You've been talking about doing that for years!
3. Have you ever thought about a career in law?

**B** 🎧 Listen and practice.

1. I love the outdoors, so I've decided to become a naturalist.
2. Tell me something about your experience.
3. What's stopping you?
4. Have you made plans to get married?
5. I just gave notice at the bank.
6. Have you decided on a career?

**C** Circle the content words.

1. It was very difficult for Dan to hide his disappointment.
2. He was rejected by two law schools.
3. What does he plan to do now?
4. He just accepted a position teaching math at the university.
5. MediLabs has an opening for a junior lab specialist.

🎧 Now practice reading each sentence aloud. Listen to compare.*

**D** Circle the last stressed content word in each of the following sentences.

1. He wants to start his own travel agency.
2. I don't really know how to get started.
3. Do I need to have experience in the tourism industry?
4. Why are you looking for a change?
5. Tell me about your plans for the coming year.
6. Do you want to become a flight attendant?
7. Have you applied for that job?

🎧 Now practice reading each sentence aloud, using the intonation patterns you have learned. Listen to compare.*

## Unit 2

### Emphatic stress and pitch to express emotion

Use emphatic stress and higher pitch on content words to indicate intensity of emotion.

I'm **SO SORRY!**          How could you **DO** that?
I'm **REALLY UPSET!**      What **GREAT NEWS!**
What do you **MEAN?**      Thank you **SO MUCH!**

**A** 🎧 Listen and practice.

1. I'm so sorry!          3. What do you mean?          5. What great news!
2. I'm really upset!      4. How could you do that?     6. Thank you so much!

*NOTE: Whenever you see a listening activity with an asterisk (*), say each word, phrase, or sentence in the pause *after* the number. Then listen for confirmation.

⌒ Practice reading each sentence aloud, using intonation to express emotion. Listen to compare.*

1. **JOHN**, what **HAPPENED**?
2. You look **WORRIED**.
3. I feel **JUST TERRIBLE**!
4. How did **THAT** happen?

5. Why didn't you slow **DOWN**?
6. We could have been **KILLED**!
7. How could you **SAY** that?

## Unit 3

### Vowel reduction to /ə/

**Remember: The /u/ sound in the function word <u>to</u> is often reduced to /ə/ in spoken English.**
We tried to cheer him up.  /tə/
They were scared to death.  /tə/
It was starting to get me down.  /tə/
You just need to give it a little more time.  /tə/

**Do not reduce the /u/ sound when <u>to</u> comes before another /ə/ sound.**
         /tə/             /tu/
She was trying to e-mail a message to a friend.

**When <u>to</u> occurs before the pronouns <u>her</u> or <u>him</u>, you can say it two ways:**
Use /tə/ and pronounce /h/  →  I sent it to her yesterday. /təhər/
Use /tu/ and drop /h/      →  I sent it to her yesterday. /tuər/

**In the phrases <u>have to</u>, <u>ought to</u>, and <u>be going to</u>, /u/ generally reduces to /ə/, and there are often other sound changes.**
I didn't **have to** walk very far.  /hæftə/
You really **ought to** be careful next time.  /ɔtə/
We're definitely **going to** take a cell phone on our next trip. /gʌnə/

⌒ Listen and practice.

1. We tried to cheer him up.
2. They were scared to death.
3. It was starting to get me down.
4. You just need to give it a little more time.
5. She was trying to e-mail a message to a friend.

6. I sent it to her yesterday.
7. I sent it to her yesterday.
8. I didn't have to walk very far.
9. You really ought to be careful next time.
10. We're definitely going to take a cell phone on our next trip.

Circle the words in the following sentences that you think contain sounds that will be reduced, according to what you learned about vowel reduction.

1. I'm learning to sail my ship.
2. They had sent an SOS text message from a cell phone to a friend in London.
3. They got several messages telling them to be strong.
4. The helicopters had been unable to take off because of the severe weather.
5. You ought to tell your brother that you can't talk to him right now.
6. Don't let it get to you.
7. I'm going to refuse to give up.
8. We have to keep trying, no matter how tired we are.

⌒ Now practice reading each sentence aloud and listen to compare.*

# Unit 4

## Shifting emphatic stress

You can shift stress within a sentence to change emphasis. Place emphatic stress on key words to get your meaning across.

**A:** I think I'm too critical of other people.
**B:** Really? I don't think I'm critical **ENOUGH**.

**A:** I don't think I'm critical enough.
**B:** Really? I think I'm **TOO** critical.

**A:** I think I'm too critical of other people.
**B:** I don't see you that way at all. **I'M** too critical.

**A:** I think I'm too critical of other people.
**B:** Really? Not me . . . At least I don't **THINK** I'm too critical.

**A** ⌒ Listen and practice.

1. I don't think I'm critical **ENOUGH**.
2. I think I'm **TOO** critical.
3. **I'M** too critical.
4. I don't **THINK** I'm too critical.

**B** Study each conversation, paying attention to emphatic stress.

1. "You know what my problem is? I'm a perfectionist."
   RESPONSE: Well, **I'M** just the opposite.

2. "You know what my problem is? I'm a perfectionist."
   RESPONSE: Not me. I'm just the **OPPOSITE**.

3. "There goes Carla again—yelling at Phil."
   RESPONSE: I'm not surprised. She's **ALWAYS** angry about **SOMETHING**.

4. "Why is Carla yelling at Phil? "
   RESPONSE: It's just the way she is. She's always **ANGRY** about something.

5. "Why was John so angry this morning?"
   RESPONSE: I don't know. I've **NEVER** seen him lose his temper like that.

6. "Can you believe how angry John was this morning?"
   RESPONSE: Not really. I've never seen him lose his temper like **THAT**.

⌒ Now practice reading each response aloud, using emphatic stress as shown. Listen to compare.*

# Unit 5

## Linking sounds

Link plural noun endings to the first sound in the word that follows.
Diamonds are very expensive. /daɪməndzɑr/
Diamonds make great gifts. /daɪməndzmeɪk/

Link third-person singular endings to the first sound in the word that follows.
It makes an impressive gift. /meɪksən/
The company promises to give you a diamond. /prɑməsɪztə/

> **Remember:** There are three different sounds for the endings of plural nouns and third-person singular verbs.
>
> | /z/ | /s/ | /ɪz/ |
> |---|---|---|
> | diamonds | results | promises |
> | superstitions | sharks | noises |
> | bottles | types | matches |
> | believes | beliefs | wishes |
> | dreams | sleeps | judges |

**A** ⌒ Listen and practice.

1. Diamonds are very expensive.
2. Diamonds make great gifts.
3. It makes an impressive gift.
4. The company promises to give you a diamond.

🎧 Practice reading each sentence aloud, paying attention to the linking sounds you learned. Listen to compare.* (Note that your choices may differ from what you hear on the audio.)

1. A frog brings good luck to the house it enters.
2. Babies born with teeth become extremely selfish.
3. An itchy nose means you will have a fight.
4. A lucky charm protects against the evil eye.
5. She keeps a large bowl of water near the front door.
6. Superstitions can be found in every culture.
7. A company claims to have invented a machine that allows people to talk with their pets.
8. Phobias are exaggerated fears.
9. My sister believes in ghosts, avoids black cats, and carries a lucky charm in her pocket.

# Unit 6

## Regular past participle endings

There are three pronunciations of the past participle ending **-ed**, depending on the final sound of the base form of the verb.

**With voiced sounds**
When the base form ends with a voiced sound, pronounce the **-ed** ending as /d/.

| moved | canceled | described | stayed | agreed |

**With voiceless sounds**
When the base form ends with a voiceless sound, pronounce the **-ed** ending as /t/.

| helped | asked | crushed | watched |

| Voiced sounds | | Voiceless sounds |
|---|---|---|
| /b/ | /i/ | /p/ |
| /g/ | /ɪ/ | /k/ |
| /ð/ | /eɪ/ | /θ/ |
| /v/ | /ɛ/ | /f/ |
| /z/ | /æ/ | /s/ |
| /ʒ/ | /ɑ/ | /ʃ/ |
| /ʤ/ | /ɔ/ | /ʧ/ |
| /m/ | /oʊ/ | |
| /n/ | /ʊ/ | |
| /ŋ/ | /u/ | |
| /r/ | /ʌ/ | |
| /l/ | | |

**With /t/ or /d/**
When the base form ends with the sound /t/ or /d/, pronounce the **-ed** ending as a new syllable, /ɪd/ or /əd/. Link /t/ or /d/ with the **-ed** ending.

| wai ted | → | /weɪţɪd/ | | nee ded | → | /nidɪd/ |
| re por ted | → | /rɪpɔrţɪd/ | | re spon ded | → | /rɪspɑndɪd/ |

## Reduction in perfect modals

The auxiliary **have** in perfect modals is generally reduced. The /h/ is dropped and /æ/ is reduced to /ə/.

/wʊdəv/
If I'd looked at the expiration date, I **would have** renewed my passport.

/maɪtəv/
If I weren't Japanese, I **might have** needed a visa to enter the country.

/wʊdənəv/
If we'd left on time, we **wouldn't have** missed our flight.

**Perfect modals**
would have ⎫
could have ⎪
should have ⎬ [past participle]
might have ⎪
may have ⎭

**A** 🎧 Listen and practice.

1. moved
2. canceled
3. described
4. stayed
5. agreed
6. helped
7. asked
8. crushed
9. watched
10. waited
11. reported
12. needed
13. responded

**B** 🎧 Listen and practice.

1. If I'd looked at the expiration date, I would have renewed my passport.
2. If I weren't Japanese, I might have needed a visa to enter the country.
3. If we'd left on time, we wouldn't have missed our flight.

**C** Circle the correct pronunciation of each –ed ending.

| | | | | | | | | | |
|---|---|---|---|---|---|---|---|---|---|
| 1. avoided | /ɪd/ | /t/ | /d/ | | 9. promised | /ɪd/ | /t/ | /d/ |
| 2. looked | /ɪd/ | /t/ | /d/ | | 10. covered | /ɪd/ | /t/ | /d/ |
| 3. summarized | /ɪd/ | /t/ | /d/ | | 11. added | /ɪd/ | /t/ | /d/ |
| 4. arrived | /ɪd/ | /t/ | /d/ | | 12. changed | /ɪd/ | /t/ | /d/ |
| 5. owed | /ɪd/ | /t/ | /d/ | | 13. reported | /ɪd/ | /t/ | /d/ |
| 6. ruined | /ɪd/ | /t/ | /d/ | | 14. discussed | /ɪd/ | /t/ | /d/ |
| 7. kicked | /ɪd/ | /t/ | /d/ | | 15. investigated | /ɪd/ | /t/ | /d/ |
| 8. refunded | /ɪd/ | /t/ | /d/ | | 16. enjoyed | /ɪd/ | /t/ | /d/ |

🎧 Now practice saying each word aloud and listen to check.*

**D** 🎧 Practice saying each sentence aloud, paying attention to reductions. Listen to compare.*

1. If I'd put the film in my carry-on, it wouldn't have gotten damaged.
2. If you'd checked the luggage limits, you might have avoided extra charges.
3. If my friend's luggage hadn't gotten stolen, he could have gone on the sightseeing tour.
4. I probably wouldn't have missed my flight if I had come on time.
5. If they'd taken a few simple precautions, their luggage might not have gotten stolen.

# Unit 7

## Intonation of sentences with subordinating conjunctions

In statements with subordinating conjunctions, it is common to use rising intonation in the first clause and falling intonation in the second clause. Pause slightly between clauses.

One's EQ can be high    even if one's IQ is low.

Even if one's IQ is low,    one's EQ can be high.

## Intonation of sentences with transitions

In statements with transitions, it is common to lower pitch after the last stressed syllable of the transition word and pause after it. Use falling intonation in the rest of the sentence.

He must have a high IQ. Otherwise, he wouldn't have gotten that job.

She achieved success. However, she doesn't do well on EQ tests.

   **1.** One's EQ can be high even if one's IQ is low.
   **2.** Even if one's IQ is low, one's EQ can be high.
   **3.** He must have a high IQ. Otherwise, he wouldn't have gotten that job.
   **4.** She achieved success. However, she doesn't do well on EQ tests.

**B** 🎧 Practice reading each sentence aloud, using the intonation you learned for sentences with subordinating conjunctions. Listen to compare. *

   **1.** You'll be given an interview as long as you get a high score on the test.
   **2.** Unless a new theory emerges, our abilities will continue to be measured with IQ and EQ tests.
   **3.** The IQ test can be an accurate measure of intelligence only if there is such a thing as general intelligence.
   **4.** Because the science of investigating the brain is quite new, no theory of intelligence has yet been proved.
   **5.** Some people have achieved extraordinary successes, although they didn't have high IQs.
   **6.** Intelligence is not easy to measure since there isn't just one kind of intelligence.
   **7.** Although good memory and creativity show intelligence, common sense is important, too.

**C** 🎧 Practice reading each sentence aloud, using the intonation you learned for sentences with transitions. Listen to compare.*

   **1.** No theory of intelligence has yet been proved. Nevertheless, many people believe success depends on high IQs.
   **2.** She has a low IQ score. However, her EQ could be high.
   **3.** The science of investigating the brain is quite new. Consequently, no theory of intelligence has yet been proved.
   **4.** He has a high IQ score. Nonetheless, he didn't get the job.
   **5.** There isn't just one kind of intelligence. Therefore, intelligence is not easy to measure.
   **6.** Good memory and creativity show intelligence. However, common sense is important, too.

## Unit 8

### Intonation of sarcasm

Saying the opposite of what you mean in order to show that you don't think a joke is funny is a type of sarcasm. When someone thinks a joke is funny, the response is usually said with raised pitch. The same response can convey sarcasm if it is said with flattened pitch and at a slower pace.

| Pleasure | Sarcasm |
|---|---|
| What a riot! (= It's funny.) | What a riot. (= It's not funny.) |
| That cracked me up! (= It's funny.) | That cracked me up. (= It's not funny.) |
| That's terrific! (= It's great.) | That's terrific. (= It's not great.) |
| I love it! (= It's great.) | I love it. (= It's not great.) |

**A** 🎧 Listen and practice.

   **1.** What a riot! / What a riot.
   **2.** That cracked me up! / That cracked me up.

   **3.** That's terrific! / That's terrific.
   **4.** I love it! / I love it.

**B** 🎧 Practice saying each statement two ways, first with intonation showing pleasure and then sarcasm. Listen to compare after you say the statement each way.* (Note that your choices may differ from what you hear on the audio.)

1. That's hysterical! / That's hysterical.
2. That's so funny! / That's so funny.
3. What a scream! / What a scream.
4. What a hoot! / What a hoot.

5. That's hilarious! / That's hilarious.
6. That's too much! / That's too much.
7. That really tickled me! / That really tickled me.

# Unit 9

## Formal pronunciation, rhythm, and intonation for reading aloud

Because it's more difficult to understand language when it is read rather than spoken in conversation, read with a regular rhythm and use fewer reductions. If there's a title, state it separately with falling intonation. Pause at all punctuation, and separate sentences into thought groups.

Rocket-delivered mail
On June 8, / 1959, / a rocket / carrying three thousand letters / was launched from a submarine in the ocean / and delivered to a U.S. naval station in Florida. / Some people believed / the age of rocket-delivered mail had begun. / But rocket-delivered mail / was a bust.

**A** 🎧 Listen to the selection. Then practice reading it aloud.

**Rocket-delivered mail**

On June 8, 1959, a rocket carrying three thousand letters was launched from a submarine in the ocean and delivered to a U.S. naval station in Florida. Some people believed the age of rocket-delivered mail had begun. But rocket-delivered mail was a bust.

**B** 🎧 Practice reading each selection aloud. Then listen to compare. (Note that your choices may differ from what you hear on the audio.)

**1. Smell-O-Vision**
In 1960, the movie *Scent of Mystery* combined visual images with releases of odors into the theater. The movie-maker predicted this technology would be used in all movies of the future. Smell-O-Vision was a flop.

**2. Cryonics for immortality**
In the 1960s, Robert Ettinger's book *The Prospect of Immortality* argued that people with fatal illnesses could have their bodies frozen before death and, once a cure for the illness was found, could then be thawed and cured. This would permit us to live beyond our natural life. This technology never took off.

# Unit 10

## Intonation in tag questions

When a tag question follows a statement to which a speaker anticipates agreement, both the statement and the tag question are said with falling intonation. The main stress in the tag question falls on the auxiliary verb and not on the pronoun. Note that there is generally no pause at the comma.

It's really shocking, isn't it?

They'll come up with a solution, won't they?

It's not really surprising, is it?

She didn't speak out against that project, did she?

It really makes you feel angry, doesn't it?

When the tag question represents a genuine question to which the speaker expects an answer, the statement is said with falling intonation, but the tag question is said with rising intonation.

It's really shocking, isn't it?

They'll come up with a solution, won't they?

It's not really surprising, is it?

She didn't speak out against that project, did she?

It really makes you feel angry, doesn't it?

**A** 🎧 Listen and practice. (Each sentence is said two ways.)

1. It's really shocking, isn't it?
2. It's not really surprising, is it?
3. It really makes you feel angry, doesn't it?
4. They'll come up with a solution, won't they?
5. She didn't speak out against that project, did she?

**B** 🎧 Listen to the following tag questions. Check to indicate if each one anticipates agreement or expects an answer.

| | Anticipates agreement | Expects an answer |
|---|---|---|
| 1. That's really appalling, isn't it? | ☐ | ☐ |
| 2. He's worried about his children, isn't he? | ☐ | ☐ |
| 3. It really makes you feel good, doesn't it? | ☐ | ☐ |
| 4. It wasn't really true, was it? | ☐ | ☐ |
| 5. They're going to do something about that problem, aren't they? | ☐ | ☐ |
| 6. It's not really important, is it? | ☐ | ☐ |
| 7. You heard that on TV, didn't you? | ☐ | ☐ |
| 8. You'll support us, won't you? | ☐ | ☐ |

🎧 Now practice saying each tag question aloud and listen to compare.*

**C** 🎧 Practice saying each tag question two ways, first to express anticipated agreement and then to express a genuine question. Listen to compare after you say each pair of questions.*

1. It really makes you stop and think, doesn't it?
2. They're concerned about global warming, aren't they?
3. It won't be easy to talk them into dropping trade tariffs, will it?
4. The president's economic policy is effective, isn't it?
5. The benefits of globalization are very clear, aren't they?
6. The benefits of globalization aren't very clear, are they?
7. There's no turning back, is there?

# Grammar Booster

The *Grammar Booster* is optional. It provides more explanation and practice, as well as additional grammar concepts and review.

## Unit 1

### Stative verbs

Stative (non-action) verbs express mental states, emotions, perceptions, descriptions, relationships, possession, measurements, and other conditions, rather than actions. They are not usually used in the continuous or perfect continuous, even when they describe a situation that is in progress.

Many people **believe** the environment should be the government's top priority.
NOT Many people ~~are believing~~ the environment should be the government's top priority.
She **has** always **understood** that job satisfaction was important to the employees.
NOT She ~~has always been understanding~~ that job satisfaction was important to the employees.

Some stative verbs have both non-action and action meanings. A stative verb that has an action meaning may be used in the continuous.

| Non-action meaning | Action meaning |
|---|---|
| That's ridiculous! (description) | You're being ridiculous! (act in a ridiculous way) |
| She has two children. (possession) | She's having another baby soon. (act of giving birth) |
| Do they have any fish? (possession) | What are we having for dinner? (act of eating) |
| We think these laws are unfair. (mental state: opinion) | We're thinking of organizing a protest. (act of planning) |
| That perfume smells beautiful! (perception) | The customer is smelling the perfumes. (act of smelling) |
| How does the soup taste? (perception) | I'm tasting the soup to see if it needs salt. (act of tasting) |
| This garden looks neglected. (description) | The child is looking at the flowers. (act of looking) |
| He's very thin. How much does he weigh? (measurement) | The nurse is weighing the patient. (act of weighing) |

NOTE: In informal spoken English, certain stative verbs, especially <u>want</u>, <u>need</u>, and <u>have to</u>, are becoming common in the continuous:

I'm really **wanting** a cup of good coffee. Let's go into that coffee bar.
John called. He says he**'s needing** to talk to you. Please give him a call.
We're so busy! We**'re having** to rewrite all these reports before tomorrow.

**For a complete list of stative verbs, see the Appendices, page A4.**

---

**A**  Decide if each stative verb in parentheses has an action or a non-action meaning. Then complete each sentence with the simple present tense or the present continuous.

action  non-action

1. ☐  ☐  Sara _____ (doubt) that she'll get a promotion since she's been here less than a year.

2. ☐  ☐  Ms. Linder's skills are excellent, and she _____ (have) experience working in the field.

3. ☐  ☐  Philip _____ (think) about moving abroad to teach for a year.

4. ☐  ☐  The training she needs to achieve her goal _____ (cost) more than she was planning to spend.

5. ☐  ☐  We _____ (have) dinner at 6:00 today so we can go to Jane Goodall's lecture on changes at Gombe.

6. ☐  ☐  Michael _____ (not remember) where the meeting will take place.

7. ☐  ☐  I _____ (include) some diagrams with my paper to explain my theory.

8. ☐  ☐  The doctor _____ (see) another patient now.

# Unit 2

## Adjective clauses: overview

| Adjective clauses | Examples |
|---|---|
| to identify or give additional information about a person<br>• relative pronoun can be subject or object of clause | The physicist { who / that } **made that discovery** } teaches at my university.<br><br>The psychologist { whom / that / who } **he interviewed** } did a study about lying. |
| to identify or give additional information about a place or thing<br>• relative pronoun can be subject or object of clause | The building { that / which } **is on your left** } was formerly a private palace.<br><br>The article { (that) / (which) } **I read yesterday** } is fascinating. |
| to show possession | The woman **whose house you admired** is a famous author.<br>Paris, **whose museums hold so many treasures,** is a favorite destination for tourists.<br>The precious stone, **whose origin is unknown,** was stolen from the gallery. |
| to modify a noun of place | The town { **where they live** / **in which they live** / **which they live in** / **that they live in** } has many beautiful parks and squares. |
| to modify a noun of time | I can't remember the year { **(when)** / **(that)** / **(in which)** } **we visited them for the first time.** |

NOTE: Words in parentheses may be omitted.

**A** Underline the best word or words to complete each sentence.

1. Parents (who / which) spend time with their children give them a sense of security.
2. The city (that / in which) my father grew up was destroyed during the war.
3. The Miller family, (whose / who) house is for sale, hopes to find a buyer soon.
4. I want to buy a cell phone (who / that) has a digital camera function.
5. The star of the film, (whom / which) we had hoped to meet, didn't come to the reception.
6. I will never forget the time (when / who) I told the truth and was punished for it.
7. The woman (who / which) used to teach English at my school is now the director there.
8. The *Sun Times*, (whose / which) is the best newspaper in town, recently published an article about the social uses of lying.

## Adjective clauses with quantifiers

**Some adjective clauses may include a quantifier that refers to a previously mentioned noun or noun phrase. These clauses are constructed as follows: quantifier + of + relative pronoun (whom, which, or whose).**

He consulted three doctors, **all of whom** confirmed the original diagnosis.
I can think of several possible explanations, **none of which** justifies their behavior.
The reporters questioned the president, **one of whose** strengths is his ability to remain calm under pressure.

**Adjective clauses that include quantifiers appear more often in written than spoken English.**

Some expressions of quantity used with of
a few of
all of
a number of
both of
each of
half of
little of
many of
most of
neither of
none of
one of
several of
some of

**B** Complete each sentence with a quantifier from the box and the correct relative pronoun. Use each quantifier only once.

> all of   each of   neither of   one of   both of

1. I know many commercials make false claims because I've bought many advertised products, only ............................................................ works.
2. He's upset with his three children, ............................................................ always makes up a different excuse to avoid sharing chores at home.
3. The teacher punished the six students, ............................................................ were caught cheating on the same exam.
4. These two articles, ............................................................ deal with the issue of honesty in the workplace, should be required reading for everyone in the company.
5. My parents, ............................................................ has ever told a lie, are the most honest people I know.

## Grammar for Writing: adjective clauses reduced to adjective phrases

| REMEMBER |
| --- |
| A <u>clause</u> is a group of words that has both a subject and a verb. A <u>phrase</u> is a group of words that doesn't have both a subject and a verb. |

**Adjective clauses can be reduced to adjective phrases.**
clause: Hawaii, **which is known for its beautiful topography and climate**, lies in the middle of the Pacific Ocean.
phrase: Hawaii, **known for its beautiful topography and climate**, lies in the middle of the Pacific Ocean.

**There are two ways to reduce an adjective clause to an adjective phrase:**

1. **When the adjective clause contains a form of the verb <u>be</u>, drop the relative pronoun and the verb <u>be</u>.**
   Herodotus, **who was the first Greek historian**, wrote about the wars between ancient Greece and Persia. →
   Herodotus, **the first Greek historian**, wrote about the wars between ancient Greece and Persia.

2. **When the adjective clause does not contain a form of the verb <u>be</u>, drop the relative pronoun and use the present participle of the verb.**
   The human skeleton, **which contains** 206 separate bones, is a strong and flexible structure. →
   The human skeleton, **containing** 206 separate bones, is a strong and flexible structure.

   Those **who tamper** with the smoke detector will be prosecuted. →
   Those **tampering** with the smoke detector will be prosecuted.

**Adjective phrases are common in writing. They often begin with an article or with words and expressions like <u>one</u>, <u>a type of</u>, <u>the kind of</u>.**
My grandmother, **a very practical and hardworking woman**, made clothes for the entire family.
The **largest city in Turkey**, Istanbul is at the point where Europe joins Asia.
They're looking for a quiet place to live, preferably **one in the suburbs**.
Chanterelles, **a type of edible mushroom with a rich yellow color**, are very expensive.
These plants are in the cactus family, **the kind of vegetation with the most tolerance for a hot, dry climate**.

**C** Reduce the adjective clause in each sentence to an adjective phrase.

1. James Bond, who is one of the best-known movie characters, often uses a fake identity when he is on a mission.
2. LaFontaine's *Fables*, which are short tales of animals behaving like people, comment on human nature.
3. Executives who fail to accept responsibility for their mistakes often lose the trust of their employees.
4. "The Boy Who Cried Wolf," which teaches the moral that liars are never believed even when they tell the truth, is a fable by Aesop.
5. Compassion, which is believed to be the source of moral behavior, develops in children at a very young age.

**D** On a separate sheet of paper, combine each pair of sentences. Use the second sentence as an adjective phrase.

**1.** Aesop wrote a lot of fables using animal characters.
(Aesop was a Greek writer living in the sixth century B.C.)

> *Aesop, a Greek writer living in the sixth century B.C., wrote a lot of fables using animal characters.*

**2.** My nephew Brian enjoys volunteering in a local hospital.
(My nephew Brian is a man of great compassion and integrity.)

**3.** Margo Farmer is an honest and independent legislator.
(Margo Farmer is one legislator never influenced by any special interest groups.)

**4.** The morality play offers moral instructions by presenting good and evil as human characters.
(The morality play is a type of play once popular in the fifteenth and sixteenth centuries.)

**5.** Making up an excuse for being late can get a person into trouble.
(Making up an excuse for being late is the kind of mistake most common among office workers.)

**6.** A lot of money was raised at last night's concert.
(Last night's concert was the biggest charity event of the year.)

## Unit 3

### Describing past actions and events: review

**The past of <u>be</u> and the simple past tense**
Use for completed actions and states and for those that occurred at a specific time in the past.
> He **was** here at 10:00 and **left** this message.

**The past continuous**
Use for one or more actions in progress at a specific time in the past.
> The baby **was sleeping** and the older children **were eating** dinner when we arrived.

**The present perfect**
Use for actions completed at an unspecified time in the past.
> She **has** already **informed** her manager about the problem.
> I**'ve stayed** at that hotel three times.

**The past perfect**
Use for an action that occurred before another past action.
> They **had** already **made** a decision when we called to discuss the matter.

**The past perfect continuous**
Use for a continuous action that had occurred before another past action.
> We **had been working** in the garden for two hours when the storm began.

**<u>Used to</u> / <u>would</u>**
Use <u>used to</u> for past situations and habits that no longer exist. Use <u>would</u> or <u>used to</u> for actions that were repeated regularly in the past.
> When she was younger, she never **used to** be afraid of anything.
> In those days, we **would take** a long walk every evening after supper.

**The future as seen from the past**
Use <u>was</u> / <u>were going to</u> + the base form of a verb to express future plans someone had in the past.
> He **was going to start** his own business, but he couldn't get a loan.

**<u>Would</u>** + the base form of the verb can also express the future as seen from the past, but only after statements of knowledge or belief.
> We always thought that she **would become** an actress, but she decided to study law.

**A** Correct the errors with past forms.

1. Florence has been walking for several hours before she realized that her wallet was missing.
2. As a child, he was practicing the piano for hours every day. Then he stopped taking lessons.
3. Eleanor's neighbor was here at noon and had left some flowers for her.
4. "I have seen that movie last year, and I thought it was great," Frank exclaimed.
5. When the power went off, I read an article in this morning's paper.
6. Before this morning, I never took a yoga class.
7. I am going to travel to Venice this summer, but I can't take time off from work.
8. He was working on the problem all morning when he finally found the solution.

# Unit 4

## Infinitive and gerund phrases in place of the subjunctive

**It is often possible to use an infinitive phrase after adjectives of urgency, obligation, or advisability with almost the same meaning as the subjunctive.**
It is essential that John **find** the time each day to relax. = It is essential for John **to find** the time each day to relax.

**It is also often possible to use a gerund phrase after verbs of urgency, obligation, or advisability with almost the same meaning as the subjunctive.**
Dr. Sharpe recommends (that) you **spend** a few moments relaxing. = Dr. Sharpe recommends **spending** a few moments relaxing.

**Note that when an infinitive or gerund phrase is used without a pronoun, it usually refers to people in general.**
It is essential **to find** the time each day to relax.
Dr. Sharpe recommends **spending** a few moments relaxing.

**A** On a separate sheet of paper, rewrite each sentence with an infinitive or a gerund phrase. Make any necessary changes.

1. It is crucial that you practice feng shui.
2. The article suggests that you carry several lucky charms.
3. The manager recommended that they finish the project before the holiday.
4. It is important that we get enough sleep every night.
5. The directions advise that you throw salt over your shoulder.
6. It is necessary that she arrive at the theater by 4:00 PM.

# Unit 5

## More phrases that make non-count nouns countable

| Natural phenomena | Foods | Drinks and liquids | Household products |
|---|---|---|---|
| **a bolt of** lightning | **a bar of** chocolate | **a bottle of** water | **a bar of** soap |
| **a breath of** air | **a clove of** garlic | **a carton of** milk | **a tube of** toothpaste |
| **a clap of** thunder | **a cup of** sugar | **a cup of** coffee | **a box of** detergent |
| **a cloud of** smoke | **a teaspoon of** salt | **a glass of** juice | **a can of** cleanser |
| **a drop of** rain | **a loaf of** bread | **a liter of** gasoline | |
| **a gust of** wind | | | |
| **a ray of** sun | | | |

Here are four common phrases that are used to make a number of non-count nouns countable.

| **a piece of** | **a sense of** | **an act of** | **a state of** |
|---|---|---|---|
| advice | achievement | anger | confusion |
| equipment | community | insanity | disrepair |
| furniture | confidence | justice | emergency |
| gossip | control | defiance | war |
| information | humor | kindness | mind |
| news | identity | generosity | |
| paper | | heroism | |

**A**  Choose the best word from the box to complete each sentence.

| |
|---|
| act |
| bar |
| cloud |
| glass |
| piece |
| sense |
| state |

1. The group's donation was a true ................ of generosity

2. My sister has an amazing ................ of humor.

3. The room was filled with a ................ of smoke.

4. The woman slipped on a ................ of soap in the shower.

5. Our town has been in a ................ of emergency since the hurricane.

6. The park just installed a new ................ of equipment in the playground.

7. I asked the waitress for a ................ of orange juice.

## More non-count nouns with both a countable and an uncountable sense

With some non-count nouns, the change in meaning is subtle: the countable meaning refers to something specific and the uncountable meaning refers to something general.

| | |
|---|---|
| **a fear** = the anticipation of a specific danger; a phobia<br>*He had **a fear** of heights.* | **fear** = a general anticipation of danger<br>*Irrational **fear** can lead to anxiety.* |
| **a victory** = a specific event in which mastery or success is achieved<br>*The battle of Waterloo was a great **victory** for the English.* | **victory** = the phenomenon of winning<br>*She led her party to **victory**.* |
| **a time** = a specific moment in the past or future; a specific occasion<br>*There was **a time** when food was much cheaper.*<br>*How **many times** did you read it?* | **time** = the general concept; clock time<br>***Time** passes so quickly!*<br>*What **time** did you arrange to meet?* |
| **a superstition** = a specific belief or practice<br>*A common American **superstition** is that Friday the 13th brings bad luck.* | **superstition** = a general attitude<br>*The prevalence of **superstition** among educated people is surprising.* |

**B**  Complete each pair of sentences.  Write a before a noun where necessary.  Write X if a noun should not have an article.

1. **a.** Will people ever learn to control their phobias?  Only ........... time can tell.
   **b.** There has never been ........... time when people didn't try to interpret their dreams.

2. **a.** If you have ........... fear of flying, you shouldn't take a job that requires overseas travel.
   **b.** Psychologists agree that ........... fear is a universal emotion.

3. **a.** Ignorance and fear may sometimes lead to ........... superstition.
   **b.** There is ........... widely held superstition that knocking on wood brings good luck.

4. **a.** The coach's tactics helped the team win ........... major victory in last night's game.
   **b.** Everyone cannot always experience the joy of ........... victory; someone has to lose.

## Article usage: overview

Note where indefinite or definite articles are used or omitted.

| | Indefinite article | Definite article | No article |
|---|---|---|---|
| General statement | Use with singular count nouns:<br>*A cat may symbolize good or bad fortune.* | Use with singular count nouns:<br>*The cat may symbolize good or bad fortune.*<br>*The telephone was invented by Bell.*<br>*The guitar is a string instrument.*<br>Use with non-count nouns:<br>*Freud called attention to the importance of dreams.* | With plural count nouns:<br>*Cats may symbolize good or bad fortune.*<br>With non-count nouns:<br>*Misfortune may strike at any time.* |
| First mention | Use with singular count nouns:<br>*I found a lucky charm.* | | With plural count nouns:<br>*I have (some) lucky charms.*<br>With non-count nouns:<br>*I bought (some) shampoo.* |
| Second mention | | Use with singular count nouns:<br>*The lucky charm was in a box.*<br>Use with plural count nouns:<br>*The lucky charms were in a box.*<br>Use with non-count nouns:<br>*The shampoo is in the closet.* | |

**C** Read the paragraph. Then correct eleven errors in article usage. Make any necessary changes.

The homes are expensive these days, but Peter got lucky and bought small house last week. A house has two bedrooms and one bathroom. It also has large kitchen and the living room. Peter will use a living room as his home office. Bedrooms are in bad condition, and Peter will need a help painting them. Then he wants to have the party so his friends can admire a house. Later Peter will buy a furniture—when he saves some money!

## Definite article: additional uses

| | Definite article |
|---|---|
| When a noun represents a unique thing | Use with singular count nouns:<br>*The sun rises in the east.* |
| With a comparative or superlative adjective to make a noun unique (or with <u>right</u>, <u>wrong</u>, <u>first</u>, <u>only</u>, <u>same</u>) | Use with singular count nouns:<br>*Telling the truth is **the best course** of action. It's always **the right thing** to do.*<br>*The robin is **the first sign** of spring.*<br>Use with plural count nouns:<br>*People in different places often have **the same superstitions**.*<br>Use with non-count nouns:<br>*That's **the only information** I was able to find on the Internet.* |
| When context makes a noun specific | Use with singular count nouns:<br>*The hospital in this town has an excellent emergency room.*<br>Use with plural count nouns:<br>*The buildings in this town are no higher than ten stories.*<br>Use with non-count nouns:<br>*The air in this city is polluted.* |

|  | **Definite article** |
|---|---|
| When an adjective clause makes a noun specific | Use with singular count nouns:<br>*The mirror that you broke will bring you bad luck.*<br>Use with plural count nouns:<br>*The mirrors that you broke will bring you bad luck.*<br>Use with non-count nouns:<br>*The progress that she made was due not to good luck but to hard work.* |
| When an adjective represents a certain group of people | Use with a noun derived from an adjective, such as the blind / the deaf / the dead / the living / the young / the old / the poor / the rich / the unemployed / the privileged / the underprivileged:<br>*The unemployed must often learn new job skills.* |

**D** Complete the paragraphs with words from the box. Use a definite article when appropriate.

| | | | |
|---|---|---|---|
| tourists | gasoline | view | world |
| wealthy | sky | ballooning | first men |

On March 20, 1999, Bertrand Piccard of Switzerland and Brian Jones of Britain were

.......................................... to travel around .......................................... in a balloon. The numerous
          (1)                                                              (2)
balloonists who had been attempting this journey for decades beforehand ran into various

problems with weather and equipment.

In the past several years, .......................................... has become a popular adventure sport.
                                      (3)
Due to the high cost of balloons and .........................................., however, it is a sport reserved for
                                                      (4)
.......................................... . .......................................... can get a taste of ballooning during their travels.
          (5)                          (6)
.......................................... of a city or landscape from .......................................... is always breathtaking.
          (7)                                                      (8)

# Unit 6

**The conditional: overview**

| Type | Use | If clause (states the condition) | Result clause (states the result) | Examples |
|---|---|---|---|---|
| **Factual conditional** | To express a general or scientific fact | **simple present**<br><br>Note: In this type of conditional, <u>if</u> can be replaced by <u>when</u> or <u>whenever</u>. | **simple present** | *If it **rains**, the gardens **close** early.*<br>*Water **freezes** if the temperature **falls** below zero degrees Celsius.* |
| | To talk about what will happen in the future under certain conditions | **simple present**<br><br>Note: Don't use a future form in the <u>if</u> clause. | **will / be going to +**<br>**base form of the verb**<br><br>Note: Use <u>can</u>, <u>may</u>, <u>might</u>, <u>should</u> if the result is not certain. | *If you **plan** your trip carefully, things **will go** smoothly.*<br>*If we **arrive** late, they're **going to start** without us.*<br>*If we **hurry**, we **may be able to catch** the train.* |
| **Present unreal conditional** | To talk about present unreal or untrue conditions | **simple past or <u>were</u>**<br><br>Note: Don't use <u>would</u> in the <u>if</u> clause. | **would + base form of the verb**<br><br>Note: Use <u>could</u> or <u>might</u> if the result is not certain. | *If I **had** the time, I **would explain** the problem to you.*<br>*If he **were** here, he **might make** a lot of changes.* |

| Type | Use | If clause (states the condition) | Result clause (states the result) | Examples |
|---|---|---|---|---|
| **Past unreal conditional** | To talk about past unreal or untrue conditions | **past perfect**<br><br>Note: Don't use <u>would have</u> in the <u>if</u> clause. | **would have** + past participle<br><br>Note: Use <u>could have</u> or <u>might have</u> if the result is not certain. | *If they **had known** about the storm, they **would have taken** a different flight.*<br>*If you **had told** us about the delay, we **could have made** other arrangements.* |
| **Mixed conditional** | To talk about past unreal or untrue conditions in relation to the present | **past perfect**<br><br>Note: Don't use <u>would</u> in the <u>if</u> clause. | **would** + base form of the verb<br><br>Note: Use <u>could</u> or <u>might</u> if the result is not certain. | *If I **had prepared** for the interview, I **wouldn't be** so nervous.*<br>*If we **had left** earlier, we **might be** on time now.* |
| | To talk about present unreal or untrue conditions in relation to the past | **simple past or <u>were</u>**<br><br>Note: Don't use <u>would have</u> in the <u>if</u> clause. | **would have** + past participle<br><br>Note: Use <u>could have</u> or <u>might have</u> if the result is not certain. | *If she **were** honest, she **would have told** us the truth.*<br>*If I **spoke** Russian, I **might have understood** the guide.* |

## Special cases

1. Use <u>should</u>, <u>happen to</u>, or <u>should happen to</u> in the <u>if</u> clause in factual conditionals when the condition is less likely.

   If you { should / happen to / should happen to } see Peter, tell him to call me.

2. Use **If it weren't for . . .** / **If it hadn't been for . . .** in the <u>if</u> clause in unreal conditionals to express regret or relief.
   **If it weren't for** the traffic, we would be at the airport by now.
   (= Without the traffic, we would be at the airport by now.)
   **If it hadn't been for** your help this morning, we wouldn't have been able to meet the deadline.
   (= Without your help this morning, we wouldn't have been able to meet the deadline.)

3. **To express inferences in conditional sentences, different combinations of tenses can be used.**
   If Julie **went** to the party last night, she definitely **saw** what happened.
   If you **don't know** the answer to this question, you **didn't do** your homework.
   If the results **didn't come out** yesterday, they'll definitely **come out** today.
   If you still **haven't finished** packing by now, you're **not going to catch** your flight.

---

**A** Underline the correct word or words to complete each sentence.

1. If Sam (does / will do) well this year, he will apply to medical school.

2. Water (boils / is going to boil) when the temperature reaches 100° Celsius.

3. If you (will / should) find my scarf, please hold it for me.

4. If it (wouldn't have been / hadn't been) for her savings, Anna wouldn't have been able to attend university.

5. If we (would have known / had known) that car insurance was so expensive, we would not have bought a car.

6. If you didn't get a reply today, you (would definitely hear / will definitely hear) from us tomorrow.

7. If I (had / would have) a garden, I would grow several types of flowers.

8. If I (would have practiced / had practiced) my speech a bit more, I might not be so worried now.

## Unit 7

### Grammar for Writing:  more conjunctions and transitions

| Purpose | Coordinating conjunctions | Subordinating conjunctions | Transitions |
|---|---|---|---|
| To add information<br><br>*Marc is working as a photographer, **and** he has experience in graphic design.*<br><br>***In addition to** working as a photographer, Marc has experience in graphic design.* | and | in addition to<br><br>besides | in addition<br>furthermore<br>moreover<br>besides |
| To clarify information<br><br>*Smaller cars are more efficient; **in other words**, they use less fuel.* | | | that is<br>in other words<br>in fact |
| To illustrate or exemplify information<br><br>*Many European cities are found along waterways. **For example**, London, Paris, Vienna, and Budapest all lie on major rivers.* | | | for instance<br>for example<br>to illustrate |
| To show contrast<br><br>*Meg does not usually perform well under pressure, **but** she gave a brilliant recital.*<br><br>*Meg does not usually perform well under pressure. **Despite this**, she gave a brilliant recital.* | but<br>yet | even though<br>although<br>though<br>while<br>whereas | however<br>nevertheless<br>nonetheless<br>in contrast<br>even so<br>still<br>despite this / that |
| To express cause or result<br><br>*They have a new baby, **so** they rarely get a good night's sleep!*<br><br>***Now that** they have a new baby, they rarely get a good night's sleep!* | so<br>for | because<br>since<br>due to the fact that<br>now that<br>so that | therefore<br>consequently<br>accordingly<br>as a result |
| To express a condition<br><br>*Pollution can be reduced **provided that** car manufacturers mass-produce cars with greater fuel efficiency.*<br><br>*Car manufacturers should mass-produce cars with greater fuel efficiency. **Otherwise**, pollution will not be reduced.* | or (else) | (only) if<br>provided that<br>as long as<br>unless<br>even if<br>whether (or not) | otherwise |
| To show similarity<br><br>*Water is necessary for life. **Similarly**, oxygen is required by all living things.* | | | similarly<br>likewise |

**A** On a separate sheet of paper, combine each pair of sentences two ways, once with the connecting word(s) in **a** and once with the connecting words in **b**. Use a semicolon before a transition. Change the wording as necessary to retain the meaning.

1. The ability to think logically is essential for making plans. The ability to think creatively is important for brainstorming new ideas. (**a.** while   **b.** in contrast)

2. Nicole has been under a lot of pressure lately. Nicole still manages to stay calm and pleasant. (**a.** although   **b.** despite that)

3. Salespeople need to know the products very well. Salespeople need to have strong interpersonal skills. (**a.** in addition to   **b.** furthermore)

4. We have to stay focused on the roots of the problems. We can't come up with effective solutions. (**a.** unless   **b.** otherwise)

5. Charlie realized that he is mechanically inclined. Charlie wants to become a mechanical engineer. (**a.** now that   **b.** as a result)

# Unit 8

## Indirect speech: review

### Optional tense changes
**When a reporting verb is in the simple past tense, backshifting is optional when:**

1. **the statement refers to something JUST said:**
   Tom just called. He said that the director **is leaving**.
   OR Tom just called. He said that the director **was leaving**.

2. **the direct speech refers to something that's still true:**
   Ann mentioned that she **needs** to renew her passport.
   OR Ann mentioned that she **needed** to renew her passport.

3. **the direct speech refers to a scientific or general truth:**
   He noted that the Earth **is** the fifth largest planet in the solar system.
   OR He noted that the Earth **was** the fifth largest planet in the solar system.

> **BE CAREFUL!** Remember that when the reporting verb is in the present tense, the verb tense in indirect speech does not change.
>
> They say an exceptionally cold winter is expected this year. NOT They say an exceptionally cold winter was . . .

### Changes in pronouns and possessives
**In indirect speech, pronouns and possessives change to reflect the point of view of the reporter rather than the speaker.**
My manager said, "**You** have to finish **your** report and give it to **me** as soon as possible." →
My manager said (that) **I** had to finish **my** report and give it to **her** as soon as possible.

I told her, "**You**'ll have it on **your** desk by noon." →
I told her (that) **she** would have it on **her** desk by noon.

### Questions in indirect speech
**Indirect questions are a kind of embedded question—a question that is included in another sentence. Indirect <u>yes</u> / <u>no</u> questions begin with <u>if</u>, <u>whether</u>, or <u>whether or not</u>. Indirect information questions begin with a question word. All indirect questions follow statement (not inverted) word order and do not usually use <u>do</u>, <u>does</u>, or <u>did</u>.**
He asked, "**Did** you **see** the movie?" → He asked **if I had seen the movie**. OR He asked **whether (or not) I had seen the movie**.
She asked, "**When are** you **planning** to go?" → She asked **when I was planning to go**.

### Imperatives in indirect speech
**When imperatives are used to report commands, requests, instructions, and invitations, the imperative form changes to the infinitive. The negative infinitive is used for negative commands, requests, and instructions.**

> **REMEMBER**
>
> Indirect questions end with a period, not a question mark. The verbs in indirect questions follow the same changes as the verbs in indirect statements.

| Direct speech | Indirect speech |
|---|---|
| "Could you please **go** to the store?" | She asked me **to go** to the store. |
| The chef said, "**Add** two eggs and stir the mixture." | The chef said **to add** two eggs and stir the mixture. |
| "Please **have** dinner with us," he said. | He invited me **to have** dinner with them. |
| She told the child, "**Don't cross** the street." | She told the child **not to cross** the street. |

**A** On a separate sheet of paper, write the sentences in indirect speech. If a sentence can be written both with and without backshifting, write it both ways.

1. Zachary mentioned, "I need a new suit, but I really want a new jacket."
2. Kate just called. She asked, "Did you enjoy your vacation?"
3. In his lecture, Dr. Taylor stated, "The Earth rotates around the sun."
4. Georgia says, "I've never seen such exciting paintings before."
5. The professor explained, "I want you to finish your essays for the next class."

**B** On a separate sheet of paper, write these conversations in indirect speech, using correct pronouns and possessives.

1. **MARIA:** Your cartoon is really good. Your drawing of the penguin is a hoot.
   **JACK:** Yours is hilarious, too! It really cracked me up!

2. **RICHARD:** My paper on the health benefits of humor has just been published in a medical journal.
   **ME:** I'm happy for you! I'd appreciate it if you could give me a copy.

3. **KIM:** I bought a new MP3 player last week.
   **BEN:** I know. I saw it on your desk. It looks much better than your old one.

**C** On a separate sheet of paper, rewrite each of the following in indirect speech.

1. The teacher asked his students, "Can you tell me what the joke is about?"
2. Don asked his wife, "Have you finished reading the book on humor?"
3. Lisa asked her boyfriend, "Why did you have to tell an ethnic joke at my father's birthday party last night?"
4. Barry sometimes wonders, "How would I react if someone made me the butt of a joke?"
5. Vivian wondered, "When is the best time to tell a joke?"

**D** On a separate sheet of paper, write the conversation in indirect speech. Begin like this: Harry asked me . . .

**HARRY:** Can I borrow your car on Saturday?
**ME:** Yes, you can. But you'll have to return it to me by 7:00 PM.
**HARRY:** Do you really need your car by 7:00? Could I bring it back by 9:00 PM instead?
**ME:** I'm sorry, but I promised to take my nephew to the movies.
**HARRY:** Oh, I understand. I'll return it to you by 7:00.

**E** On a separate sheet of paper, write each sentence in indirect speech.

1. The patient asked the nurse, "Could you please bring me a funny movie?"
2. Dr. Baker advised, "Don't let emotional tension make you sick."
3. She told me, "Be a good sport and laugh about it."
4. "Don't laugh at that joke," Fred instructed his son. "It's disgusting," he said.
5. "Laugh first, cry later," an old saying advises us.
6. Lucas told us, "Never touch the green button on the printer."
7. "Take the penguin to the zoo tomorrow," Mr. Franklin's neighbor told him.
8. Nick said, "Please don't ask how the meeting went."

# Unit 9

## Grammar for Writing: when to use the passive voice

Sentences in the passive voice can have the same meaning as those in the active voice. However, the word order in passive sentences gives a different emphasis to the information. Passive sentences focus the reader's (or listener's) attention on the result of the action rather than on the performer of the action (the agent). Writers prefer the passive voice in the following situations:

1. **To emphasize the result of an action, or if the agent is unimportant or unknown. This use is common in academic writing, scientific articles, and news reports.**
   A number of sophisticated treatments for heart disease **have been developed** in the last decade. (The writer emphasizes the treatments rather than the people who developed them.)
   Hundreds of people **were made** homeless by yesterday's floods. (The writer emphasizes the result of the floods rather than the floods themselves.)
   The Parthenon **was built** in the fifth century BC. (The builder is unknown or unimportant.)

2. **To describe a process. This use is found in technical and scientific writing.**
   There are four basic steps in the production of juice. First the oranges **are unloaded** from the trucks and **placed** on a conveyor belt. Then they **are washed** and **sorted**. Next they **are put** into machines that remove the juice and put it into cartons. Finally the juice **is distributed** all over the world.

3. **To use an impersonal or indirect tone, which suggests formality, impartiality, or objectivity. This use is favored in official documents, formal announcements, and signs, or to avoid placing blame.**
   Their wedding **will be celebrated** in June.
   Walking on the grass **is prohibited**.
   A mistake **has been made** in your account. It **will be corrected** on next month's statement. (The writer avoids mentioning who made the mistake and emphasizes the fact that it will be corrected, rather than who will do the correcting.)

4. **To keep the reader's attention focused on a previously mentioned noun, because it is the central topic of the paragraph.**
   They caught the thief later that evening. He **was placed** in jail and **was allowed** to call a lawyer. (The topic of the paragraph is the thief. By using the passive voice in the second sentence, the writer keeps the reader's attention focused on the thief.)

5. **To avoid using a general subject, which is considered weak. General subjects include the impersonal <u>you</u>, <u>we</u>, and <u>they</u>; <u>people</u>; <u>one</u>; <u>someone</u> / <u>somebody</u>; <u>anyone</u> / <u>anybody</u>. This use is common in formal documents, in official signs, and in newspaper editorials and other texts that express an opinion.**
   People must show their IDs before boarding. PREFERRED: IDs **must be shown** before boarding.
   We have cut prices on all merchandise. PREFERRED: Prices on all merchandise **have been cut**.
   Someone should inform voters of their rights. PREFERRED: Voters **should be informed** of their rights.

6. **To avoid clumsy sentence constructions. This is a common solution when the agent has a long or complex modifier.**
   The Tigers, whose new strategy of offense and defense seemed to be working, defeated the Lions.
   PREFERRED: The Lions **were defeated** by the Tigers, whose new strategy of offense and defense seemed to be working.

**A** On a separate sheet of paper, write each sentence in the passive voice.

1. Construction workers built the museum in less than six months.
2. People must present their passports at the border.
3. The company hired Ben Jones to replace the executive director. They gave Jones the corner office and offered him a very generous salary.
4. First engineers perfect the design for the new product. Then workers build a prototype. Next engineers test the prototype. After engineers approve the design, the factory begins production.
5. We have credited the sum of eighty-five dollars to your VISTA account.
6. The reporter, whose investigation uncovered many shocking facts and a pattern of corrupt behavior, exposed the official for taking bribes.

# Unit 10

## Phrasal verbs: expansion

### The passive form of phrasal verbs

Transitive phrasal verbs are always inseparable in the passive voice, even when they are separable or always separated in the active voice.

The TV couldn't be **turned on** this morning. (I couldn't **turn** the TV **on** this morning.)

The empty lot has been **turned into** a beautiful garden. (They **turned** the empty lot **into** a beautiful garden.)

### Transitive and intransitive meanings

Some phrasal verbs have both a transitive and an intransitive meaning.

He went to bed without **taking off** his clothes. (transitive meaning: remove)

What time does your plane **take off**? (intransitive meaning: leave)

Thieves **broke in** and stole her jewelry. (transitive meaning: enter by force)

She **broke in** the new employees by showing them the procedures. (intransitive meaning: train someone)

**For a complete list of transitive and intransitive phrasal verbs, see the Appendices, pages A4–A5.**

### Three-word phrasal verbs

A three-word phrasal verb consists of a verb, a particle, and a preposition that together have a specific meaning.

The verb and the particle in three-word phrasal verbs are inseparable.

As a result of his controversial ideas, the senator **came up against** members of his own party, who opposed him vigorously.

Does society have an obligation to **look out for** people who are disadvantaged?

Temper tantrums are not uncommon in young children. As they mature, they **grow out of** this behavior.

I'm going to close my door and not take any calls today; I've just got to **catch up on** my work.

**For a complete list of three-word phrasal verbs, see the Appendices, page A6.**

**A** On a separate sheet of paper, write each sentence in the passive voice. Use a <u>by</u> phrase, if necessary.

1. We have to call the meeting off.
2. He talked the client into a better deal.
3. The president covered the mistake up.
4. She dropped the children off in front of the school.
5. One of the applicants filled the form out incorrectly.
6. I paid the balance off last month.
7. Someone threw the document away by mistake.
8. The speaker handed pamphlets out at the end of the presentation.

**B** Underline the phrasal verb in each sentence. Then decide if it has a transitive or an intransitive meaning.

transitive  intransitive

1. ☐ ☐ The photographer blew up the photo 200 percent so we could use it for the poster.
2. ☐ ☐ The plane blew up shortly before it was supposed to land.
3. ☐ ☐ The workers won't give up until they're paid fair wages.
4. ☐ ☐ She has tried to give up smoking several times, without success.
5. ☐ ☐ Phil has to wake up at 5:00 AM every morning to get to work on time.
6. ☐ ☐ The children played quietly in order not to wake up their parents.
7. ☐ ☐ He works out three or four times a week in order to keep in shape.
8. ☐ ☐ World leaders are meeting to work out a plan to eradicate poverty.